# SPINNING
## and weaving
## with WOOL

*by Paula Simmons*

**Pacific Search Press**

Pacific Search Press, 222 Dexter Avenue North, Seattle, Washington 98109
Printed in the United States of America

Second printing 1978
Third printing 1980
Fourth printing 1981

Figures 5, 78, and 99 reprinted by permission from Phyllis
Bentley's *Colne Valley Cloth* (issued by The Huddersfield and District
Woollen Export Group). Drawings by Harold Blackburn.

Designed by Pamela Hoffman
Edited by Betsy Rupp Fulwiler


Library of Congress Cataloging in Publication Data

Simmons, Paula.
    Spinning and weaving with wool.

    Continues the author's Raising sheep the modern way.
    Bibliography: p.
    Includes index.
    1. Hand spinning.   2. Hand weaving.   I. Title.
TT847.S57        746.1        77-76137
ISBN 0-914718-28-2
ISBN 0-914718-23-1 pbk.

# Acknowledgments

*Without the photos, drawings, and technical advice offered by
a number of people, this book would not have been complete. My thanks
go to Levi Ross, Noel Rockwell, Ann Meerkerk, Phyllis Lennea Mason, Lew Turner,
and Michael Baehr for their drawings; to Charles R. Pearson, Lew Turner,
and Ruth Richardson for their photographs; and to Ernest Mason
for his technical advice. I would especially like to thank
my darling friends at Pacific Search Press for making the
production of this book not a chore, but a pleasure.*

# Contents

# Preface

This book was first conceived as a sequel to my 1976 book *Raising Sheep the Modern Way*. I wanted to continue where that one left off — to show how to use the wool in spinning and the handspun yarn in weaving and knitting. But once I began the project, I forgot my original aim. While the book does exclusively treat the spinning of wool, it is not so much related to sheep as it is to the spinner and the spinner's problems. It is designed to be used as a reference book, so some information is repeated in order to make each chapter, as much as possible, complete in itself.

I found that I had to go into greater detail about spinning wheels than I had intended, because faulty equipment (or just the choice of the wrong wheel for the job) hinders the learning process and makes spinning a less than pleasurable pursuit. In over twenty years of spinning, this is the first time I have given much conscious thought to the actual theory of spinning wheel operation. As long as our wheels worked reasonably well, I did not even wonder why. Now, in trying to see why and then write about it, I have learned a lot of things that I should have known all along.

I have tried to use plain and nontechnical language, and have made the equipment plans as simple as possible (many can be made with only hand tools). The floor loom is an exception because to be truly valuable, it must be more complicated than the other equipment.

I see the purpose of this book as not just to show "how to spin," but how to spin better, and faster, and how to produce plenty of yarn for weaving and/or knitting. In short, how to spin in a way that affords real satisfaction.

To begin at the beginning, you must consider the sheep. The breed most desirable for spinning depends on the individual, but spinners generally agree about certain qualities to seek in a good spinning fleece. Whether you are choosing a fleece from your own flock or buying part of a fleece in a shop or at a livestock show, you want to consider:

1. How clean is it? Dirt, sand, and grease all wash out readily, but contamination by weed seeds, burrs, and hay and grass cuttings are more of a problem. They do not wash out or card out, and those that do not shake out must all be removed by hand.

2. How strong is it? Test a lock for evidence of *tender* wool, which can be caused by illness or undernourishment during the animal's pregnancy, by stretching a small tuft of wool between both hands. Strum it with the index finger of one hand. A sound staple emits a faint, dull twanging sound and does not tear or break.

3. Are the tips overly weathered? Tippy wool dyes poorly because it takes dye unevenly. Some tips come off in washing and carding, which causes conditions similar to second cuts and short, broken fibers.

4. How well was it sheared? There should not be lots of *second cuts* (cuts in the middle of the staple), which are caused by the shearer going over the same place twice, overlapping his strokes, or using the shears to push back the wool. These second cuts do not shake out easily once the fleece has been compressed by rolling and tying.

5. Are there heavy dung tags wrapped with the fleece? If you are paying by the pound, these can be expensive.

6. Is the fleece matted? *Cotty* wool is matted or felted, which is sometimes the result of a two-year growth without shearing, or unusual weathering conditions.

7. Does it smell musty? A fleece that is sheared when the

# 1
## Choosing and Washing Wool

**1.** *Black sheep, half sheared. Short wool from the top of the head and some neck wool are already discarded in the small pile at the right.*

sheep is wet, then stored damp, has damaged, weakened fibers.

8. Does the wool grease appear to be caked and hardened? When sheep are sheared too late in the spring, hot weather can cause coagulation of the *yolk* (the combination of lanolin and sweat found in unprocessed sheep wool), which causes yellowing of a white fleece and is difficult to wash out. Dark wool appears dandruffy after washing.

Since these conditions are more or less within the control of the sheep raiser, spinners who raise their own sheep have a decided advantage. By taking proper care of the animal, they can avoid illnesses that weaken the wool, and eliminate ticks and parasites that cause rough, lusterless fleece.

Doing your own shearing gives you control over that preliminary process, also. More careful shearing can minimize second cuts. You can also save time by now discarding the tags and belly wool, and the neck wool if it is seedy. Shaking the fleece well after shearing eliminates most second cuts you do have, along with seeds, short leg wool, and other undesirable materials that would get imbedded in the fleece when it is rolled and tied.

## SHEEP BREEDS

There are other things that determine your personal choice of a fleece, and most of these are related to the breed of sheep. A spinner's preference is influenced by fineness, handle (feel), crimp, luster, and length of fiber. The choice of fiber length varies depending on the kind of yarn to be spun. For fine yarn, you can use a shorter wool than is convenient for spinning either a medium-heavy or a bulky yarn. Fineness is also related to the use of the yarn and to personal taste. The following chart shows a general classification of the major sheep breeds according to wool type.

| WOOL GRADES | | |
|---|---|---|
| American Merino | 64s to 80s | FINE WOOL BREEDS |
| Rambouillet | 58s to 70s | |
| Debouillet | 60s to 70s | |
| | | |
| Corriedale | 50s to 60s | CROSSBRED WOOL BREEDS |
| Columbia | 50s to 56s | |
| Montadale | 56s to 58s | |
| Polypay | 58s to 62s | |
| Romeldale | 58s to 60s | |
| Targhee | 58s to 60s | |
| Panama | 50s to 58s | |
| | | |
| Southdown | 56s to 60s | MEDIUM WOOL BREEDS |
| Clun Forest | 56s to 60s | |
| Finnsheep | 54s to 60s | |
| Hampshire | 49s to 56s | |
| Dorset | 48s to 56s | |
| Shropshire | 48s to 56s | |
| Suffolk | 48s to 56s | |
| Dorset | 48s to 56s | |
| Cheviot | 48s to 46s | |
| Oxford | 46s to 40s | |
| Ryeland | 48s to 56s | |
| Tunis | 58s to 56s | |
| | | |
| Romney | 46s to 50s | LONG WOOL BREEDS |
| Cotswold | 36s to 40s | |
| Lincoln | 36s to 46s | |
| Leicester | 40s to 48s | |
| | | |
| Karakul | Coarse outer coat and | COARSE WOOL BREEDS |
| Scottish Blackface | fine under coat | |

2. *"Vanilla," a Corriedale ewe. She was raised for spinning wool by the Oldebrook Spinnery.*

## WITHIN THE GRADES

Among the long wool breeds, the Romney is the most outstanding fleece for spinning as it is silky, lustrous, and not as coarse as the others. The Lincoln has longer wool and is strong, lustrous, long-wearing, and therefore good for use in rugs and outer sweaters. The Lincoln lambswool, sheared at six to eight months, is much softer and more versatile.

Of the medium wool breeds, Cheviot is easy to spin and a little scratchy, but ideal for men's tweedy, woven fabrics. Southdown, Suffolk, and Hampshire are short wools, but easy to spin into fine-weight yarn. The Dorset, Oxford, Tunis, and Clun Forest all have nice fleeces for spinning into a variety of yarn.

The crossbred wool breeds include the Corriedale, which is fine, long, silky, and one of the most versatile and useful of all wools. Ranking very close to it is the Columbia, and then the Panama.

The three breeds that have fine wool — the Merino, Rambouillet, and Debouillet — all spin into soft, wearable yarn, but they are difficult to card properly and are not easy to spin.

Almost any breed or wool type is ideal for some particular use. For example, the low quality wool from sheep of the Scottish coast is made into the durable Harris Tweeds.

## SKIRTING

The easiest way to sort a whole fleece is to lay it out in one piece like a rug, with the sheared side down. To remove the least desirable wool first, *skirt* it by removing a strip about three inches wide from around the edge of the fleece. This takes in many of the dirtiest tags, the back leg wool, belly wool, front leg wool, and neck wool. The rest of your fleece, if fairly clean, is usable wool. In some countries, a good handspinning fleece is expected to be not only skirted, but so clean and of such high quality that it can be easily spun without either washing or carding.

## SORTING

After skirting, the fleece can either be all blended together or sorted by quality and used accordingly. Black sheep fleeces, which are seldom a solid shade, can be sorted into several distinct shades to give you a variety of colors with which to work or they can be blended together to make a more heathery mixture.

In general, a skirted fleece can be separated into various groups:

Shoulder: good wool unless unduly contaminated with vegetable matter

Sides: good spinning wool

Back: good unless weakened by weathering

Flanks: good strong wool that is longer and often coarser than the rest of the fleece, but usually cleaner

The skirtings are:

Neck: shorter, and may be matted and filled with undesirable material

Legs: short and coarse

Belly: short, and may be matted or dirty; if not, it is probably usable

Tail: usually dirty, coarse, and short

## SORTING BY CRIMP

If you are working with fleeces of several breeds having different amounts of crimp, you may want to keep these separate during all the processes. Yarn is difficult to use in knitting if fibers with differing crimp are spun into the same yarn unless it is well blended in drum carding and is also mixed together prior to carding.

You can have difficulty with different elasticity in yarns, also, if you combine two that are spun from different kinds of wool (and crimp) in a warp or use them together in a knitted item. Yarn elasticity is a combination of several factors: the

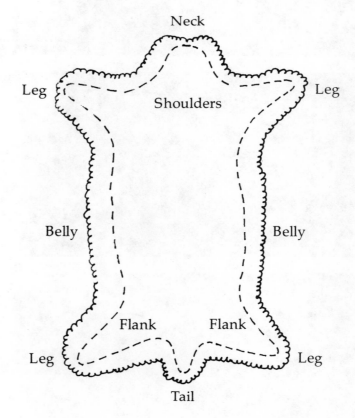

**3.** *Skirting. Removing wool at the dotted line eliminates leg, belly, neck, and tail wool (in approximately a three-inch strip).*

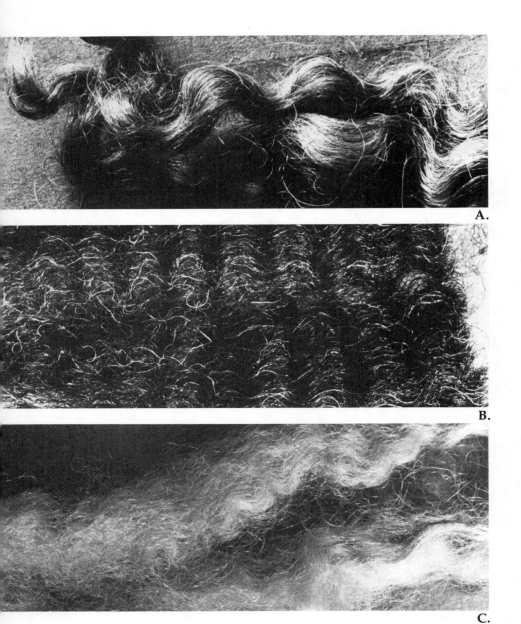

**A.**

**B.**

**C.**

amount of twist in the yarn, the crimp in the individual fibers, and the uniquely elastic property of all wools. The variations of crimp among the different breeds of sheep can be recognized most easily before any processing has begun.

## GREASE WOOL

Some people prefer spinning *in the grease* — that is, without washing the fleece. Aside from enjoying the feel of the grease wool, they find it easier to have it hang together as they spin. It also eliminates the need to wash the fleece before spinning. Washing only the finished yarn causes less mess than washing whole fleeces.

However, it is practical only if you begin with wool that is fairly clean. For spinning in the grease, select, if possible, a fleece that is not only clean but one that has been sheared early in the spring. It will ordinarily have less of the coagulation of yolk that is caused by warm weather.

## WASHED WOOL

As a rule, it is easier to control yarn size and irregularity with clean, fluffy wool. It is also possible to get more done in the long run. I have found that most unwashed fleeces have a certain gumminess that makes it difficult to card them into an even web, and thus harder to eliminate unwanted lumps in the yarn. Also, some parts of the fleece are dirtier and more weathered than others, as is, for example, the area right along the backbone. These dirtier and more weathered areas are particularly hard to spin unless they have been washed and oiled. Then, too, wool grease and *suint* (sweat) are not evenly distributed in all parts of a fleece, which makes your wool draw out

**4A–C.** *Examples of different crimp in three fleeces. It is not important to be able to identify the sheep breed,*
*but only to recognize the varying crimp. Loose wavy crimp produces yarn with less elasticity than does a tight crimp.*

unevenly when you are spinning it.

Most parts of an average fleece warrant at least a minimum of washing prior to carding and spinning, if you have the facilities. But if the fleece is to be dyed before spinning, you *must* wash it thoroughly before dyeing, because it will not take the dye properly if it is at all greasy. After dyeing, lubricate the dyed wool by adding water-soluble oil. Without lubrication, the dyed wool might be damaged in carding or become harsh and difficult to spin.

When yarn is to be spun first and then dyed, there is still a better penetration of the dye into the yarn if you wash the fleece well instead of just washing the yarn after it is spun. Otherwise, in places of even slight overtwist, the dirt and lanolin will not wash out of the yarn completely and these overtwisted areas will not dye evenly.

## PREPARING FOR WASHING

Any fleece that has many weed seeds benefits, after sorting, from being shaken against a wire mesh to remove as many seeds as possible. Some are almost too small to see. (To stretch your patience while doing this tedious work, place a piece of newspaper under the rack so you can hear the seeds continuing to hit the paper.) This same process can be repeated after the wool is washed and dried, or you can lay the wool out on the wire rack and beat it with a flexible stick. Later, teasing removes its share of any remaining undesirable vegetation.

## WOOL WASHING

Wool washing is called *scouring,* but this does not mean that it is rubbed, scrubbed, or twisted. It should be washed gently, by hand. The actual choice of a washing agent is not as important as the method used. Many spinners have their own choice of a certain soap, washing soda, Basic H, or Woolite.

If you use soap, it should be dissolved in hot water and then added to the wash water, as any undissolved soap particles are almost impossible to rinse from the wool. Washing in soap necessitates more than one rinse because it is difficult to wash out.

For many years, we have used a *mild* detergent and have been happy with the results. It does a very good job with only one wash water, and rinses out well enough with one rinsing, leaving no dulling film on the wool. It is also available at the grocery store. Since the spun yarn will be washed for preshrinking and our wovens are washed right after they come off the loom, the wool still has one or two washings ahead of it, so we keep this stage as simple as possible.

One way of washing two large fleeces (up to twenty pounds) is to fill a twenty-gallon laundry tub to within about four inches of the top with water as hot as is comfortable for your hands. Ten cups of mild detergent are dissolved in this before adding the wool. The fleeces should be pulled apart to shake out some of the seeds and dirt and to prevent matting of the shorn ends. Push as much wool into the wash water as the tub holds. It will seem to be solid wool with no water when you have as much wool in it as possible. Cover the tub and allow the wool to soak a few hours. Remove the wool while the water is still warm. With the tub packed so full, it will not cool as quickly as it would with less wool.

As you remove the wool, souse it up and down, squeezing it between your hands a few times. If you are washing white fleeces, you may want to give a little special attention to any stained portions at this time. Badly stained locks that are not markedly improved by the wash water can be laid aside or discarded.

## WATER EXTRACTION

One of our most valuable pieces of equipment is a centrifugal extractor. We use it in fleece, yarn, and yardage washing to remove the wash and rinse water. You have probably seen one at a coin laundry. It is a circular, steel contraption that opens at the top and removes excess water from the clothes before you put them in the dryer. The smaller extractor, still made for commercial use, is wonderful for wool. It is easy on the fibers and removes so much moisture that the wool dries quickly, all fluffed up. Since extractors are made for industrial use, they are sturdy and last almost indefinitely. If you are planning on doing a lot of spinning (and thus wool washing), you might consider one.

A similar way to remove wash water before rinsing is with your washing machine if it can be turned on only to the spin cycle. Place the squeezed wool in pillowcases (to protect your washing machine), put them in the washer, and start the spin cycle to whirl the water out of the wool.

Another way to remove sudsy water is with a wringer, either the hand-operated type, which can still be purchased as clamp-on equipment (see "Sources" chapter), or with an old wringer washing machine. The tub of such a machine, with the gyrator removed, can be used instead of the twenty-gallon laundry tub.

## RINSING

Having soaked the wool and extracted the wash water, you are now ready for rinsing. To avoid *felting*, caused by a drastic change in temperature, the rinse water should be about the temperature of the slightly cooled wash water.

You need not pack all your washed wool into one twenty-gallon rinse bath; it rinses better if you put only part of it in at once. Squeeze out a double handful at a time, removing water by either the pillowcase/spin cycle method or by a hand wringer. The advantage of spinning out the water is that the wool is easier to fluff up for drying, and drying time is shortened if the wool is well fluffed, separated, and free of matted clumps.

## DRYING

We use chicken-wire racks for outdoor drying in the favorable times of year, but keep permanent wire racks indoors for the rest of the year. These are arranged so that they can be filled at a convenient height and then raised up to the ceiling, where they are out of the way and get the warmest air in the room.

You can wind chicken wire between the horizontal bars of a folding, wooden clothes-drying rack to make mesh bins for drying wool in any convenient, warm place in the house. You can also cover the ends of each of these "bins" with wire to keep the wool from spilling out from the ends, and thus accommodate a larger load of wool for drying.

## TEASING OR PICKING

The purpose of teasing is to separate the fibers by opening up the tips to remove any vegetation, and to disentangle any matted locks so that they will not be damaged in carding. You may have some choice fleeces, or parts of fleeces, that need only a minimum of teasing after washing and drying. These can be kept separate from the others.

The most effective way of teasing the wool is to pull the fibers between the fingers of both hands with a quick picking motion, which causes the seeds literally to fly out. This need not be done roughly. Rough handling can damage the fibers and is not necessary since a gentle washing should not have matted them.

This is the time for making the initial mixing of various portions of a fleece, or blending of two fleeces, that you want to card together for a whole project. They need a lot better mixing when you use hand cards than when you use the drum carding machine. The layering of the drum carder makes a more uniform mix, and you can also card the fleeces twice for an even better blending.

There are a number of different systems or techniques of using hand cards. Any of these processes will be easier on both the fibers and the cards if the wool has been well teased in order to open up any matted or tangled portions. If the fleece has been washed, it can be sprayed with water-soluble oil (mixed with water to form an emulsion) either before or after teasing. The purpose of using this emulsion is to add both moisture and oil, which prevents damage during carding, as well as to lubricate fibers, which allows more control of yarn size and texture during spinning. If the fleece is to be carded and spun reasonably soon after drying, there is a water-soluble oil that can be added to the last rinse water (see "Sources" chapter). Very clean fleeces may not need washing before carding and spinning, and some extremely nice ones may not even need carding.

Ideally, more than one pair of cards should be used in preparing fibers thoroughly. Coarse cards, once called *breaker cards,* can be used first and then finer cards, once called *roll cards.* When using two sets of cards, the wool is removed from the coarse cards in a loose batt and not rolled. It is ordinarily removed from the fine-tooth cards in a roll called a *rolag.*

The following illustrations are of one standard method for using hand cards, but there are many variations of this. How well the wool must be carded depends both on the type of fleece and the evenness of the yarn that you wish to spin from it.

NONSTANDARD METHOD

An untraditional, short method of carding, often used with clean fleeces, is called the *fluffy cloud.* It is a cross between teasing and carding, and results in a fluffy mass of semicarded wool. You start it by filling the lower card with a thin layer of wool, just as in the usual method.

2

## Hand Carding

**5.** *Children carding wool*

**6.** *Standard method*
*Step 1. Hold the bottom card in your left hand and the wool in your right hand. Draw the wool down across the bottom card so that it pulls fibers from your hand and holds them on the teeth of the card. The card should be filled evenly with a thin layer of wool.*

*Step 2. With one card in each hand and the handles pointing in opposite directions, prepare to make the first stroke of the top card over the bottom card.*

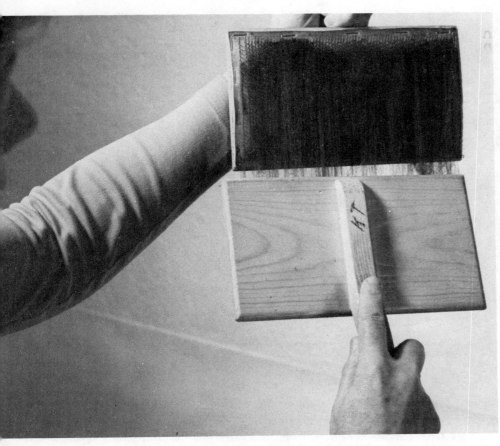

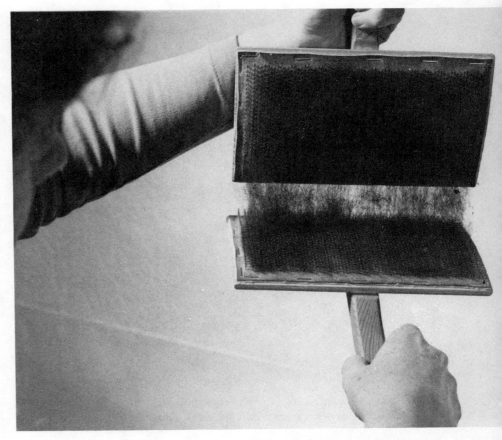

Step 3. In the first stroke, draw the top card across the bottom card. The teeth of the two cards should not touch as they are stroked across.
Repeat this stroke several times, but not beyond the stage where you are no longer transferring fibers to the top card.

Step 4. Now, transfer the wool back to the original position on the bottom card. The handles should be pointing in the same direction in this action.
Then, repeat strokes of step 3.

Step 5. Remove the carded wool with both handles pointing toward you. A looser, little batt of wool is obtained by making one stroke of the upper card; a more compact, whole roll is formed if several short strokes are used. Some spinners remove the wool with one forward stroke and two short, backward strokes.

Step 5*. Another way to remove the wool is by having only the teeth on the lower edge of the top card lifting the fibers from the bottom card.

Step 6. Here, wool is rolled lightly for ease in spinning. On very large hand cards, you can make two or three rolls from one carding.

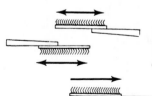

Step 6*. You can roll wool between the backs of the cards for a more compact roll, or roll it across one card with your fingers to consolidate the roll.

**7.** *Nonstandard (fluffy cloud) method*
*Step 1. For the first stroke of the card, lightly draw the upper card across the lower card, but with a lifting motion, moving the card in a semicircle rather than in straight strokes.*

*Step 2. This is the second stroke, also a lifting motion. The wool is now about half carded.*

*Step 3. The wool is completely carded.*     *Step 4. The wool is removed.*

## FLICK OR FLICKER

This is a single, small card with a carding surface about two inches by four inches and a handle about six inches long. (There are some made with short handles, but they are not as easy to use because your hand slips off.) These are not used in pairs, and are a less expensive and more convenient alternative to hand card pairs.

This kind of card provides a way of teasing, separating, and fluffing the wool without greatly disturbing the general parallel arrangement of the fibers. It is not drawn *through* the wool as you do hand cards and so it is especially convenient with fleeces of a longer staple, which are not otherwise easily carded.

If you want to spin a particularly nice fleece in the grease, this is a good way to prepare it, since using your drum carder with greasy fleece leaves a coating on it that is almost impossible to remove. The small area of the flick carding surface is much easier to clean; or you can reserve one flick for use only with grease wool.

To use a flicker, hold a fairly good size lock of wool in one hand and "flick" at it, using a fast series of downward strokes, moving your hand up and down quickly from the wrist. It is most efficient when the wool is held against a board or heavy piece of leather, or you can just hold the wool against an *old* towel on your lap. When one end of the lock is flicked and fluffy, with fibers separated and vegetable matter removed, turn the wool, hold it by the other end, and repeat the operation.

You can spin wool directly from this preparation. Flicked locks laid crisscross in a basket are easily removed for spinning. They can be attenuated into a strip, or just folded over your

**8.** *Flick carder and board*

leader yarn and spun from the center of the fold. I have found that flicked wool works quite well on the great wheel, which normally requires better-prepared wool than does other spinning.

Use of the flick, instead of normal teasing, is one way to ready wool for the drum carder when you want a semiworsted carding that leaves the fibers mainly parallel.

### WORSTED FLICKER

This single card has about a three and one-half by two-inch combing surface, and a short, three and one-half inch handle that is set at a right angle to the base. Its carding teeth are coarse.

To use it as a comb for worsted spinning, hold the flicker in one hand, facing upward, and "flick" a lock of wool onto it to comb it out. Turn the lock and repeat the process on the other end. The short fibers are removed by the flicker, and can be saved for another use. The lock of fleece that is left in your hand is now prepared for spinning a worsted yarn in which all the fibers lie parallel to each other.

### MAKING HAND CARDS

You can make hand cards for somewhat less than you can purchase them, but the savings is not substantial because of the cost of the carding material.

The single flick carder and the worsted flicker both require less card clothing than do hand card pairs, and provide more savings for the effort. The dimensions shown in the drawings are typical.

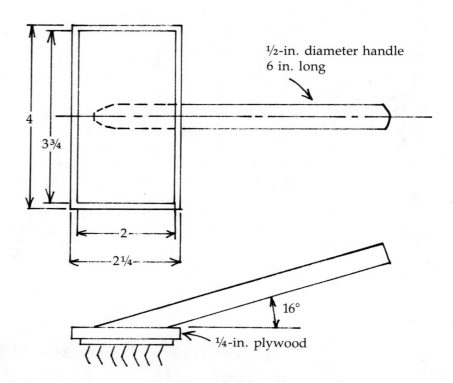

½-in. diameter handle
6 in. long

4

3¾

2

2¼

16°

¼-in. plywood

**9.** *Flicker*
*Note: Dimensions are in inches except where marked.*

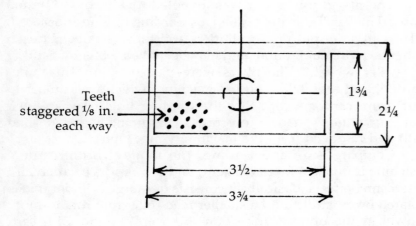

Teeth
staggered ⅛ in.
each way

1¾

2¼

3½

3¾

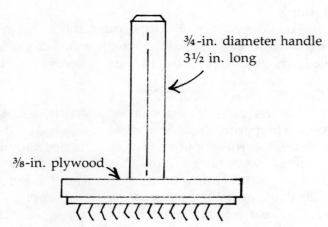

¾-in. diameter handle
3½ in. long

⅜-in. plywood

**10.** *Worsted flicker*

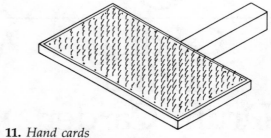

**11.** *Hand cards*

**A.** *Tack on card clothing;*
*space tacks three-fourths inch apart (bottom view).*

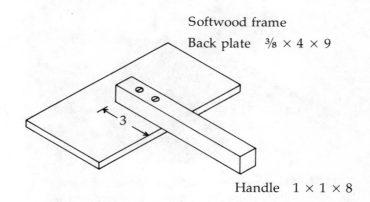

Softwood frame

Back plate   ⅜ × 4 × 9

3

Handle   1 × 1 × 8

**B.** *Hand card (make 2)*

# 3
# Carding with a Drum Carder

**12.** *The Spinning Wheel Factory's "Mark IV" carder has a heavy duty chain drive, fine-toothed carding cloth, zinc bearings that can be oiled, adjustable action for light or heavy carding, and kiln-dried wood.*

The first drum carder was invented in 1748 by a London shroud maker. The patent called it a Carding Engine and stated: "The cards are put upon cylinders and these act against each other by a circular motion, and may be moved either by hand or by water wheel." The fibers were placed on the machine, carded, and then taken off the machine, which was similar to our drum carder except that the Carding Engine was wider. Later inventions made the process continual, with wool fed into and removed from the machinery mechanically.

Compared to hand carding, the modern drum carding machine is quicker, more efficient, and can produce varied and interesting effects. Basically, it consists of a large cylinder that is rotated by a handle, and a smaller feed roller that rotates more slowly in the opposite direction. Both are wound with card clothing.

To make your own drum carder, follow the building plans provided at the end of this chapter or purchase one of the ready-made carders listed in the "Sources" chapter.

TEASING FOR CARDING

*Teasing,* or picking the wool apart, is necessary whether you are preparing the wool for use with hand cards or the drum carder. This process pulls apart both the tips and the cut ends of the fibers, separating them so they are not broken in carding. Opening matted areas permits removal of weed seeds, straw, and other vegetable matter either by hand or by shaking the wool. I like to tease the wool over a newspaper, not for tidiness, but so that the sound of the small particles hitting the paper gives me patience to keep at it. Seeds you can barely see still make noise against the paper. Shaking the wool against a wire frame also helps remove fine seeds and sand, and the wire mesh prevents the wool from dropping into the accumulation of dirt.

At this stage, unwashed wool is harder to work with than washed wool. More foreign matter drops out of washed wool because there is less grease to which the debris may stick. And no matter how clean the unwashed wool, using it on the drum carder will leave a grease residue on the carding cloth that is difficult to remove.

## OILING THE WOOL

After the fleece is washed, it benefits from the addition of water-soluble oil (see "Sources" chapter), diluted with as much as four parts water, to form an emulsion. For best mixing, add the water to the oil. It takes only a small amount of oil to facilitate both carding and spinning, and it washes out easily from the finished yarn.

For maximum ease in carding and minimum strain on fibers, spray the wool lightly with the emulsion the day *before* carding, then wrap it (preferably in an old wool blanket), and keep it in a warm place until the fibers are uniformly penetrated. Research has produced impressive statistics on the rapid increase of wool plasticity with such a rise in temperature and humid conditions. (Even another resting period, which can be compared to the resting of fabric after the stress of weaving, can be helpful to the fibers after carding.)

When the wool is unwrapped, the fibers will shine with their coating of oil, and then a light teasing will ready them for carding. More wool than you plan to use in the immediate future should not be oiled at one time. Oiling has its most beneficial effect on the wool if done within a few days prior to carding and spinning.

## ADJUSTING THE DRUM CARDER

The efficiency of the drum carding machine depends on its being in good working condition. Keep in mind the following points:

1. The teeth of the smallest carding roller should just barely touch the carding pan from which the wool is

**13.** *The Hedgehog carder has a hardwood main frame, an easily adjustable drum, one central screw, and either fine or coarse card clothing. Replacement drums are available if the clothing is changed.*

fed into the carder. If there is not a slight noise made from the touching of the pins against the pan, then the pan should be removed and its end adjusted upward so there is some slight touching.

2. The teeth of the two carding rollers, on the other hand, must *not* touch each other. Here the adjustment can be made by loosening the bolts controlling the large cylinder and tightening or loosening the side screws or other mechanisms that adjust its location. The closeness can vary from one sixty-fourth to one sixteenth of an inch depending on the fiber being used, but for average conditions one thirty-second of an inch is suitable. The distance can best be determined by the use of a feeler gauge, purchased from a hardware store or the Sears Roebuck catalog, inserted between the cylinders. Being an exact distance apart, however, is not so important as being an *equal* distance apart. An ordinary table knife can be used to make sure there is uniform spacing between the rollers.

3. The belt must be tight enough to get good traction if you are using a belt-type model instead of a gear-sprocket model. Most carders have a wing-nut-and-bolt adjustment for tension on the drive belt.

4. Places that need oiling should be oiled frequently. Dirt can clog the oil holes that lubricate the large drum, so it is a good practice to clean them periodically, as well as to oil them.

5. The carder should be kept in a dry place to prevent the carding teeth from rusting.

## DOUBLE CARDING

Wool can be *double carded;* that is, carded once, removed from the large drum, and recarded. When deciding whether or not to double card, consider the condition of the fleece, the thoroughness of the teasing, the length of the fiber, and whether two wool types are being combined to obtain a particular blend for spinning. There is also the question of what degree of carding is necessary to allow spinning of the type of yarn planned. Carding twice gives a more thorough preparation of the wool, and allows better control over the yarn when it is spun.

For the recarding, you can change the ratio between the speeds of the two rollers to a higher ratio by using a larger pulley on the small cylinder.

## FEEDING IN THE WOOL

Place the well-teased fibers on the feed pan of the carder, covering it with only a thin layer so that too much is not drawn in at one time. When you turn the crank, the fibers are drawn in by the smaller roller (called the *taker-in* on old carding machines and the *licker-in* on modern industrial ones) and fed onto the large drum.

With correct adjustment of the machine, proper teasing, and the right amount of wool fed into it, there will be little piling up of fibers on the smallest roller. When you are working with short wool, placing a half-inch steel rod that is the width of the drums in the angle between the drums can help keep the wool from picking up around the small roller. (This procedure is not too helpful with long wool, however.) Any tendency of the wool catching on the small roller can be corrected by using an ice pick or strong knitting needle to flip up fibers from the small roller and add them to those still being carded.

The wool that accumulates around the large cylinder forms the batt, and the amount of wool that can be carded into one batt is limited by the length of the carding teeth on the drum. You get better carding results, and the process actually goes faster, if you card thinner batts and remove them more often.

## REMOVING THE BATT

The layer of carded fibers (called a *batt, lap,* or *web*) is removed from the large drum by lifting it up with an ice pick or knitting needle so that it separates across the width of the large cylinder. On some carding machines, the carding teeth are set in a solid blanket of leather that is wrapped around the cylinder. On these machines, pry the batt up at the juncture of the ends of the carding cloth, which forms a bare strip across the drum. On models that have *card fillet* (a long strip of card clothing encircling the drum), there is no special place to separate the wool.

To remove the carded batt after you have pulled it apart, slowly rotate the handle of the carder counterclockwise while peeling off the wool. It is important that it not be cut, for cutting gives you short fibers at both ends of the batt, which are crucial places for joining while spinning.

## CARDING MACHINE DOFFER NET

Shawn Higgins of Portland, Oregon, has devised a *doffer net* that can be adapted to any make of drum carding machine. It is a netting that fits over the large roller and is held in place by rods fastened to each end of the netting. When the carded batt is ready to be removed, one of the end rods can be lifted up. As the drum is reversed, the net neatly lifts off the carded batt.

## MOTOR-DRIVEN CARDER

Drum carders lend themselves to motorization as long as they can be kept at a slow speed (60 to 80 rpm). The advantage of the motor is not that the carder rotates faster, but that its operator can use both hands to tease the wool and feed it in.

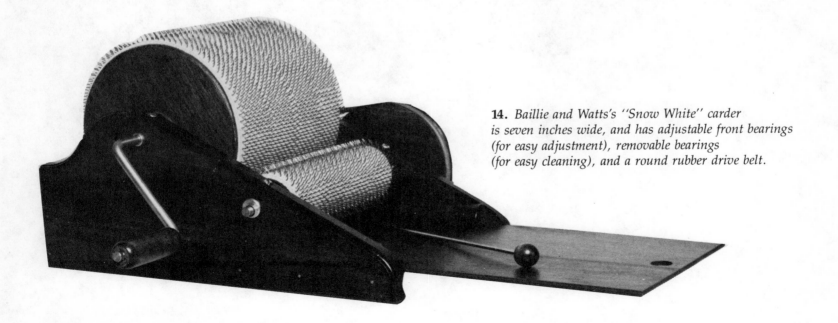

**14.** *Baillie and Watts's "Snow White" carder is seven inches wide, and has adjustable front bearings (for easy adjustment), removable bearings (for easy cleaning), and a round rubber drive belt.*

 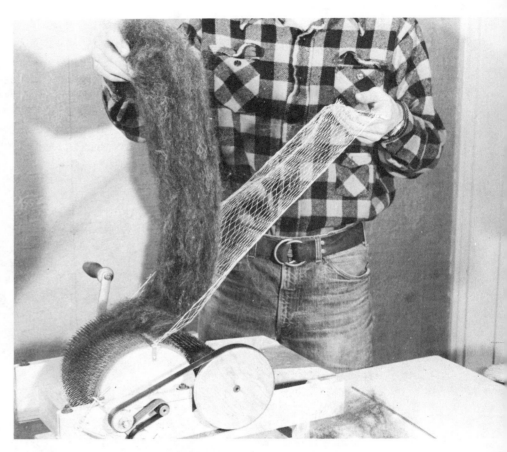

**15.** *Doffer net.* **A.** *Applying net with a brush (prior to carding)*     **B.** *Using net to peel off the batt*

## ARRANGING WOOL FOR SPINNING

There are several methods of attenuating or dividing the fiber web after it is removed from the carding drum. The following are the most common:

**Method 1:** Draw it out, thin it, and lengthen it carefully by hand until it is triple its original length and consequently only one third as wide. Repeat this process to make a roving that is six times as long and one sixth as wide as it was originally. Preparing it this way requires fewer joinings and less drawing out during spinning, thus making it ideal for beginners.

**Method 2:** This consists of dividing the web lengthwise into a number of narrow strips. Its disadvantage is in the number of joinings it requires in spinning which, for the inexperienced spinner, may result in the same number of lumps or weak spots in the yarn. The joining is made easier for beginners if each new strip is lapped against the last strip while it still has a sizeable portion unspun. With more practice, very little of the unspun wool need be left for joining. Because of the speed and simplicity of tearing strips, this method is a useful way to divide several carded webs for special recarding or spinning effects.

**Method 3:** This is done by dividing the web into one long strip by *Z-shaping* it, back and forth, dividing not quite to the end each time, and making it into a single long roving. This is obviously fast, but the strip is a bit harder for beginners to spin than the one in Method 1, for it requires a fast hand manipulation of fibers in action when passing the turning-back places of the Z strip. If spun well, you cannot detect the places where the Z strip was turned back.

**Method 4:** Cross sections of the batt can be torn off for a handful of spinning fibers. This is particularly useful when a long strip of carded fibers is inconvenient, such

**16.** *Wool batt*

**A.** *Shape of wool batt when just removed from drum of carder*

**B.** *Shape of batt made into Z strip, divided for spinning*

as in spinning on the great wheel (see "Learning on the Great Wheel" chapter).

## CARDING EFFECTS

By using the drum carder, you can create many special effects that are difficult or impossible to do with hand cards. The short snips, those second cuts that occur in poor shearing, can be saved and used for unusual, nubby yarn textures. For example, you can use white wool snips in white wool or as contrasting nubs in dark wool, or you can dye the short snips and card them with longer fibers to make a tweedy dyed yarn. Belly wool or skirtings can be utilized this way.

The machine is also ideal for blending two or more types of fibers for better spinning results, such as by adding a portion of lambswool to a crisper wool to produce a softer yarn. Or you can use the carder for blending two shades of wool to produce a third shade. Some of our most interesting black sheep shades are made this way. It permits the combining of separate shades without blending them in order to make variegated tweeds.

## VARIEGATED EFFECTS

There are two distinct methods for obtaining random but controlled variegations. Each way uses two or more colors, either vegetable-dyed or natural black sheep shades, or both. For better results, card each color once prior to using either of these methods. The amount of precarding to be done can be decided by considering the degree of irregularity in texture that is intended in the finished yarn.

**Tandem Method:** Alternately feed a quantity of each fiber color, one after the other, into the carder. If you want regularity within the variations, control the quantities (weight) of each color being alternated.

**Team Method:** Feed the fibers into the carder at the same time with the two colors side-by-side, half on the left side and half on the right side. Colors can be re-

versed midway through the carding of this web. When removed, either tear it in strips for spinning or fold it over and attenuate it to make another type of variegated yarn.

When removed, the batts or webs done in these two ways will differ considerably. Even within each method, there are variations. With the tandem, for instance, you could get four different effects in carding up a combination of only two colors. Taking one and one-half ounces of white and one and one-half ounces of brown, you could:

1. Alternate one-half ounce of brown, then one-half ounce of white, and so on to make a mottled tweedy yarn.
2. Layer one and one-half ounces of brown, then one and one-half ounces of white to make a variegated yarn that shows each color equally.
3. Layer three-fourths ounce of brown, one and one-half ounces of white, and three-fourths ounce of brown to make a variegated yarn that is predominantly brown.
4. Layer three-fourths ounce of white, one and one-half ounces of brown, and three-fourths ounce of white to make a yarn that shows more of the white.

Also, the finished effect of both the tandem and team methods can be varied by the way you divide the batts for spinning, and draw out and manipulate the wool during spinning.

## DRUM CARDING MACHINE PLANS

This portable carding machine should be clamped or fastened down securely to a bench or a table when used. It is intended to be turned by hand but can be motorized, using a ¼ to ⅓ hp motor (1750 rpm) geared down to 60 to 80 rpm. The reason for using the motor is not to speed up the process, but to leave the operator with both hands free to tease the wool and place it on the feed tray. The slow speed of the machine is important in order to avoid damaging both the wool and the card clothing. It is composed of 3 subassemblies:

1. Frame, outlet tray, and bearing supports
2. Large and small diameter carding drums covered with card clothing (fillet or sheet)
3. Adjustment bolts, drive mechanism, and general assembly

## LIST OF MATERIALS

Soft wood
Metal rods
Bolts and nuts: ¼ in.
Tacks
Flat head wood screws
Sheet metal: 16 gauge
Card clothing
Wooden cylinders

The exact amounts and sizes of each are not mentioned to allow for substitutions, and it is best to use what is available locally. You need different quantities of the various materials if you decide to make a carder of double width or double all the dimensions. There is also some advantage to a narrower carder that makes a narrower strip of carded wool. In this instance, it might be more efficient not just to make it narrower, but to double the diameter of the drums in order to make a narrow and much longer strip of carded wool.

Card clothing used may be either card fillet or card sheet. The fillet, available by the foot from a number of sources (see "Sources" chapter) comes in both a 1½-in. and 2-in. width, depending on the fineness or coarseness desired. The amount needed to cover the drums (allowing for tapered lap at both sides of the drum) is different depending on the width. Card sheet is also available in an 8-in. width, so for the 8-in. wide

drum, you need only a single strip of this width for the circumference of each wooden drum.

Some card fillet can be ordered either "ground" or "unground," and unless you are sure of the quality of this sharpening or grinding, it might be safer to purchase the unground. We know of one instance in which a homemade carder used ground

**17.** *The Cascade carder has a cherry wood base with dovetail joints, rubber belt drive, and commercial card fillet on the drums.*

fillet in which the grinding had left almost invisible burrs at the edge of each wire, making it difficult to strip the wool off cleanly after it was carded.

### Sheet metal outlet tray

The sheet metal outlet tray is provided with 2 tabs, which are to be fitted between the bearing supports for the small carding drum and the frame. The curved portion fits under and around the lower portion of the small carding wheel. Note that this curved portion should not touch either carding drum. Some commercially made drum carding machines do not have a bent sheet metal outlet tray, so study the carder photos if you do not want to bother with forming a bent metal tray.

### Frame

The frame is merely a rectangle, as shown. Drill the holes as straight as possible where indicated.

### Outlet tray

The outlet tray is made of 12- to 16-gauge sheet metal and is cut to the dimensions shown. The lower diagram shows where and by how much the tray is bent to shape. The two ⅛-in. diameter holes are for subsequent mounting to the frame. Bevel the corners 45° and to about ⅜ in. across the face of the bevel.

### Bearing supports

Of the 2 sets of hardwood bearing supports, the larger is slotted to permit adjustment of the gap between larger and smaller carding drums. If you have the material handy, the bearing supports can be made more durable by providing bushings for the ⅜-in. and ⅝-in. shaft holes. Be sure to fit the bushing (brass tube, G.I. pipe section, or other) tightly into the holes in the bearing supports.

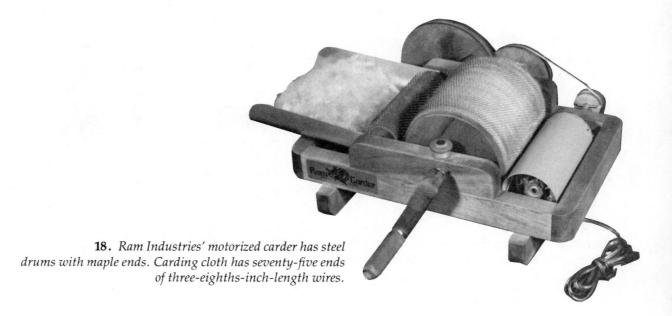

**18.** *Ram Industries' motorized carder has steel drums with maple ends. Carding cloth has seventy-five ends of three-eighths-inch-length wires.*

### Large and small carding drums

These are softwood cylinders of the radii indicated. The ¼-in. hole shown is for securing the wood cylinder to the wheel shaft. Tap in a nail of suitable length to permit a secure anchor in the cylinder. Then wrap each cylinder with card fillet strips tapered at the beginning and end, to fully cover the cylinders with 1½-in. or 2-in. wide fillet, or with 8-in. wide card sheet. Tack the fillet or sheet in place with ¾-in. to 1-in. nails. Note: The metal shafts for the 2 wheels are of different lengths and diameters, and the larger shaft should be long enough to permit you to form a crank at one end, as shown.

### Card clothing, sheet or fillet

If you use 8-in. wide card sheet, you need about a 21.98-in. length to go around the large drum, and a 6.28-in. length to go around the smaller drum. The cut ends butt and are tacked across those edges, as well as around the drum.

If you are using 1½-in. or 2-in. wide card fillet and are measuring the length needed to wind around each drum until each is covered with the fillet, add 1 extra diameter of it. This will allow for the long taper that you should have at the beginning and end of the spiral of card fillet. It must be stretched taut, and tacked around both outside edges. With a 2-in. width, allow about 9 ft. of fillet for the large drum and about 2½ ft. for the small drum. That leaves enough fillet for the long, tapered ends.

### Drive mechanism, adjustment bolts, and final assembly

The drive mechanism of the assembly is attached to the longer, straight protrusion of both carding wheel shafts. Note the direction of the teeth. Several variations of the drive mechanisms can be used.

The ratio between the pulleys is 1 to 6, with the large carding

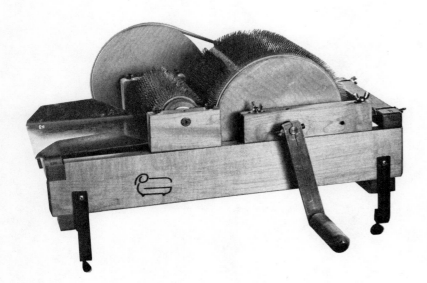

**19.** *Patrick Green's heavy-duty carder has a maple frame and drums laminated from solid wood, and is available with fine, medium, or coarse carding cloth as well as a swift-change feature. Available with teeth at thirty, seventy-five, or ninety-six per square inch.*

drum turning 6 times for every 1 revolution of the small carding drum. The carding drums are adjusted by 2 brackets. One way of making the adjustment bolt is to flatten the head of a ¼-in. bolt, bend it off to 1 side, and drill the flattened head out for the result shown. Bolts are mounted with 1-in. wood screws.

### Chain drive mechanism details

Attach the sprockets to the shaft by any means available. Weld the sprockets directly to the shaft, or bolt the sprockets to a mounting collar (hardwood or metal), which can be fixed to the shaft in a manner similar to the method used for fixing the wood cylinders to their shafts (fig. 20D).

If a standard large bicycle sprocket is used for the small wheel, it may be necessary to make your own small sprocket for the large drum. To do this, first determine the required diameter of the smaller sprocket by dividing the diameter of the larger sprocket by 6. Bear in mind that the spacing of the teeth will have to be the same on both sprockets. If this spacing cannot be maintained with the 1 to 6 ratio, it will be necessary to increase or

**20.** *Drum carder. The basic plans, with some alterations, originated with VITA (Volunteers in Technical Assistance) at 3706 Rhode Island Avenue, Mt. Rainier, MD 20822.*

*Note: Dimensions are in inches except where marked.*

**A.** *Frame (top view)*

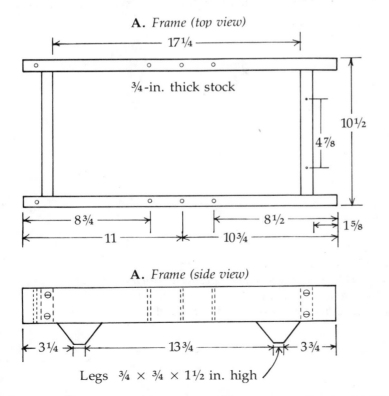

**A.** *Frame (side view)*

Legs ¾ × ¾ × 1½ in. high

**B.** *Outlet tray (top view)*

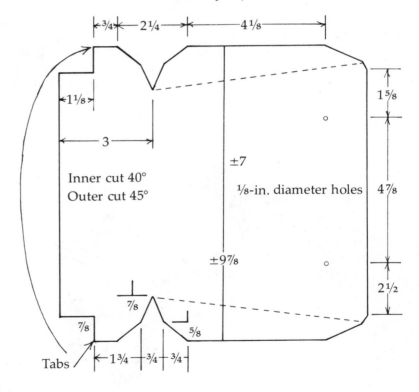

**B.** *Outlet tray (side view)*

This face turned 90° along dotted line

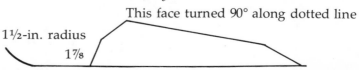

decrease the diameter of the smaller sprocket. Increasing or decreasing the diameter by 1 unit increases or decreases the circumference by 3.14 units. The best way to make such a sprocket is to draw the full-size sprocket on paper with a compass. Cut out the finished drawing and fix it onto the ⅛-in. thick metal plate. Then cut the form out of metal. Finish the task by filing the teeth to the shape of those on the large spocket.

The final step is to attach a bicycle chain of suitable length.

## OPERATION AND MAINTENANCE

Wool should be washed and sprayed with water-soluble spinning oil, for best results (see "Sources" chapter). After careful teasing, lay it on the outlet tray and feed it into the carder while cranking the large wheel clockwise. Tangled or matted wool must not be put into the carder, as this bends the wires or loosens them so that the carding material becomes damaged and does not function properly. Do not feed in too much at a time,

and do not allow too much to build up on the large cylinder at once. It is better to remove thinner batts than to allow them to become so thick that portions of the wool are not sufficiently carded. Read the instructions for using the machine and removing the carded batt that are provided in this chapter.

After the carding machine is used for some time, it may be necessary to move the drums a little closer together. The carding wires of the large drum and the small drum should *not* touch, but just exactly how close you want them depends on the type of wool you use most of the time.

To move the drums closer after a period of use, notice the two small slots on each side. Loosen the nuts in these slots and slide the big drum closer by adjusting the adjustment bolts, which are located on each side near the front of the carder. These bolts each have two nuts that can be tightened.

Lubricating with a heavy oil and cleaning wool fibers from the bearings is all that should ordinarily be needed to maintain the machine.

**C.** *Small bearing support*

**C.** *Large bearing support*

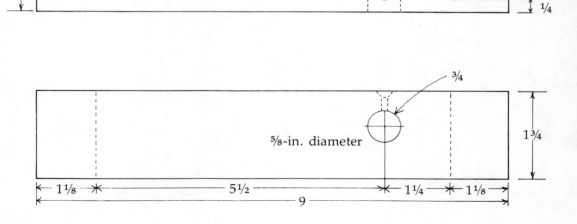

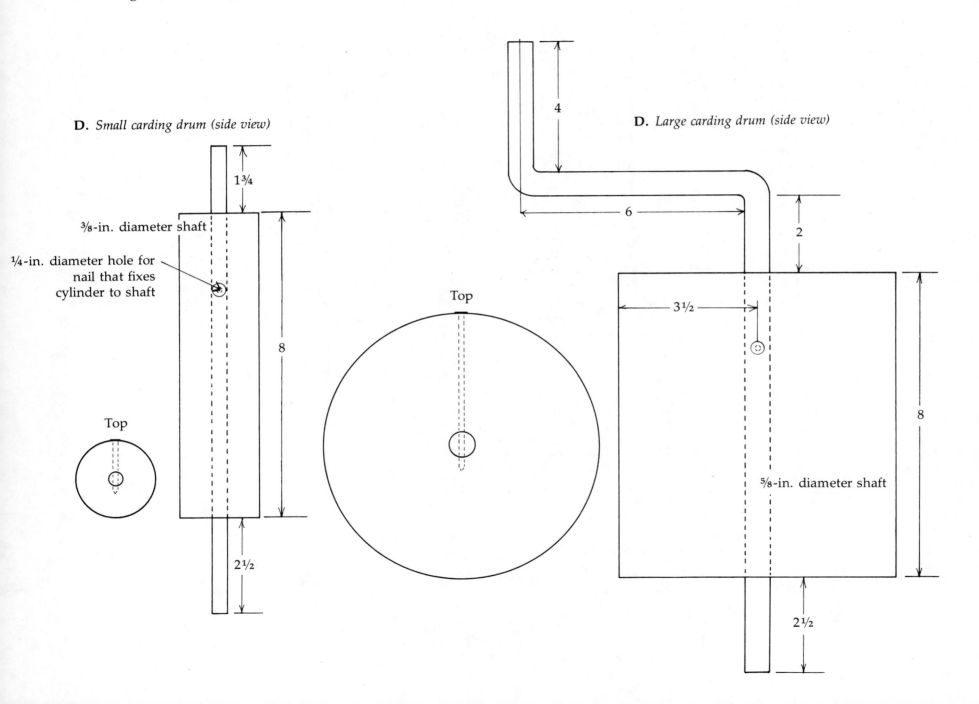

**D.** *Small carding drum (side view)*

**D.** *Large carding drum (side view)*

1¾

⅜-in. diameter shaft

¼-in. diameter hole for
nail that fixes
cylinder to shaft

8

Top

2½

Top

4

6

2

3½

8

⅝-in. diameter shaft

2½

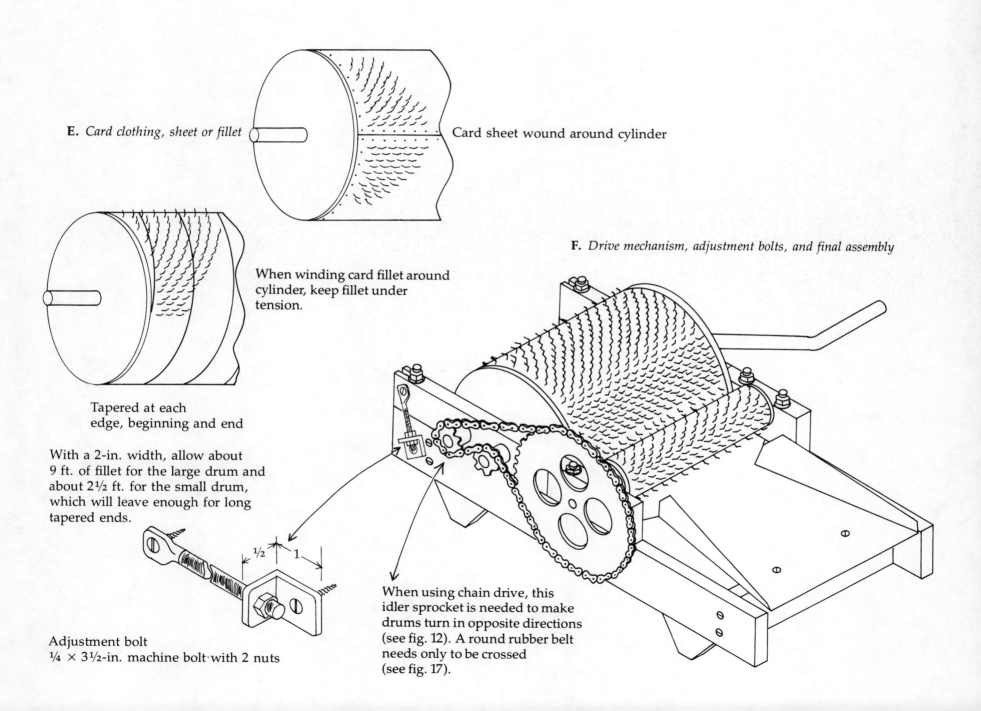

**E.** *Card clothing, sheet or fillet*

Card sheet wound around cylinder

When winding card fillet around cylinder, keep fillet under tension.

Tapered at each edge, beginning and end

With a 2-in. width, allow about 9 ft. of fillet for the large drum and about 2½ ft. for the small drum, which will leave enough for long tapered ends.

½   1

Adjustment bolt
¼ × 3½-in. machine bolt·with 2 nuts

**F.** *Drive mechanism, adjustment bolts, and final assembly*

When using chain drive, this idler sprocket is needed to make drums turn in opposite directions (see fig. 12). A round rubber belt needs only to be crossed (see fig. 17).

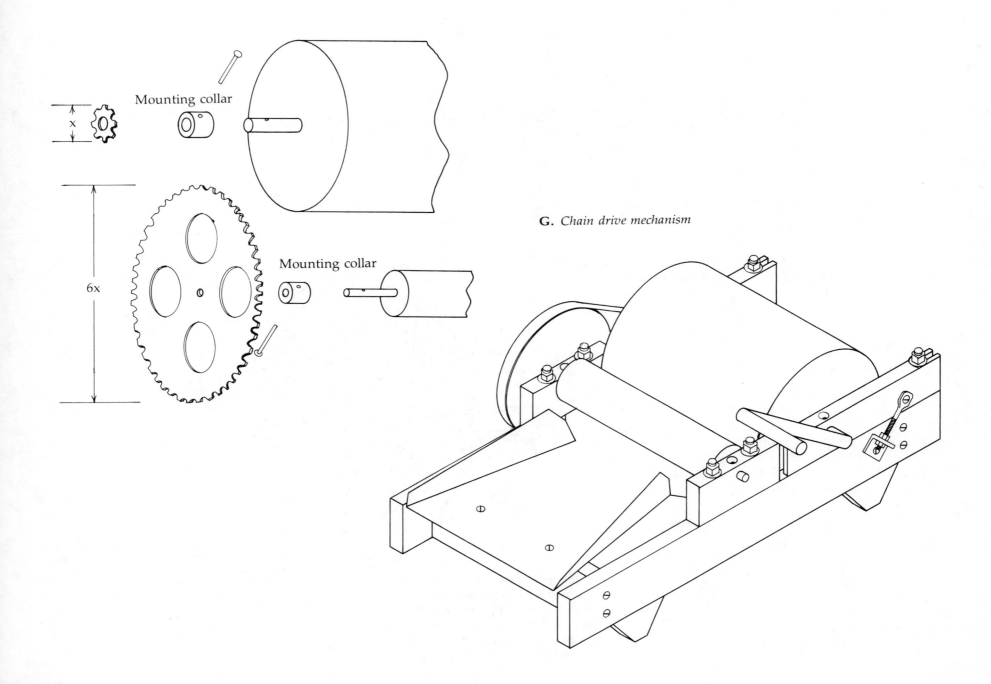

Mounting collar

x

6x

Mounting collar

**G.** *Chain drive mechanism*

## WHEEL PERFORMANCE AND STYLE

Beginners want some assurance of a wheel's efficiency so they can be confident that any trouble they have is not the fault of the wheel. Understanding the advantages and disadvantages of how different wheels operate will help them decide which wheel is best suited to their needs.

Some things about spinning wheels are mainly a matter of taste, such as the *style* of the framework that holds the working parts. There are four-legged "chair" wheels, upright castle wheels, three-legged Saxon or colonial wheels, and many newer pedestal wheels. The choice of style, as long as the wheel has stability, balance, and efficiency, is influenced by personal preference and often by price.

## PROPER MOVEMENT OF SEPARATE PARTS

Regardless of the style, the working parts should be considered carefully. Certain parts must move freely:

1. The spool should move freely on the spindle when the belt (or brake) is removed.
2. The flyer should rotate easily in its maiden bearings.
3. The treadle should move easily (and without undue noise) in its bearings or on its pivot.
4. The drive wheel should rotate easily and smoothly and be well balanced.

## FLYER ASSEMBLY

This is the "heart" of the spinning wheel and if it does not work efficiently, you will not be happy with your wheel. With the drive belt disengaged, test to determine if the flyer moves easily in its bearings and if the bobbin moves freely on its spindle. Some bobbins turn freely enough for spinning fine yarn, but not easily enough, with the belt removed, to wind off this fine yarn into a skein without breaking it. With a new wheel,

# 4
# Spinning Wheel Operation

**21.** *Spinning wheel*

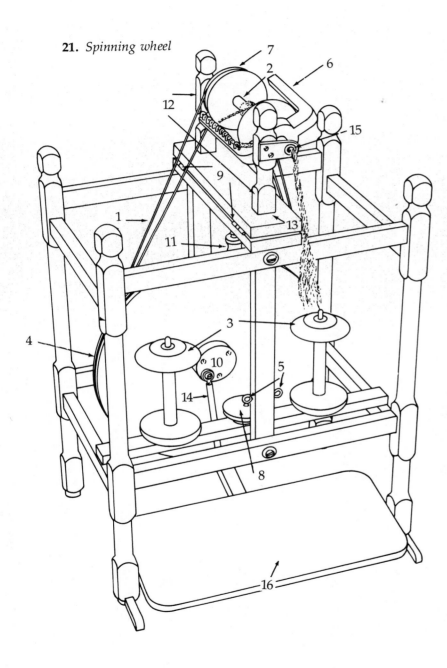

this is a serious defect; with an old wheel, it probably means that the shaft and bobbin bearings need cleaning and lubrication.

If the fork has hooks on only one arm, the weight of the hooks should have some compensation, for good balance, in the design of the other flyer arm. This can mean slightly more thickness in the arm without the hooks or the insertion of a metal slug, with the same weight as the hooks, into the arm without the hooks.

## YARN CAPACITY

The length and depth of the bobbin, the diameter of the bobbin's core, and the width of the fork are what limit the yarn capacity or the size of the skein that can be spun. If your flyer has a large orifice, then you should expect it to have a generous yarn capacity. This means having at least four and one-half inches in fork width and a bobbin length of at least four and one-half

### PARTS OF A SPINNING WHEEL

1. *Drive belt – doubled*
2. *Bobbin – in use on spindle*
3. *Extra bobbins*
4. *Drive wheel*
5. *Eyelets – carry yarn ends for plying*
6. *Flyer – with hooks*
7. *Large flyer whorl – for heavy yarn with looser twist*
8. *Small flyer whorl – for fine yarn with tighter twist*
9. *Hinges – spinning head folds down inside frame*
10. *Hub – with 2 ball bearings on axle*
11. *Knob on screw – adjusts belt tension*
12. *Maidens – with leathers*
13. *Mother-of-all*
14. *Pitman – with ball and socket bearings on each end*
15. *Spindle – with orifice*
16. *Double-action treadle – for both feet*

inches. Anything smaller than this should be considered as suitable primarily for fine-weight yarns regardless of the orifice size.

A wide-angle flyer (fig. 23) allows the bobbin to be filled to a greater than normal capacity by using small dowels stuck in three or four places at the end of the filled bobbin. The "Thumbelina" flyer (fig. 54) tapers from three and one-eighth inches to five and one-half inches.

## FLYER HOOKS

The hooks used on the spinning fork should be well placed to allow the bobbin to be evenly filled, and not so close to the end of the bobbin that they encourage the yarn to slip off and wind around the spindle. They should be smooth so they do not catch on the fibers and their size should be matched to the size of the yarn that can be spun with the orifice size. Some wheels, such as the Columbine, have small, closely spaced hooks on one arm for fine yarn, and larger, more widely spaced hooks on the other arm for heavy yarn. Flyers built by Alden Amos have hooks on each arm, staggered for efficient filling of the bobbin.

## BOBBIN BEARINGS

The full length of the bobbin core should not ride on the flyer spindle. Bearings are needed in each end, not just to prevent wear on the bobbin, but to eliminate surface friction. With a close-fitting bobbin, this surface drag is particularly noticeable when winding off fine yarn. It does not allow the bobbin to unwind as freely as it should, even though the fit of the bobbin

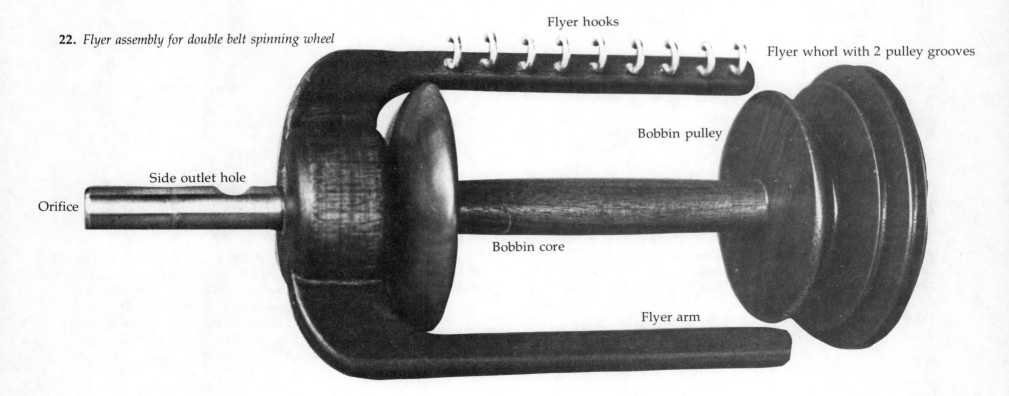

**22.** *Flyer assembly for double belt spinning wheel*

Flyer hooks

Flyer whorl with 2 pulley grooves

Bobbin pulley

Side outlet hole

Orifice

Bobbin core

Flyer arm

**23.** *Wide-angle flyer with dowels inserted for greater yarn capacity*

appears to be perfect. This is helped a little by using a silicone lubricant spray on the flyer shaft, but the only permanent solution is to ream out the bobbins and install bearings.

## FLYER, FOR SPEED

The slender, rounded arms of a metal flyer (such as the Made Well sold in Canada and the Columbine sold in the United States) allow a different arrangement for the yarn feeding in from the orifice through the side exit hole and over the hooks onto the bobbin. By coming through the orifice, up over the *back* of the flyer arm, and down through only one hook at the point where you want it to wind onto the bobbin, you can spin fast without the yarn hooping up as it draws in at fast speed (fig. 118). This airborne action of the yarn causes it to catch occasionally on the hooks or skip over and under hooks, which completely defeats the purpose of fast spinning. Because of the space required to accommodate a three-eighths-inch or larger orifice, many wooden flyer arms are not slender enough to do this.

The placement of the side exit hole for the yarn coming through the orifice toward the bobbin also determines whether this method may be used. If the exit hole is midway between the two flyer arms, it is not easy. But if the exit hole is close to the flyer arm, or directly in line with it, you have a choice of going behind the flyer arm or directly through the hooks, as is usually done.

Sometimes just the bending of the first (front) hook into a more closed loop helps correct the yarn hooping.

## ORIFICE

Most spinners agree that an orifice smaller than three-eighths inch is not practical for general all-purpose use and causes special difficulties for beginners who are still experiencing overtwist. An orifice size of one-half inch is better and allows a soft, heavy yarn to be spun if desired. An even larger size can be used for spinning thick-and-thin weaving textures.

There is a disadvantage to a large orifice (larger than one-half inch) for the spinning of fine yarn because you get a kind of wobbling feel as the twist is transferred to the fibers from the large-diameter orifice.

To make the large orifice serve double duty, I have wondered about the possibility of an optional insert to change the orifice from large to small. The insert would have a flat edge in front, would taper toward the far end, and could be used when spinning finer yarn.

The height of the orifice from the floor is a matter of comfort for the spinner. While you can adjust this to some extent by the height of the chair you use, if your spinning habits are already well formed, you want a spinning wheel with a height that is comfortable for the direction you draw out your yarn.

The height of the orifice is more important with styles where the front of the spinning fork rests in an open, U-shaped maiden. Here, if the orifice height combined with the height of your chair causes you to pull upward as you draw out the yarn, it can contribute to a chattering of the fork as it bounces up and down in its cradle. The front tension band of the Indian-head spinners counteracts any tendency for the fork to pull upward.

## YARN HOOK

Except with a large, one-inch orifice, you need a yarn hook to pull your yarn through the orifice. To make such a hook, unbend a small, flexible hair pin, then bend a loop in one end for attaching string, and make a hook in the other end.

An even better hook can be made from a wire heddle. Cut it on each side of the heddle eye to make two pieces of wire. Make a sharp bend in the cut end, and use the looped end to attach string with which you can hang the hook on your spinning wheel, in easy reach.

## THREE TYPES OF PULLEY ACTIONS

There are three types of pulley power arrangements (fig. 25):

1. **Double belt, bobbin lead (pronounced "lēd")** has power on both the flyer pulley and the bobbin pulley. The flyer causes twist and the bobbin causes pull (with a slipping clutch action when not pulling in).
2. **Single belt, flyer lead (Scotch tension)** has power on the flyer pulley and brake on the bobbin pulley. The flyer causes both twist and pull (slipping brake).
3. **Single belt, bobbin lead (Indian-head tension)** has power on the bobbin whorl and brake on the flyer shaft or pulley. The flyer causes twist and the bobbin causes pull (slipping brake).

## PULLEY RATIO ON DOUBLE BELT WHEELS

With a double belt wheel, the ratio between the pulley groove diameter (or diameters) on the spinning fork, and the pulley groove diameter on the bobbin is very important as it (plus drive belt tension) controls the speed with which your yarn is drawn in.

Many of the Saxony-style spinning wheels being built are

**24.** *Staggered hooks on flyer arms. This single belt, bobbin lead has a clamped leather brake on the flyer.*

replicas of colonial wheels, with a low ratio between the bobbin pulley diameters. To determine pulley diameter ratio, divide the fork pulley diameter by the bobbin pulley diameter. A pulley ratio of about 1.21 to 1.66 would be suitable for spinning fine yarn, but would not draw in heavy yarn hard enough, or fast enough, even with the drive belt adjusted to a tension that makes treadling difficult. On these wheels, just the addition of a large orifice would not make them capable of spinning heavy yarn. On top of the beginner's usual problem of overtwist, a wheel with a low ratio would add too much additional twist while it was slowly drawing in the yarn.

If you intend to spin a medium-heavy yarn, you should have a possible ratio of about 2.0, meaning that the largest flyer pulley is twice the size of the small bobbin pulley. If the ratio on

**25.** *Pulley power arrangements*

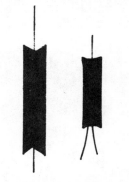

**A.** *Double belt, bobbin lead*

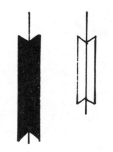

**B.** *Single belt, flyer lead*

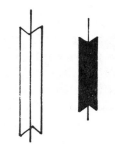

**C.** *Single belt, bobbin lead*

your wheel is not suited to the heavy yarn you want to spin, a woodworker can sometimes make the size of the bobbin pulley smaller (within certain size limitations). If the wheel is being made-to-order for you, ask for an alternate fork whorl, with larger pulleys, to use when you want to spin heavier yarn.

If there are two pulley grooves on the fork, the larger of the two could be about a 2.0 ratio for heavy yarn, and the smaller one a ratio of 1.21 or up to 1.66 for use with finer yarn. Two examples of such all-purpose wheels are Ernest Mason's wheel, with two different flyer whorls giving ratios of 1.33 and 1.66 when using the smaller one, and ratios of 1.83 and 2.16 when using the larger whorl on the spinning fork. The Columbine wheel has three pulley grooves on the fork, giving ratios of 1.21, 1.64, and 2.16.

For spinning finer yarns, which requires less force to draw them in and more twist, you will probably use some combination of the lesser pulley ratios, as well as a looser drive belt tension. For *high speed* with fine yarn, I find that I prefer the 2.0 ratio, but with a loose belt tension.

### DRIVE BELT ON DOUBLE BELT WHEELS

On a double belt wheel, the drive belt is not two separate bands, but one continuous belt, wound around twice. It goes once around the drive wheel and the fork pulley and once around the drive wheel and the bobbin pulley.

The style of some wheels allows for splicing the belt prior to installation (when the flyer and drive wheel are removable) and some require the belt to be in place (twice around the drive wheel and flyer assembly pulleys) before joining the two ends of the band.

### CROSSING THE DOUBLE BELT

Since it is a continuous cord going around twice, it must be crossed. Loop a rubber band twice around your hand and note how it crosses.

There is some advantage to installing a belt on the wheel

before making the permanent splice (splice instructions to follow), because you can more easily see and plan the *direction* of this cross for the way you intend to spin.

When the wheel is in use, the cross is in one constant position — just where the belt moves from the drive wheel toward the flyer pulleys. The larger pulley diameter of the fork and the smaller pulley diameter of the bobbin prevent the cross from rubbing *if*, when you splice it together, it is crossed (lapped) in the correct direction for the drive wheel rotation that you commonly use.

If you are installing a continuous belt, such as a dental motor belt, on your wheel, you have to double it before placing it on the wheel, and you have to determine the direction of the cross at that time. Of the two motor belt brands, Emesco and Parkell, the Emesco has a more durable surface and lasts longer.

A clockwise motion of the drive wheel (for Z twist) will bring the belt cross toward the flyer pulleys from the ''left'' on chair and upright wheels and from ''below'' on Saxony or colonial wheels. It works just the opposite with counterclockwise motion of the drive wheel for S twist.

The main thing to remember is that the belt portion that is traveling over the larger pulley on the fork must be lapped over, not under, the belt portion that is traveling over the bobbin pulley when you are operating the wheel.

While not vital, it is interesting that if the drive wheel has double grooves for the belt, they hold the crossed portion well apart as it comes off the drive wheel, thus eliminating any friction and lessening subsequent wear on the belt. Even with the belt crossed in the correct direction, there can still be a slight rubbing of the crossed portion when using the minimum pulley ratio or with some styles of wheels.

When you are not spinning, leave the belt slack, either by lowering the belt tensioner or by changing the belt to the smallest pulleys on the flyer. This is much better for your wheel. There is an Irish fairy who puts a hex on people who do not release the tension on their looms or spinning wheels when they are not using them. I understand she gets a little miffed, too, if you have not wound your yarn off the bobbin, but that sounds unreasonable.

## DRIVE BELT SPLICE

A knotted belt causes a slightly jerky pull each time it passes over a pulley. You may want to knot it temporarily to check the correct length, and then splice and sew it. When spliced, it should have very moderate tension when the tension device is at its minimal adjustment. If the belt tension is too slack then, you have not allowed for some eventual belt stretching.

With the tension device at the lowest point, run the drive belt cord around the bobbin pulley, around the drive wheel, over the small flyer pulley, and back around the drive wheel again. Pull to make it snug and mark where the two ends meet. Slip the belt off the pulleys to provide slack for working on it.

Cut the drive belt cord three inches too long. Untwist the three plies (or the twenty-ply if using soft heavy cord). Make a staggered splice by cutting one ply back three inches and one ply back one and one-half inches at each end. (With twenty-ply, divide it into three sections and treat it as three-ply.) Twist the plies back together at each end, tightly and evenly. Lap them over and hand sew, stitching through the plies. Then wind the stitched cord with thread. Tom Wertenberger, maker of the Columbine wheel, suggests that a little Elmer's Glue-All rubbed on the splice area makes stitching easier when the glue is dried.

The size of the cotton cord that you use depends on the size, width, and depth of your pulleys. Some very old wheels have narrow pulley grooves, and cord should be smaller for these to allow it to rest firmly in the grooves and to slip as necessary in the spool pulley. Ideally, the fork pulley should be a bit more wedge-shaped so that the belt gets very good traction there. While a hard finish cotton cord wears longer, I like the feel of a soft finish heavy cotton.

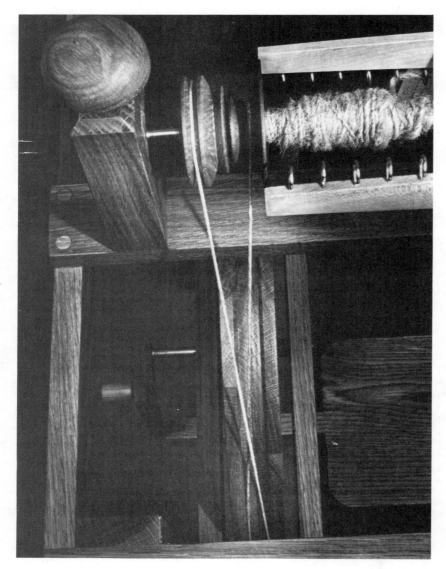

**26.** *Proper lap in the crossing of a double belt (for Z twist)*

Some people like to use beeswax (or belt dressing) to increase traction. This is effective on a single belt wheel, but with a double belt style it has the reverse effect of not allowing as free a slippage at the bobbin pulley and can cause a gummy deposit to build up on the pulleys. For use on the belt of the great wheel, however, which operates on a different principle than the flyer wheel, beeswax is very useful.

DRIVE BELT TENSIONER

The type of drive belt tensioner is not vital to the success of the spinning process as long as it does the job, but some kinds are more convenient. Some hold the tension better than others, some can be adjusted more accurately, and some can be operated with only one hand. The easier and more quickly the adjustment can be made while spinning, the more likely the adjustment will be made when it is necessary. The more sensitive the adjustment, the less likely you will be to overadjust.

As the bobbin fills, the yarn on it increases its diameter, which does affect the tension, as does the weight of the yarn on the bobbin. For beginners, this may necessitate setting a bit tighter tension as the spool fills in order to obtain the same pull-in action. With a tension arrangement where there can be a measured amount of tightening or loosening (one-half turn or one whole turn on a knob), you can regain the previous tension more easily. However, if you are hesitant to change what appears to be a "perfect" tension, just wind off the yarn into a skein and start again with an empty spool.

The norm is to make the adjustment, but as you become more proficient, you are able to adjust your spinning technique to the small change in bobbin diameter and weight. If you have to adjust the tension halfway through each bobbin, and adjust it back again to start the next skein, it is a little harder to spin a number of skeins all the same size, such as for sweater knitting.

The mid-bobbin adjustment is not the same thing as adjusting the drive belt tension for spinning a different size of yarn.

You want a looser tension for finer yarns and a tighter drive belt tension for spinning heavy yarn.

## SCOTCH TENSION (SINGLE BELT, FLYER LEAD)

With *Scotch tension*, the power is on the flyer pulley and the brake is on the bobbin pulley, so when properly adjusted, the flyer goes faster and wraps the yarn around the bobbin. Actually, it wraps around the bobbin in the opposite direction from that of double belt spinning. This arrangement for tension makes it somewhat harder to regulate the working of the wheel, and with a beginner, the tendency is to overadjust.

Successful spinning on any wheel having Scotch tension depends on the *coordination* of the tension on the drive band and the brake. They both need to be looser than you would think if you have been accustomed to the standard double belt wheel.

Start with both bands so loose that no spinning action takes place when you treadle. Tighten the drive belt first, a *very* small amount at a time, until that engages the fork. Then tighten the Scotch tensioner until the yarn winds around the bobbin nicely. Adjust just a fraction of an inch at a time. When your bobbin is half full, you may need to adjust either the brake or both bands to compensate for the added diameter of the bobbin, but adjust only if necessary and only as much as is absolutely necessary.

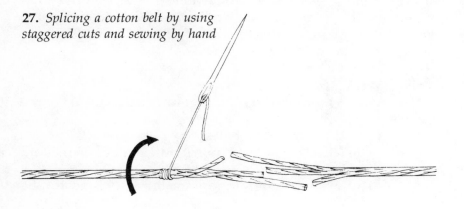

**27.** *Splicing a cotton belt by using staggered cuts and sewing by hand*

Most spinners who have been at it for a while do not need to make this mid-bobbin tightening.

## INDIAN-HEAD TENSION (SINGLE BELT, BOBBIN LEAD)

With power on the bobbin and the brake on the flyer, this was once considered only a variation of Scotch tension, but the distinction should be made that the so-called *Indian-head tension* is bobbin lead rather than flyer lead. It is a bit easier to adjust correctly than Scotch tension. While it has been used on many Swiss and other alpine styles, its nickname comes from its use on the large-head, bulk yarn spinners associated with Northwest Indian spinning.

The speed of the Indian-head wheel is dependent on the size of the drive wheel in relation to the bobbin pulley diameter, and the draw-in/twist is controlled by the tension (brake) on the flyer. Swiss wheels usually have a very large drive wheel for great speed, while bulk spinners have a small drive wheel for slow spinning of thick yarn.

In the case of the bulk yarn spinners, using the tension band is not always necessary. The drive is on the bobbin. The flyer is turned partly by friction of the large bobbin on the spindle, and partly by the force of the yarn and other factors. The tension band is sometimes needed to slow down the flyer if it is moving too fast (relative to the pull of the bobbin) and causing overtwist. The flyer tends to move faster as the bobbin fills up and causes greater friction on the spindle.

There are a couple of disadvantages to a production-type spinning wheel (large drive wheel) with a single belt arrangement. While you can achieve a high speed, you cannot stop as easily as with a double belt style, especially when spinning fine yarn that needs very little brake action on the flyer. When you try to stop, the flyer keeps right on rotating, out of your control. Actually, the moment you slow down to stop, even while the bobbin is still turning, you lose the drawing in action on your yarn. This can be offset somewhat by spinning right up to the

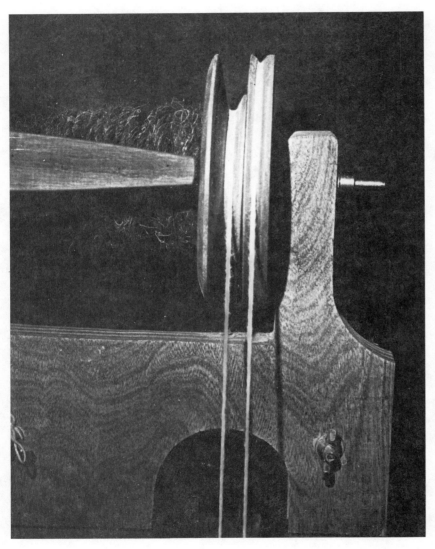

**28.** *The flyer whorl pulley is wedge-shaped for traction; the bobbin pulley is U-shaped to allow slippage when needed.*

orifice before you try to stop, then drawing back sharply on the yarn as you stop. That will prevent any snarling of the yarn as the flyer rotates without pulling in the yarn.

### DRIVE WHEEL: MOMENTUM

The upright castle wheel, often called a cottage wheel, has its drive wheel directly under the flyer, as do the chair-type wheels. The Saxony or colonial style has the drive wheel placed horizontally from the flyer. The momentum of the drive wheel is assisted by a heavy wheel, a large diameter wheel, a weighted wheel, or a double-action treadle.

### DRIVE WHEEL: SIZE AND DRIVE RATIO

In general, the smaller size drive wheel is not as efficient as a larger size, except on bulk yarn spinners. It can give a choppy action if the treadle and its connections are not well engineered. However, a drive wheel with larger than a twenty-inch diameter can have a drive ratio a little too fast for most beginners, depending on the bobbin pulley size. The drive ratio is the drive wheel diameter divided by the bobbin pulley diameter in wheels having bobbin lead, and the drive wheel size divided by flyer pulley diameter in flyer lead systems. For beginners, a drive ratio as low as 6:1 gives their hands time to handle the yarn in keeping with the speed of the wheel. For production spinning, a drive ratio of 20:1 to 30:1 is suitable, depending on the size yarn being spun. Most spinners find a ratio of about 10:1 to 12:1 is a comfortable speed.

### DRIVE WHEEL PROBLEM

If the wheel throws the belt off, it can be due to one of the following:
1. The drive wheel wobbles.
2. The wheel is not lined up with the pulleys on the fork and bobbin.
3. The whole maiden-fork assembly is twisted to one

side.
4. The pulley grooves are too shallow or the belt is too heavy for them.
5. The drive wheel groove is too shallow and/or the wheel itself is slightly warped.

## ALIGNMENT OF THE DRIVE WHEEL

The pulleys on the flyer assembly must line up with the groove or grooves on the drive wheel before spinning can proceed or else the belt will be repeatedly thrown off as you spin.

There are some instances where it has turned out that parts of more than one antique wheel have been pieced together to make one salable one, and in that case it is not always possible to get it aligned and in working operation. In an antique, it is usually the drive wheel that is out of alignment, and this can be corrected by using wedges at the bottom of the upright support posts where they fit into the bench. Even if the wheel lines up well, it may still need small wedges in the base to prevent the slight wobble that shows up because the wood parts are so dry from age.

If the axle of the drive wheel is not exactly centered, the spinning action may be intermittent due to the tightening and loosening of the belt as the wheel goes around. This is a fault that is not easily detected nor easily corrected.

## SOLID DRIVE WHEELS

Many of the drive wheels being made now are solid, rather than open with spokes. They thus have more weight for a smaller diameter and, if well constructed, are not apt to get warped through years of use. Before laminated wood was used, spokes were the only means of providing any assurance that the wheel would not warp. (Although a few solid wheels were made in the 1800s, they were unusual.)

One of the most practical models is the *chair style* (four legs with drive wheel below the flyer), usually having a solid wheel

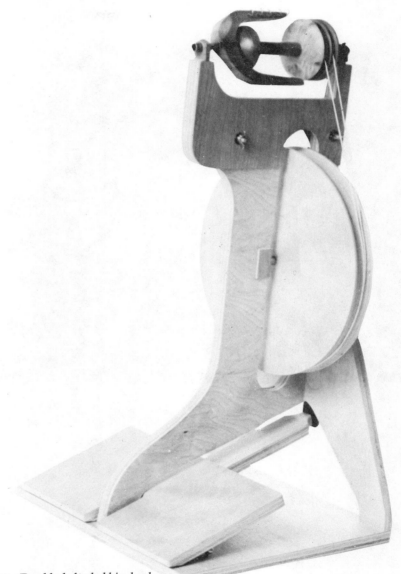

**29.** *Double belt, bobbin lead.*
*Turning wing nut raises or lowers the whole flyer assembly, and thus adjusts drive belt tension.*

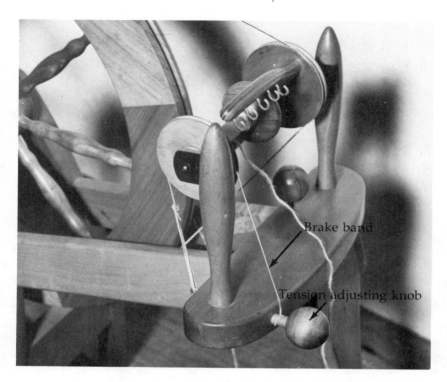

**30.** *Single belt, flyer lead. The rubber band and nylon line tensioner are used for a brake on the bobbin.*

that is often braced between two crossbars for greater stability with long usage. Good bracing prevents it from ever getting out of alignment or wobbly. One disadvantage of the front crossbar is that it makes it harder to replace a worn-out belt or to put the belt back in place if you slip it off for any reason. Good engineering can make this crossbar unnecessary.

## SAXONY TREADLE

The typical Saxony or colonial treadle hinges or pivots at the very front end of the treadle to give a down-stroke control only. This treadle must be depressed only when the axle crank is at the top and traveling downward in order to avoid inadvertent reversal of the direction of the drive wheel. Once you have learned to unconsciously stop the wheel with the treadle in a position to press downward again (just barely over the highest point), you do not need to use your hand to start the motion of the drive wheel. This points out the need for practicing treadling before you start to learn the actual spinning process. With the Saxony-type treadle, practice slowing down so that the actual stopping place of the treadle is in a position to start again. You should never allow it to stop on "dead center," with the treadle at either its highest or lowest position.

On Saxony wheels, the footman is usually attached to the treadle with a leather thong or leather hinge, and the curved drive wheel crank fits into a hole in the top of the footman, held on with a wooden ball or the equivalent.

Whether this crank is curved or straight makes no difference as a matter of physics. It has been said that the curved crank will keep the pull off dead center, but this is not so. Whether it stops at the top or the bottom in its revolution, the pull of the footman, or pitman arm as it is sometimes called, is still at dead center. There is some speculation that the reason some cranks were made curved was so that the effective length could be changed by bending, which makes some sense. Shortening the crank does make the wheel run faster, but also requires a harder pressure to operate it.

## PIVOTED DOUBLE-ACTION TREADLE

Many upright, castle, and chair-type wheels have the treadle pivoting more toward its middle, similar to an old sewing machine treadle, for a heel-and-toe action. (Not all treadles with an overhang in front are true double-action treadles.) This is easier for a beginner, for there is control of both the up-stroke and the down-stroke as you turn the crank on the drive wheel. Its action is more like a dual reciprocal treadle, but it is easier to learn. Also, I feel it is less tiring for long spinning sessions than a treadle that requires the use of only one foot. It can be done with a lighter touch, with less effort producing more momentum, because it gives two power impulses per revolution.

The pivoted treadle has a footman or pitman arm that is usually attached to a *straight crank* on the drive wheel with a *permanent bearing.* It is also hinged, usually with a bearing but sometimes with a fixed leather joining, at the point where the footman joins the extended arm of the treadle.

With its double action, a pivoted treadle minimizes the likelihood of the treadle stopping in a position where you cannot easily start it by using only your feet. It does sometimes stop in a position where foot pressure can start it in *reverse.* In that case, hold back on your yarn so that it does not lift off the hooks and snarl. Then, with gentle foot movement, turn it backward one-fourth turn or less to the place where a reversal of your foot treadling direction will start it up correctly. You can practice this treadling trick when you are not spinning so that it becomes easy (and fast) for you to do as needed.

## TREADLE-TO-CRANK RATIO

With the upright wheels, there are two places where a pivoted treadle can attach to the drive wheel, and it makes little difference in the *way* power is applied to the crank as long as the leverage ratio is adequate. When the crank of the wheel is on the

Leather thong tensioner for brake on bobbin

Idler arm tensioner on drive belt →

**31.** *Single belt, bobbin lead, and solid drive wheel*

Knob at the end of the bench moves the whole flyer assembly (mother-of-all) to adjust drive belt tension.

Saxony-type treadle

**32.** *Double belt, bobbin lead, and spoked wheel*

front or treadle side of the wheel, the distance from the pivot point of the treadle to the bottom of the pitman (footman) arm and thence to the crank of the wheel, is shorter than if the bar from the treadle passes under the drive wheel and connects to a crank on the back side of the wheel. Since the foot applying the power is in the same relative position in both instances, to transmit the same turning effort to the drive wheel, the crank on the far side would have to be longer than if it were on the front side.

In his *Spinning Wheel Primer*, Alden Amos suggests that a suitable treadle has an effective length of at least six times the length of the crank. This *effective treadle length* is measured at right angles to the treadle pivot axis, from the pivot line to the attachment point of the footman or pitman arm. This ratio is applicable to either the double-action treadle or the Saxony-type treadle.

There is much advantage in having easy treadle action, so consider this carefully when buying a spinning wheel. A lot of effort is required in treadling for any extended period of time. You treadle more strokes per inch or per yard of fine yarn, but you have to treadle with more strength for heavier yarn, since it is against a harder tension on the drive belt.

## LUBRICATING OLD WHEELS

When the leather bearings in the maiden need lubrication, use neat's-foot oil because it makes the leather last longer. Replace these leathers if they are so worn that the flyer fits too loosely. Do not make the new ones so snug that the flyer does not turn freely. If they are too tight, this not only interferes with the spinning action, but requires extra treadling effort. Oil only until the leather becomes pliable, because too much oil can make it too soft to do its job.

Remove the spinning fork and take off the bobbin. Clean the spindle well, using fine steel wool and cleaning solvent if necessary, and clean and oil the shaft hole in the bobbin. It is important that the bobbin turns freely, not just for ease in spinning and efficient drawing in of the yarn, but even for winding off a skein of yarn once the bobbin is full. The inner bearings of the bobbin should have a heavier oil than the faster-moving parts of the wheel. Actually, the bobbin rotates on the spindle only when the yarn is pulling into the wheel, not when the yarn is just twisting.

## LUBRICATING NEW WHEELS

The maker of the wheel should advise you about the points that need oil or grease. Some of the new wheels have teflon or nylon bearings that need little or no lubrication. As a general rule, it is usually necessary to lubricate the main wheel bearings, the treadle bearings, the point where the treadle meets the footman, where the footman joins the crank (depending on the type of joining), the tension device (depending on its material), the maiden leathers or bearings, and the flyer spindle and/or bearings in the end of the bobbin.

## POINTS TO CONSIDER WHEN BUYING A WHEEL

While you can hardly expect to find any one wheel that embodies *every* desirable point, you can check a wheel against the things that you consider most important, thus anticipating your problems. Not all the items mentioned in the following list are crucial, but they are some of the things to be considered, *especially in relation to the wheel's cost:*

1. Is it easy to oil the places that need oil? The maker should give a list of the points to lubricate.
2. Does it have an easily adjustable drive belt tensioner? A measured adjustment is most useful — the kind in which you can make a half-turn or a whole turn on a screw and then regain the previous tension when desired.
3. Does the drive wheel have good momentum and balance? Test it by removing the drive band from the fork, treadling, and then letting it revolve by it-

Screw raises hinged flyer stand to adjust belt tension

Double-action treadle

**33.** *Double belt, bobbin lead*

self. A perfectly balanced wheel does not always stop in the same place.

4. Note the grooves in the pulleys. They should be deep enough to hold the belt well. On a double belt wheel, the standard design has a V shape on fork pulleys for traction and a U shape on bobbin pulleys where slippage is needed part of the time. However, the reverse of these pulley shapes, with a very deep V on bobbin pulleys, provides more efficient drive for fast spinning of fine yarn.

5. On a single belt style, the brake tensioner should be durable and allow for delicate adjustments.

6. The size of the fork hooks should be compatible with the orifice size. A large orifice means you can spin large yarn, but only if the hooks accommodate it (and the side exit hole is the same diameter as the orifice). They should be placed so that they fill up the bobbin evenly.

7. Pulley ratio should also relate to orifice and hook size. This means a low pulley ratio for small orifice and hooks (fine yarn) and a greater pulley ratio for large orifice and hooks.

8. The bobbin should have ample yarn capacity so that you can spin at least 100 yards of yarn of the size allowed by the orifice. Size four and one-half inches by four and one-half inches is needed for 100 yards of a medium-weight yarn such as could be spun with a three-eighths-inch orifice.

9. Does the bobbin have bearings in each end? This feature may depend on the price you pay. However, a close-fitting bobbin without bearings has the full length of the bobbin core rubbing against the spindle, which creates an undue amount of surface friction.

10. The drive wheel groove should be deep enough to hold the belt well, and not smooth, for here you want constant traction.

11. If you are buying a wheel for production work, consider if the drive ratio is fast. Ordinarily, it takes an eighteen- to twenty-four-inch drive wheel to allow sufficient bobbin pulley/drive wheel ratio, especially for spinning fine yarn.

12. How is the treadle hinged? If it is double action, pivoting in the center or just front of center, does it pivot on a rod or is it rigidly attached to a rod that pivots in bearings? Are they bearings or just holes that will enlarge later, causing noise?

13. Is the treadle action easy? A short or choppy treadle action can be almost as tiring as a treadle that requires actual exertion.

14. Does it have some effective way of keeping the belt in place while you remove the spool so it is easy to replace the belt on the pulleys?

15. Is there some easy way to remove the spool from the flyer to oil the inside bearings of the spool (unless they do not need oil), or to remove the spool for plying, or to unsnarl yarn that has slipped off the end of the bobbin?

16. Are there any bearings that may eventually wear out, or become so loose that they are noisy? If so, can they be easily replaced?

17. If possible, make some agreement with the seller that if the wheel is not entirely satisfactory, some adjustments will be made.

Consider how quietly the wheel operates when new, and also the eventualities. After many years of use, will it still be an efficient, smoothly running piece of equipment? While learning to spin, a few rattles and squeaks may not bother you, but later the noise can make spinning a less pleasant occupation than it is otherwise. If possible, learn to spin on a borrowed or rented wheel before deciding what wheel you want to buy.

This chapter shows a representative selection of the spinning wheels now being made. Not all available wheels are shown because space limitations do not allow numerous duplications. As many specifications as possible are given for each so that their potentialities may be assessed with regard to the information in the preceding chapter on spinning wheel operation. Many of the features listed at the end of the previous chapter are important only in relation to the price you are paying, and prices shown here are only approximations. When a feature is listed as optional, it may indicate availability at additional cost. If you are interested in more specific information, send your inquiries and a self-addressed, stamped envelope to the distributors.

# 5
# Available Spinning Wheels

**34.** *DIXON DOUBLE TREADLE PRODUCTION WHEEL*

*Paul Dixon Woodworking*
*P.O. Box 295*
*Hamilton, Massachusetts 01936*

*Orifice $^{1}/_{4}$, $^{5}/_{16}$, $^{3}/_{8}$, $^{7}/_{16}$, and $^{1}/_{2}$ in. (choice of 2),*
*    25 in. from floor*
*Double belt, bobbin lead*
*Bobbin length 5$^{3}/_{4}$ in.*
*Bobbin width 4 in.*
*Flyer drive ratios 10:1 and 17.85:1*
*Pulley ratios 1.27, 1.68, 2.19, and 3.00*
*Drive wheel diameter 30 in., with sealed ball bearings*
*Saxony-type double treadle*
*Black walnut or native cherry*

**35.** *HEMLOCK HILL HANDSPINNER*

*Hemlock Hill*
*28405 Honeysucle Drive*
*Damascus, Maryland 20750*

*Brass orifice $1/2$ in. $31\,1/2$ in. from floor*
*Double belt, bobbin lead*
*Bobbin length 6 in.*
*Flyer width 7.5 in., with brass slide*
*Pulley ratios 1.4 on small whorl and 1.9 on larger whorl;*
*    extra flyer whorls available*
*Solid drive wheel 18 in., supported by 2 enclosed,*
*    sealed ball bearings*
*Drive ratios 13.5 and 9.3*
*Heel-toe treadle wide enough for both feet*
*Weight 23 lb.*

**36.** *CASTLE WHEEL*

*Alden Amos*
*Straw into Gold*
*P.O. Box 2904*
*Oakland, California 94618*

*Orifice ½ in., 28 to 32 in. from*
*  floor depending on tension*
*Single belt, bobbin lead, brake on flyer*
*Bobbin length 3⅞ in.*
*Flyer width 4½ in.*
*Staggered hooks, 6 on each arm*
*Drive wheel 18 in., drive ratio 14:1*
*Screw drive belt tensioner*
*Saxony-type treadle, effective treadle length 6:1*
*3 bobbins and Lazy Kate*
*Maple or beech*

### 37. SWISS STYLE PRODUCTION WHEEL

*Ernest L. Mason*
*3033 Northeast Davis Street*
*Portland, Oregon 97232*

*Orifice ⅜ in. (larger to order), 33 in. from floor*
*Single belt, bobbin lead, brake on flyer*
*Bobbin length 5¼ in.*
*Flyer width 4 in. (wider to order)*
*Leather bobbin bearings*
*Bobbin whorls – 1 bobbin with 2 in.*
    *for 12:1 drive ratio, 1 bobbin with 1½ in.*
    *for 16:1 drive ratio (optional 1 bobbin*
    *with 1¼ in. for 19.2:1 drive ratio)*
*Extra bobbins available*
*Drive wheel 24 in.*
*Double-action treadle (choice of narrow for*
    *1 foot or wider for both)*
*Effective treadle ratio 6:1*
*Positive screw-controlled friction brake*
*Precision screw drive belt tensioner*
*Ball bearing drive wheel axle*
*Oak*

**38.** *WALNUT TYROLEAN*

*Alden Amos*
*Straw into Gold*
*P.O. Box 2904*
*Oakland, California 94618*

*Orifice ½ in.*
*Single drive, bobbin lead, brake on flyer*
*Bobbin length 3¹/₁₆ in., lignum vitae bearings*
*Fork width 3¼ in.*
*2 different bobbin speed whorls –*
 *fast 17.9:1 drive ratio, slow 11.1 drive ratio*
*Drive wheel 18 in.; groove 17¹³/₁₆*
*Matching distaff, Lazy Kate, skein winder, and bobbins*
*Screw, maidens, flyer, and wheel are english walnut*
*Base and treadle are american black walnut*
*Wheel posts and pegs are south american rosewood*

### 39. CHAIR-TYPE WHEEL

Ernest L. Mason
3033 Northeast Davis Street
Portland, Oregon 97232

Orifice ⅜ in. (larger to order), 29 in. from floor
Double belt, bobbin lead
Bobbin length 4¾ in., leather bearings,
    3 bobbins furnished
Flyer width 4 in. (larger to order)
2 flyer whorls, giving pulley ratios
    of 1.33, 1.66, 1.83, and 2.16
Optional large 5 in. whorl for soft twist yarn
Small hooks on 1 flyer arm, large hooks on other arm
Perfectly balanced flyer arm and bobbins;
    bobbins are turned and balanced after they
    are assembled with bearings
Pivoted double-action treadle; treadle rod
    rides in Nylatron bushings,
    so it is noiseless and oilless
Effective treadle ratio 6:1
Drive wheel 15½ in., drive ratio 10.3:1,
    ball bearings in hub
Exit hole may be requested in line
    with flyer arm for speed position
Endless, knotless dental engine belt,
    easily replaced if necessary
Easy one-handed drive belt tensioner
Each wheel broken in (run by
    motor power for 30 min. on each bobbin)
Optional bobbin pulley 1¼ in. for 12:1 drive ratio
Flyer folds down for easy transport and shipment
Built-in bobbin storage, Lazy Kate, with plying loop
Walnut or cherry

**40.** *CASCADE SHAKER CHAIR WHEEL*

*Cascade Looms*
*7364 Conifer Northeast*
*Salem, Oregon 97303*

*Orifice ½ in.*
*Double belt, bobbin lead or with Scotch tension*
*Bobbin length 4 ³/₁₆ in., leather bearings*
*Fork width 4 in.*
*Bobbin pulley 1 ¾ in.*
*Fork pulleys 2 ¼ and 2 ½ for pulley ratios of 1.28 and 1.42*
*Drive wheel 16 in., drive ratio 9:1, sealed ball bearings*
*Double-action treadle, ball joints to pitman arm*
*Effective treadle ratio 6:1*
*Rock maple and eastern cherry*

**41.** *AMERICAN TRAVELER*

*Doloria Chapin*
*49 Wilshire Boulevard*
*Milford, Connecticut 06460*

*Double belt, bobbin lead, or single belt with brake on*
*bobbin or on flyer*
*Drive wheel 16 in., drive ratio 7.4:1 with large flyer,*
*13.5:1 with small flyer, sealed bearings*

SMALL FLYER ASSEMBLY
*Orifice ½ in., 27 in. from floor*
*Bobbin length 3 in., flyer width 3½ in., drive ratio 13.5:1*
*Bobbin pulley 1.185 in.*
*Flyer pulley — 1 size 1.76 in. for pulley*
*ratio of 1.48, 1 size 1.6 in. for pulley ratio of 1.35*

LARGE FLYER ASSEMBLY
*Orifice 1 in., 27 in. from floor*
*Bobbin length 3½ in.*
*Flyer width 5 in.*
*Flyer pulley 2.875 in.; bobbin pulley 2.150 in.*
*for pulley ratio of 1.33*
*Drive ratio 7.4 (not too fast for beginners)*
*Oilite bearings in treadle bars and tensioner*
*Steel treadle plates, double treadle arrangement*
*Accessories — large head, spindle head, carrying cases for wheel and*
*accessories, extra bobbins, portable chair, distaff, hook, water*
*cups, Lazy Kate, etc.*
*Walnut, cherry, maple, and oak with lacquer finish*

**42.** *JOURNEY WHEEL*

*Reeds Weeds and Whistles*
*29 Main Street*
*Acton, Massachusetts 01720*

*Open orifice, yarn up to ½ in., 29 in. from floor*
*Double band, automatic tension*
*Spool length 3 in.*
*Fork width 3½ in., 2 hook sizes*
*Easy bobbin changing, pulley ratio 1.37*
*      (suitable for fine yarn)*
*2 spare bobbins, mounted for plying*
*Drive wheel 11 in.; accelerating wheel*
*      makes equivalent of 18-in. wheel*
*Pivoted double-action treadle*
*Portable, folds into 14 × 16 × 6½-in. cherry*
*      box with leather shoulder strap*
*Cherry and rock maple*

**43.** *DOUBLE FLYER WHEEL*

*Vernon Joslin*
*Box 2470, Dee Highway*
*Hood River, Oregon 97031*

*Orifice ¼ in., 30 in. from floor*
*Double belt, bobbin lead*
*Bobbin length 2 ¾ in.*
*Flyer width 3 ½ in.*
*Pulley ratio 1.28*
*Drive wheel 16 in., drive ratio 9:1*
*Saxony treadle*
*White oak, eastern maple, walnut, or cherry*

**44.** *WENDY*

*Pipy Craft Limited*
*228 Wellington Street*
*Howick, Auckland, New Zealand*

*Also available from U.S. dealers*

*Orifice ³/₁₀ in., 24 in. from floor*
*Double belt, bobbin lead*
*Bobbin length 3 ⅝ in., 3 bobbins furnished*
*Flyer width 4 in., with hardened steel replaceable hooks*
*Pulley ratios of 1.11, 1.19, and 1.29 (suitable for fine yarn)*
*Drive wheel 16 ½ in., drive ratio 9.42, counterbalanced wheel*
*Metal-screw drive belt tensioner*
*Pivoted double-action treadle*
*Heart rimu with linseed oil finish*

**45.** *COLUMBINE*

*Columbine Machine Shop*
*518 Sunnyside Court*
*Newton, Kansas 67114*

*Orifice size ⅝ in., 28 in. from floor*
*Double belt, bobbin lead*
*Fork width 4½ in.*
*Bobbin length 7⅜ in., with nylon bearings in bobbin*
*Flyer pulley has 3 grooves for ratios of 1.21, 1.64, and 2.16*
*13 fine, narrowly spaced, small, stainless steel*
    *hooks on 1 flyer arm, with small exit hole*
*9 heavy, wider spaced hooks on other arm, with large exit hole*
*Exit holes close to arms for speed position (yarn over back of arm)*
*Drive wheel 14 in., drive ratio about 8½:1*
*Pivoted double-action treadle,*
    *pitman with aircraft ball joint*
*Precision drive belt tension knob*
*Nylon bearings throughout wheel*
*All metal wheel — flyer is bright nickel-plated and*
    *the rest is bright orange*

**46.** *WIND MOUNTAIN SPINNER*

*Steven J. Gray*
*514 East Davis*
*Bozeman, Montana 59715*

*Orifice ⅜ in., 28 in. from floor*
*Double belt, bobbin lead*
*Bobbin length 5½ in.*
*Flyer width 4 in.*
*Pulley ratios of 1.5 and 1.84 (or as requested)*
*Drive wheel 22 in., in ball bearings, drive ratio 14.5:1*
*Drive wheel can be aligned with flyer assembly*
*Pivoted double-action treadle*
*Size when folded—23 × 24 × 10 in.*
*Lazy Kate with 3 bobbins, will hold up to 6*
*Can be shipped by U.P.S.*
*Oak with walnut trim*

*JUMBO HEAD*
*Orifice ⅞ in.*
*Bobbin length 8 in.*
*Flyer width 6 in.*
*Pulley ratios of 2.0 and 2.22 (or as requested)*
*Drive ratio 5:1*

*SPINDLE HEAD*
*Spindle 7 in.*
*Drive ratios of 5:1, 7:1, or 14:1*
*May be ordered with ball bearings*

**47.**

*Woodspin Industries (NZ) Limited*
*107 Daniell Street Newton*
*P.O. Box 9637*
*Wellington, New Zealand*

*Orifice ³⁄₈ in., 33 in. from floor*
*Single belt, brake on bobbin*
*Bobbin length 4 in.; optional larger whorl 6 in.,*
  *for slow spinning of heavier yarns*
*Fork width 4 in.*
*4 bobbins, all nylon bushings*
*7 hooks on each flyer arm*
*Drive wheel 18 in., heavily lead-weighted and counterbalanced*
*Drive wheel shaft in "no lubrication" bearings*
*Saxony-type treadle*
*Mahogany or walnut stain, lacquer finish*

### 48. NORWEGIAN PRINCESS

Robin and Russ Handweavers
533 North Adams Street
McMinnville, Oregon 97128

Orifice ½ in., 32 in. from floor
Double belt, bobbin lead
Bobbin length 2½ in.
Flyer width 3⁹⁄₁₆ in.
Bobbin pulley diameter 1½ in.
Flyer pulleys 2 in. and 2½ in., pulley ratios of 1.33 and 1.66
Drive wheel diameter 18 in., drive ratio 12:1
Precision screw drive belt tensioner
3 extra bobbins and built-in Lazy Kate
Shipped assembled
Beech with lacquer finish, trimmed in red

### 49. BAYNES SIMPLEX WHEEL

Baynes Woodcrafts Limited
P.O. Box 227
Ashburton, New Zealand

Orifice ³⁄₈ in., 31 in. from floor
Single belt, flyer lead
Jumbo flyer with ⁵⁄₈-in. orifice and drive ratio of 3.5:1
"Spinning Jenny" flyer with jumbo pulley for medium-thick yarn
High-speed flyer with drive ratio of 8.5, fully balanced
Drive wheel diameter 16 in., graphite-impregnated
      nylon self-lubricating bearings
Heel-toe double-action treadle
New Zealand beech

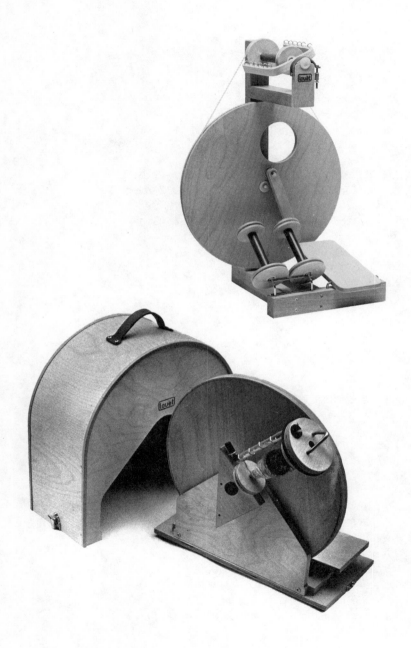

**50.** *LOUËT WHEELS*

*Dutch Canadian Spinning Wheel Company*
*Box 70*
*Carleton Place, Ontario, Canada*

*LOUËT*
*Orifice ½ in., 28 in. from floor, slanted toward side exit hole*
*Single belt, bobbin lead*
*Simple and precision brake adjustment*
*Bobbin length 5¼ in., with nylon bearings*
*3 bobbins, reversible for choice of 2 pulley diameters*
*Flyer width 4¾ in., with staggered hooks*
*Drive wheel 20 in., drive ratios of 5:1 or 7:1*
*Faster bobbin available for drive ratio of 10:1*
*Drive wheel counterbalanced, in ball bearings*
*Built-in Lazy Kate*
*Optional attaching swift (yarn winder)*
*Assembled weight 20 lb.*
*Rock maple and laminated birch, nonskid feet*

*TRAVELING "BABY" LOUËT (S40)*
*Orifice loop 15 in. from floor (which does not*
*    limit height of chair in which spinner sits)*
*Beltless direct drive, flyer lead*
*3 bobbins, bobbin length 4¼ in.*
*Flyer width 3 in.*
*Double-action treadle*
*Size, when in case, 15 by 16 by 7 in.; fits*
*    under airplane seat*
*Carrying weight 9 lb.*
*Sturdy wooden case*

**51.** *SHETLAND CASTLE BY HALDANE*

*The Hidden Village*
*4650 Arrow Highway G1 and 2*
*Montclair, California 91763*

*Orifice ¼ in., 30½ in. from floor*
*Double belt, bobbin lead*
*Bobbin length 2⅞ in., pulley ratios of 1.42 and 1.52*
*Fork width 3½ in.*
*Drive wheel 16½ in., drive ratio 13.9*
*Tension screw on crown of rear maiden*
*Saxony treadle*
*Built-in Lazy Kate*
*Kiln-dried oak and beech*

**52.** *CLEMES CASTLE WHEEL*

*Clemes and Clemes*
*650 San Pablo Avenue*
*Pinole, California 94564*

*Orifice ⅜ in., 28¼ in. from floor*
*Double belt, bobbin lead*
*Bobbin length 3⅛ in., pulley ratio 1.85*
*Flyer width 3⅝ in.*
*Drive wheel 16 in., drive ratio 10.6*
*Saxony-type treadle*
*Weight 50 lb. (can be shipped by U.P.S.)*
*Maple, with fruitwood, walnut, or natural finish*

*Baillie and Watts Limited*
*P.O. Box 1512*
*Auckland, New Zealand*

**53.** *SLEEPING BEAUTY WHEEL*
*Orifice ⅜ in., 38 in. from floor*
*Double belt, bobbin lead*
*Bobbin length 3 in.*
*Fork width tapers from 3⅛ in. to 5½ in.*
*Standard pulley size gives 1.52 ratio*
*Heavy yarn whorl (5 in.) for 3.2 ratio (optional)*
*Replaceable graphite bobbin bearings*
*Drive wheel 20½ in., drive ratio 12.8:1*
*Saxony-type treadle*
*Shipped in kit form*
*Hardwood*

**54.** *THUMBELINA KIT WHEEL*
*Also available from Hide n' Hair,*
    *Clemes and Clemes, and other U.S. dealers*
*Orifice 35 in. from floor*
*Same flyer and bobbin as the Sleeping Beauty*
*Double-action treadle*
*Drive wheel 15 in., drive ratio 9.6:1*
    *(not too fast for beginners)*
*Unfinished hardwood kit*

*JUMBO FLYER*
*Fits either wheel; photo appears*
    *later in this chapter*
*Orifice ⅞ in.*
*Bobbin 5½ in. long*
*Fork 6 in. wide, counterweighted*
*Indian-head tension*

**55.** *POLY WHEEL*

*Pipy Craft Limited*
*228 Wellington Street*
*Howick, Auckland, New Zealand*

*Large orifice hook for all yarn sizes, 25 in. from floor*
*Single belt, flyer lead*
*Bobbin length 6¼ in., ball bearings*
*Bobbins double ended with choice of braking surface*
*Flyer width 7¼ in.*
*Drive ratios of 3:1, 4:1, 5½:1, 7:1 (faster on request)*
*Elasticized drive band*
*Double-action treadle*
*Weight 12 lb.*
*New Zealand rimu wood frame, heavily oiled*

**56.** *GREEN SPRING SPINNER*

*Whitehorse Mountain Woodworks*
*P.O. Box 23*
*Green Spring, West Virginia 26722*

*Orifice 7/16 in., 30½ in. from floor*
*Double belt, bobbin lead*
*Bobbin length 3¼ in.*
*Pulley ratio 2.0 (for variety of*
*   yarn sizes), large hooks*
*Flyer width 3¼ in.*
*Larger bobbin and flyer (optional and at*
*   slight additional cost)*
*Drive wheel 14¾ in., drive ratio about 11.8:1*
*Idler arm belt tensioner*
*Pivoted double-action treadle*
*Built-in Lazy Kate*
*Lifetime guarantee*
*Shipped fully assembled*
*Oak, cherry, and black walnut;*
*   birch-faced ply wheel*

### 57. *SIEVERS SPINNING WHEEL*

*Sievers Looms*
*Jackson Harbor Road*
*Washington Island, Wisconsin 54246*

*Brass spindle with $^3/_8$-in. orifice, 28 in. from floor*
*Double belt, bobbin lead*
*Bobbin length 3 $^1/_8$ in.; will hold from 3 to 4 oz. of spun yarn*
*Drive wheel diameter 18 in.*
*Drive ratios 9:1 and 10.3:1*
*End-grain maple wheel bearings*
*Leather spindle bearings*
*11 staggered flyer hooks*
*Extra bobbins available*
*Weight 18 lb.*
*Size 18 × 34 × 36 in., with distaff 48 in. high*
*Rock maple*

### 58. *ASHFORD KIT WHEEL*

*Ashford Handcrafts Limited*                    *Under $100*
*P.O. Box 180*
*Ashburton, New Zealand*

*Also available from many U.S. dealers*

*Orifice $^3/_8$ in.*
*Single belt, flyer lead, brake on bobbin*
*Bobbin length 3 $^1/_2$ in.*
*Flyer width 3 $^1/_4$ in.*
*4 bobbins (sometimes need a little reaming*
    *out to fit well); no bearings*
*Drive wheel 22 in.*
*Silver birch*

*Jumbo Flyer with $^5/_8$-in. orifice available to fit this wheel*

**59.** *CLEMES KIT WHEEL*

*Clemes and Clemes*
*650 San Pablo Avenue*
*Pinole, California 94564*

*Orifice ⅜ in.*
*Double belt, bobbin lead*
*Bobbin length 4¼ in., pulley ratio 1.73*
*Flyer width 4 in.*
*3 bobbins*
*Drive wheel 16 in., drive ratio 8.5, ball bearings*
*Double-action treadle*
*24 lb.*
*Unassembled and unfinished (5 pages of assembly instructions included)*
*Maple and multi-layered hardwood (fine sandpaper sent with wheel)*

**60.** *RIO GRANDE WHEEL*

*Rio Grande Weaver's Supply*
*P.O. Box 2785*
*Santa Fe, New Mexico 87501*

*Drive wheel diameter 38 in., height 51 in., length 60 in.*
*Aluminum spindle 12 in. long*
*Three pulley sizes provide speeds from 200 to over 2,000 rpm*

**61.** *CALIFORNIA BULK SPINNING WHEEL*

*Lydia Hillier*
*Weaving-Spinning Supplies*
*P.O. Box 85*
*Manhattan Beach, California 90266*

*Orifice ¾ in. for heavy yarn, 31½ in. from floor*
*Single belt, bobbin lead, brake on flyer*
*Spool length 9 in.*
*Fork width 7 in.*
*Drive wheel 14 in. (low drive ratio for heavy yarn)*
*Pivoted double-action treadle*
*Black walnut*

**62.** *INDIAN VALLEY SPINNER*

*Indian Valley Spinner*
*Route 2, Box 17*
*Bradfordsville, Kentucky 40009*

*Also available from Hide n' Hair and other dealers.*

*Orifice size ¹¹⁄₁₆, 30 in. from floor*
*Single belt, bobbin lead, brake on flyer*
*Bobbin length 10¾ in.*
*Fork width 6½ in.*
*Flyer assembly mounted in leather bearings*
*Heavy, cast iron drive wheel mounted in bronze bearings*
*Leather drive belt*
*Extra bobbins and Lazy Kate available*
*Spinner head can be purchased separately*
*Black walnut with hand rubbed oil finish*

### 63. *PIRTLE SPINNER*

*Pirtle Spinner*
*21501 St. John Lane*
*Huntington Beach, California 92646*

*Orifice 1 in., 31½ in. from floor*
*Single belt, bobbin lead, brake on flyer (leather drive belt)*
*Bobbin length 10¼ in.*
*Fork width 6½ in.*
*Balanced flyer, sliding yarn guides*
*Optional high-speed head available*
*Drive wheel 12 in. and 1¾ in. thick,*
*    solid wood, sealed bearings*
*Idler arm tensioner*
*Pivoted double-action treadle*
*Shipped fully assembled, with orifice on the left or right*
*Oak, maple, or zebra*

### 64. *HEDGEHOG BULK SPINNER*

*Hedgehog Equipment*
*Forest Craft Centre*
*Upper Hartfield*
*East Sussex, England*

*Large orifice*
*Single belt, bobbin lead, brake on flyer*
*Bobbin 10 in.*
*5 large hooks*
*Drive wheel 14 in., drive ratio 5:1*
*Head may be mounted on an old treadle*
*    sewing machine or used with a motor,*
*    or mounted on a base constructed*
*    from plans sold by Hedgehog*
*Beech wood with teak oil*

**65.** *KLIOT WALKER KIT*

*Some Place*
*2990 Adeline Street*
*Berkeley, California 94703*

*Removable spindle (can also be used*
*    with a drop spindle)*
*Ball bearings in spindle assembly*
*Filled spindles can be removed for storage or plying*
*Turn ratio 50:1*
*Drive wheel — use 26-in. front bicycle wheel*
*    (any size from 20 in. on up will*
*    work satisfactorily)*
*Distaff (for flax) available*
*Extra spindles available*
*Lazy Kate available, to hold 3 spindles*
*Weight 12 lb.*
*Vertical grain Douglas fir*
*Patent 3776055*

**66.** *PENGUIN QUILL WHEEL*

*School Products Company*
*1201 Broadway*
*New York, New York 10001*

*Quill length 11 in., 24 in. from floor*
*Drive wheel diameter 15 in.*
*Pulley diameter 4 1/4 in.*
*Drive wheel and pulley have ball bearings*
*Birch-faced plywood with sealer finish*

**67.** *SARAH GREAT WHEEL*

*Obadiah Tharp Company*
*8406 Southwest 58th Avenue*
*Portland, Oregon 97219*

*Spindle 7 in., sturdy*
*Accelerating Minor's head for speed; change to direct drive*
*    without disturbing Minor's head arrangement*
*Head and wheel both swing 180 degrees for either*
*    right-handed or left-handed spinning position*
*Easily adjusted metal tension devices*
*Double-grooved, 48-in. diameter hickory wheel rim*
*Lifetime bronze bearings*
*2 skeiners that mount on wheel hub*
*    for skeining and/or plying*
*Plying loop on bench*
*Assembles and disassembles in minutes*
*Hard eastern maple and hickory;*
*    hand rubbed with wild honey oil finish*

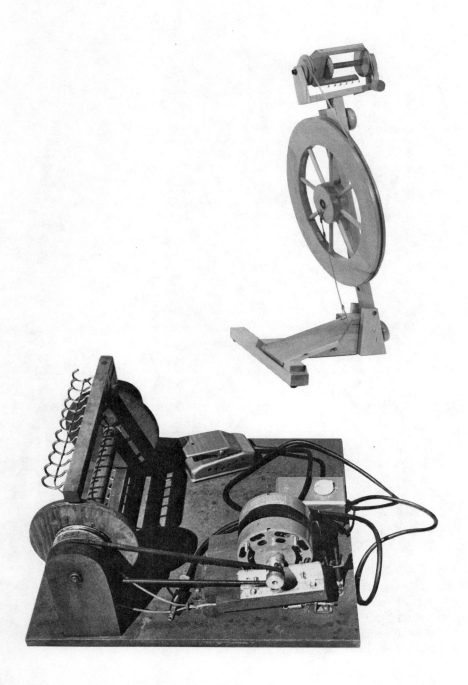

**68.** *LENDRUM FOLDING WHEEL*

*Something Special*
*5400 Park Lake Road*
*East Lansing, Michigan 48823*

*REGULAR HEAD*
*Orifice $7/16$ in., $30 1/2$ in. from floor*
*Single belt, flyer lead*
*Fork width $3 1/2$ in.*
*Bobbin length 4 in.*
*Drive ratios —regular flyer 6:1 and 8:1;*
  *high-speed flyer 10:1 and 12:1*

*LARGE (JUMBO) HEAD*
*Orifice $7/8$ in.*
*Single belt, flyer lead*
*Fork width $5 1/4$ in.*
*Bobbin length $8 1/8$ in.*
*Drive ratios 3:1 and 5:1*

*Drive wheel diameter 19 in.*
*Nylon flyer bearings*
*Single-action treadle*
*Maple*

**69.** *ELECTRIC BULK SPINNER*

*Sam Noto*
*6504 39th Avenue*
*Kenosha, Wisconsin 53142*

*Orifice $7/8$ in.*
*Single belt, flyer lead*
*Bobbin length 10 in.*
*Flyer width $6 1/2$ in.*
*Choice of 2 motors: serving machine motor —5,000 rpm,*
  *$1/15$ hp, with variable-speed dial foot control; heavy duty,*
  *continuous use motor —1,550 rpm, $1/15$ hp, 3-speed switch foot control*

### 70. *SPINDLE HEAD*

*Handcraft Wools, Distributor*
*Box 378*
*Streetsville, Ontario L5M 2B9*
*Canada*

*Steel spindle shaft, 10½ in. long*
*Available in 4 different speed ratios – to spin easily the*
*yarn sizes mentioned, the chart below shows which head*
*to order for particular drive wheel sizes*

*Chart Showing Wheel to Spindle Head Ratio*

| Head Size Number | For Yarn Size | Use with Wheel Having Diameter of |
|---|---|---|
| 1 | fine | 16 to 20 in. approx. |
| | very fine | 24 to 30 in. approx. |
| 2 | medium | 16 to 20 in. approx. |
| | fine | 24 to 30 in. approx. |
| 3 | bulky | 16 to 20 in. approx. |
| | medium | 24 to 30 in. approx. |
| 4 | giant | 16 to 20 in. approx. |
| | bulky | 24 to 30 in. approx. |

*The spindle head attaches to most spinning wheels with the use*
*of a C clamp, usually after removing*
*the flyer assembly. Make new drive cord of necessary length.*
*Instruction sheet is provided with spindle head.*
*Spindle is operated by the treadle wheel,*
*so both hands can be used for spinning.*

**71.** *GOOD KARMA*

*Good Karma Looms*
*440 West 4th*
*Chadron, Nebraska 69337*

*Orifice ⅜ in.*
*Double belt, bobbin lead*
*Bobbin length 2 ⅜ in.*
*Flyer tapers from 4 in. to 5 in.*
*2 flyer pulley grooves for 1.2 and 1.3 pulley ratio*
    *(suitable for fine yarn)*
*Drive wheel 21 in., drive ratio 17.7:1, on ball bearings*
*Saxony-type treadle, leather footman*
*1 leg removable to lubricate treadle easily*
*Extra bobbins available*
*Maple, with danish oil rub finish, or unfinished*

**72.**

*Nilus Leclerc Incorporated*
*L'Islet, Quebec*
*Canada*
*(and their many dealers)*

*Orifice ½ in., 23 in. from floor*
*Double belt, bobbin lead*
*Bobbin length 3 ⅛ in.*
*Fork width 3 ⅛ in.*
*Pulley ratio 1.46*
*Drive wheel 21¾ in., drive ratio 18:1*
*Bearings in wheel and bobbin; nylon*
*Extra bobbins and Lazy Kate available*
*Birch or canadian maple*

**73.**

*John White*
*39918 North Ruby Loop*
*Scio, Oregon 97374*

*Orifice ⅜ in., 27 in. from floor*
*Double belt style or single belt on request*
*Bobbin length 2¾ in.*
*Flyer width 3½ in.*
*2 whorls, for pulley ratios of 1.3 for fine yarn*
    *and 2.0 for heavy yarn (other whorl ratios to order)*
*Drive wheel 20 in., drive ratio 7.2*
    *(not too fast for beginners)*
*Saxony-type treadle*
*Walnut or maple*

*BULK SPINNER HEAD*
*Available to fit the wheel*
*Orifice ¾ in.*
*Scotch tension*
*Spool length 8 in.*
*Fork width 4¼ in.*

**74.** *HALL TRADITIONAL'S NONPAREIL PRODUCTION SPINNER*

*Norman Hall*
*R.D. 3, Box 185 A*
*Oxford, New York 13830*

*Orifice ¹/₂ in., 27 in. from floor*
*Bobbin length 6 in.*
*Flyer width 5 in.*
*Double band, convertible to Scotch brake band*
*Drive wheel diameter 27 in.*
*Drive ratios 10:1, 15:1, 20:1*
*Heel-toe double-action treadle*
*Oak, rock maple, cherry, walnut, etc.*

**75.** *PARAGON WHEEL*

*Craig Rehbein*
*2309 Laguna Road*
*Santa Rosa, California 95401*

*Orifice ³/₈ in. (¹/₂ in. on request)*
*Double belt, bobbin lead*
*Bobbin length 4 ³/₈ in.*
*Fork width 3 ⁵/₈ in.*
*2 fork pulley grooves for ratios of 1.36 and 1.86*
*Slip-on flyer whorl for easy bobbin changing*
*Drive wheel 20 in., drive ratio 14.5:1,*
*       permanently lubricated ball bearings*
*Saxony-type treadle*
*Built-in Lazy Kate with 2 extra bobbins*
*Oil-finished hardwood*

**76.** *ELECTRIC SPINNER*

*Clemes and Clemes*
*650 San Pablo Avenue*
*Pinole, California 94564*

*Orifice ⅜ in.*
*Double belt, bobbin lead*
*Bobbin length 3 ⅛ in., pulley ratio 1.85*
*Flyer width 3 ⅝ in.*
*Motor, with foot control for variable speed*
*Base 8 × 14 in.*
*Weight 9 lb.*

**77.** *TYROLEAN WHEEL*

*Crisp Woodworking Concern Limited*
*333 Southeast 3rd*
*Portland, Oregon 97214*

*Orifice ½ in., 25 in. from floor*
*Double belt, bobbin lead*
*Bobbin length 3 ¾ in., bronze bearings*
*Flyer width 3 ¾ in., with speed hooks,*
*    pulley ratios 1.75 and 2.75*
*Drive wheel 25 in., drive ratio 25:1*
*Saxony treadle*
*Lazy Kate with 3 bobbins*
*Can be taken apart for shipping; assembles with locking pegs*
*Maple or walnut*

Handspinning can be considered as three distinct operations: attenuation (for yarn size and length), twisting (for strength), and winding on.

One of the earliest forms of spinning was done without even a spindle, rolling wool on the lap with one hand and drawing it out into yarn with the other hand. This is one of the simplest examples of attenuation and twisting combined, which is speeded up considerably by using a spindle.

In some parts of the world, spinning is still done with a small, rough stick, hooked at the tip (the shorter the fibers, the finer the stick). It is twirled to draw wool out of a teased fiber supply, which is weighted down with a stone. Considering the amount of cloth produced this way, one can only be amazed at the dexterity with which the "spindle" must be handled.

Whatever spindle you use to start with, it might be a good idea to practice "spinning" with commercial yarn before you use fibers, in order to learn how to twirl the spindle effectively and get the feel of its weight and balance.

NAVAJO SPINDLE

The long, Navajo-type spindle has a simpler spinning style than other spindles; you do not need to loop the yarn under the whorl and hitch it over the tip. Also, it does not hang from the yarn being spun, so you can attain the right amount of twist without the yarn parting because of the weight of the spindle. In addition, you do not have to cope with the pull from the spindle as it gets progressively heavier (from more and more yarn being added to it).

The long hip spindle provides good training in the drawing out (*drafting*) process since the handling of the wool is done entirely with one hand. This prevents you from getting into "inchworm" habits, inching the wool out of the fiber supply into the twist, as is often done with a drop spindle, and carrying that slow technique into wheel spinning.

To make a Navajo spindle, you need a length of three-

# 6

## Learning on a Spindle

**78.** *"Wuzzing" wool in the seventeenth century. "Bobbins of weft were dipped into the nearby stream, then to shake out the water they were 'wuzzed' round in a basket slung from a stick, one end of the stick being inserted into a 'wuzzing hole' in the nearest field wall."*

eighths inch dowel about thirty or thirty-two inches long, and a wooden disk about five inches in diameter, which is fitted onto the dowel about six to ten inches from the bottom. (Indian spindles had a whorl of clay instead of a wooden disk, so if you know a potter, or have some children's modeling clay or a clay bank nearby, you can make a flat, clay whorl for your spindle.) The top end of the dowel should be tapered and sanded to a rounded point.

**79.** *Schacht spindles. Navajo—30-in. shaft, 5-oz. weight (center); 3 drop spindles—1 with 3-in. whorl, thin shaft, 2-oz. weight (bottom right); 1 with 3-in. whorl, thick shaft, 3-oz. weight (upper); 1 with 4-in. whorl, thin shaft, 3-oz. weight (bottom left)*

Take a length of yarn of about one and one-half yards for the leader yarn, and tie or tape it to the spindle just above the whorl. Wind it around the spindle a few times (clockwise for spinning on the right thigh), then spiral it up the spindle, ending with a few turns around the tip of the spindle. About six inches of the leader yarn should extend past the spindle tip. The last few turns around the tip are not really necessary, but make it easier for a beginner to join on the wool to get started.

Sitting on the floor, or on a low stool, rest the spindle base on the floor and lean the spindle against your right thigh. You may need to rest the base in a small bowl, if you have a slippery floor, to keep the spindle from scooting around as you spin. Your right hand rotates the spindle by rolling it along your thigh toward your hip, causing the twisting action, while your left hand draws the twisting fibers out into yarn.

This sounds as though the spindle is turning *only* while your hand is rolling it along your thigh, but the heavy whorl actually gives it enough momentum so that it does not stop turning until you want to wind on the yarn. At the end of each stroke, scoop it up with your thumb under it (your palm still downward to start the next rolling motion) and carry it back to its starting point, where you can roll it upward again with no interruption of its rotation.

The wool spins off the tip of the spindle, each flip off the tip causing one twist in the yarn. This spindle prepares you for using the great wheel (colonial walking wheel), which ordinarily requires a left-handed drafting and also spins the yarn off the spindle tip. To gain practice that will later be useful with a treadle wheel, you can reverse your hand and spindle positions and spin the fibers with your right hand. This alternate use of either hand is a useful skill to acquire.

It is easier with this spindle than with a drop spindle to attach your wool fibers to the leader yarn. The handspun yarn need not support the weight of the spindle at the joining. It is then less apt to pull apart as you try to spin that first length. As the twist from the rolling spindle travels into the wool, draw it out with the hand that is holding the fibers. When you have drawn your hand back as far as you can spin comfortably, wind this length of yarn onto the spindle above the whorl. The last yard of it spirals up the dowel to reach six inches past the tip, and you then repeat the spinning process. To wind the spun yarn onto the spindle, reverse the spindle about one and one-half to two turns in order to uncoil the spiral of yarn so that the newly spun yarn can be wound onto the base next to the whorl. With a crisscross motion to keep it firm, gradually build a tapered, cone-shaped ball of yarn against the whorl. Once you become proficient with it, the long draw can make the hip spindle nicely suited to fine yarn, especially if the wool is well prepared.

As an alternative to drawing out with only one hand, you can roll the spindle and then use both hands to draw out this twist. This method is slower, and you also have to prevent the spindle from rolling back and untwisting.

The hip spindle can be used to make yarn in two steps, as is usually done by the Navajos for warp yarn. The first spinning makes a loose, heavy yarn, twisted only enough to hang together well. When a large ball of this is spun on the spindle, it is wound off or taken off onto a rod, which is hung by both ends. This yarn is then respun into finer yarn that has more twist. The second spinning goes much faster, as all the splicing or joining on of new fiber has been done.

In spinning a smooth warp yarn, the farther you can work from the tip of the spindle, the easier it is to spin an even yarn, for it takes a certain amount of distance to even out the thick and thin places by drawing them.

## HAND-ROTATED AND DROPPED SPINDLE

There is a modified way of using a drop spindle that utilizes some of the Navajo spindle techniques. This is usually done with a spindle having a hook at the top and the whorl a few inches below it. Yarn is wound around the spindle below the

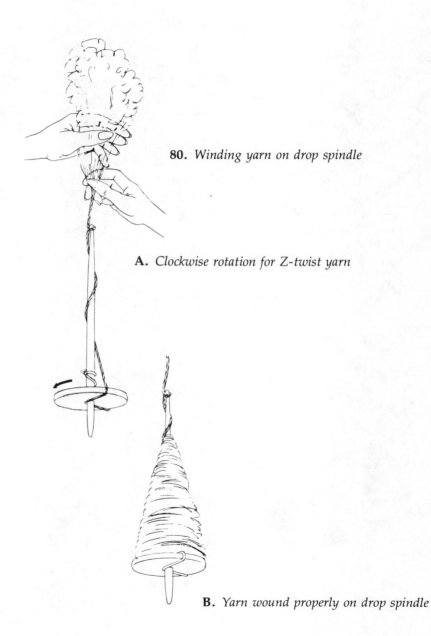

**80.** *Winding yarn on drop spindle*

**A.** *Clockwise rotation for Z-twist yarn*

**B.** *Yarn wound properly on drop spindle*

whorl, crosses over the whorl, and is twisted from the hook. To start spinning, hold and rotate the spindle in one hand while the other hand draws out the yarn. This is done for *part* of the process, to put the twist into the yarn so that it will bear the weight of the spindle. Then roll the spindle against the hip and drop it. While it is twirling and inserting more twist, draw the yarn out to the exact size and evenness desired, using both hands. Then wind the yarn onto the spindle next to the whorl, catch it under the hook, rotate it by hand, and then roll it against the hip and drop it. It gains a much faster rotation when rolled against the hip than if it is just twirled by the fingertips.

The length of the spindle below the whorl provides the right amount of space to rest your hand when rolling the spindle to

**81.** *Joyous Song spindles*

get it started twirling, while also providing the place where it is grasped by the hand for rotating.

## DROP SPINDLE

Yarn spun with a drop spindle is attenuated both by your hands drawing the wool and by the weight of the spindle. To begin spinning with a drop spindle, tie or tape leader yarn to the spindle just above the whorl, pass it over the whorl, catch it over the bottom of the spindle, and then bring it up to make a half hitch around the spindle tip. Many spindles have a notch there, but that is not necessary to hold the loop around the tip. Your fibers are laid against the leader yarn, and the spindle is twisted in a clockwise direction until the twist grabs into the wool. Then the right hand twirls the spindle (also clockwise) and lets go, assisting the other hand in drawing out and controlling the twist as the spindle is rotating and inserting more twist. More fibers must not be pulled from the fiber supply than can be held together by the twist; as more twist enters, more fibers can be pulled out. Reach down and twirl the spindle again when it slows down. Otherwise, it will reverse and start to untwist your yarn.

The weight of the whorl greatly helps the momentum of the twirl, and as the weight of the spindle increases from yarn wound onto it, it will rotate longer each time you twirl it.

## WINDING ON

When the yarn is so long that the spindle reaches the floor, it is time to wind up the yarn. It is sometimes advised that you wrap some of this yarn around your hand in order to shorten it to a more manageable length for winding neatly. This overlong yarn can be sufficiently shortened by just looping it over your bent elbow until you have wound enough of it onto the spindle to handle the rest easily. Rather than winding the yarn on by circling the spindle with the hand carrying the yarn (which adds more twist), you may find it more convenient to twirl the spindle with its base against you, winding the yarn around it as it turns.

Yarn should be wound into a cone shape, with the widest end against the whorl. The occasional zigzagging back and forth, as you are winding it, prevents it from embedding itself in the already wound yarn.

## DISTAFF AND SPINDLE

To spin while walking, prepare your wool by drawing out Z-shaped strips from the drum carder into attenuated rovings, or attenuate and twist rolags sufficiently to make a long strip. Wind these back and forth onto one end of a *distaff* stick until they form a large, soft ball of roving. The stick is held under your arm and turned slowly to unroll the fibers as you spin them.

Another style of distaff can be made to hang from your arm. Take a long, supple switch and bind the ends together for six to ten inches up from the ends. The wool strips are wound loosely onto the joined ends, and the looped switch goes over your wrist.

## TURKISH SPINDLE

A turkish-style spindle is made up of three pieces, the whorl being two separate crossarms. The spindle fits together so that the shaft goes through the two parts of the whorl. Winding the yarn around the crosspieces results in a center-pull ball when the spindle is slipped apart. If using yarn directly from this ball for knitting, you have to allow for some shrinkage in washing the finished article. In things like scarves, where there is no exact size needed to fit properly, this can be a convenient system.

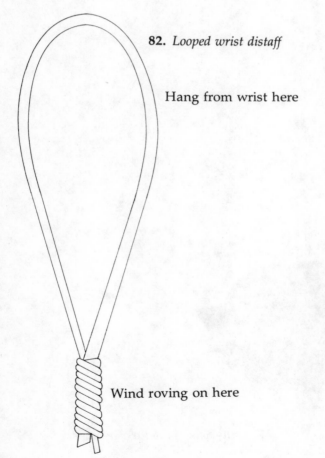

**82.** *Looped wrist distaff*

Hang from wrist here

Wind roving on here

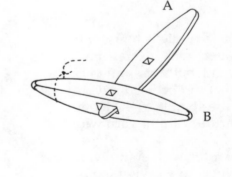

**83.** *To begin spinning on the turkish spindle, slip A through B; then slip these crossed pieces on spindle C down to D. Take about one yard of yarn for a leader, form a yarn loop around the end of B, as indicated, and tie a knot. Transfer the knot to C and slip it down to D. Wind a few turns of the leader around the crossed whorl made by A and B and then loop the yarn around the spindle tip. Spin as with any drop spindle.*

## WINDING YARN ON THE TURKISH SPINDLE

Each time you get a length of yarn spun, wind it onto the spindle, across the whorl arms rather than above the whorl. Wind on rather loosely so that when you have a sizeable quantity spun and wound onto it, you can disassemble the whole spindle, leaving a center-pull ball.

To wind each length of yarn, find the balance point on the spindle and hold the spindle there, with one hand. Turn the spindle clockwise while the other hand holds the yarn. Move the hand holding the yarn back and forth so that the yarn winds in and out between the crosspieces.

There is also a more deliberate winding pattern that can be followed. Turning the spindle clockwise with one hand and holding the yarn in the other hand, wind the yarn over two adjacent cross-tips several times. Then skip to the third tip, wind around it and the one next to it several times, and continue in that fashion. Each change moves the yarn to encircle one of the points used in the previous winding, along with the point next to it. You end up with a nicely balanced center-pull ball.

## WEAVING QUILLS

One way to get the most out of your spindle is to use it to spin weaving weft. Wrap a brown paper quill several times around the spindle shaft, and wind each length of spun yarn onto it in an elliptical shape, of a size that can be used in your shuttles, so that it can go directly from the spindle to the loom. This does not, however, give you preshrunk yarn or yarn with the twist "set" by washing.

In the Middle Ages, it was common for weavers to wind their yarn directly from the spinning wheel to weaving quills, then wet these quills and let them dry to set the twist. This can also be done with your spindle quills if you make them of a middle-weight, plastic sheeting of about a four-millimeter thickness (called "four mil.").

**84.** *Yarn wound onto turkish spindle*

Before you start to work with actual fibers, there are two procedures that can make spinning easier for you from the beginning.

## PRACTICING TREADLING

This is as monotonous as practicing scales on the piano, but the learning process goes more smoothly when your feet can do their work automatically. You want them to do their part without accidentally reversing the drive wheel just when you think your hands are getting the hang of it. Practice stopping and starting without using your hands to start the drive wheel. You must learn to treadle slowly, for your hands will be slow at handling the fibers and will not keep up with fast feet. Try to see how slowly you can treadle and still keep the wheel turning evenly and clockwise. It is well to spin all your yarn with the same twist (Z twist being the norm) and use the reverse twist only when you are plying. Keep in mind that the drive wheel goes clockwise for Z twist and counterclockwise for S twist. Be careful not to combine both S- and Z-twist yarns in warp or in weft for weaving, or use both in an article being knitted.

## PRACTICING SPINNING

Spin up a ball of store yarn to experience the feel of the twisting action and the drawing in movement before you have to cope with the problem of fibers. Place the ball of yarn on the floor beside you in a box, jar, or can. Feed the loose end of it through the orifice at the front of the flyer, over several hooks, and wind it clockwise a few times around the bobbin. Fasten it there with a snip of tape. Then treadle slowly, holding the yarn lightly with one hand nearer the orifice and one hand quite a bit farther away from the orifice. (If you are right-handed, keep the right hand, which will be doing most of the work, farther from the orifice.)

Treadling slowly, let the yarn slip through the fingers of your hands. Hold it back, from time to time, by pinching the yarn with the hand nearest the orifice. Let some twist build up;

# 7

## Learning on a Spinning Wheel

then release the twist into the yarn and let it draw into the bobbin.

*If the wheel does not pull the yarn in* when you move it toward the orifice, then you may need to make some adjustments. First, make certain that your yarn is not caught up on one of the hooks. Then consider if your bobbin moves freely on its spindle. If it is a new wheel, it may need a little oil here. If it is an old wheel, the bobbin shaft may need both cleaning and lubrication. If the bobbin does not rotate freely with the belt off the pulley, it will not spin well.

With a double belt wheel, see that your drive belt is over the largest whorl of the fork pulley and the smallest whorl of the spool pulley (this may vary depending on the size and number of pulley grooves). This larger ratio between them gives you the maximum drawing in.

If your problem is none of the above, then tighten the drive belt.

*If the yarn pulls in too hard,* your drive belt is too tight. Loosen its tension until the bobbin draws in your yarn when you want it to, but does not take it away from you.

*If the yarn seems to pull in too fast* when you are just practicing with already spun yarn, you are probably treadling too fast. If you are already working with unspun wool, it is more likely that you are using too large a pulley ratio for spinning a fine yarn, and you should probably change your drive belt to a smaller flyer pulley. If the yarn pulls in too hard on a *single belt* wheel, it means that you need less tension on the brake.

## SPINNING CLASSES

One nice thing about classes is the stimulus of all that spinning enthusiasm. It can have a more tangible advantage, too, if you are able to learn on a class-provided wheel before you invest in one. You are in a better position to judge what kind you want to buy after you have spun on several different makes. Even if people have to bring their own wheels, it still gives you the chance to see wheels other than your own. By trading wheels during the class, you might get a better idea about how many of your problems are wheel related.

A class is not without disadvantages, however. It can be distressing to sit next to someone who appears to be learning faster, but that *may* be due to differences in your spinning wheels. Lessons can also give you a preconception of the only "right" kind of yarn to spin. None of us is without a preference, which can be easily conveyed no matter how unbiased we try to be. Opinions about yarn size, plying, and texture should not be formed for you as that limits your freedom to discover the type of yarn best suited to your own use and enjoyment. There are many possible styles of spinning and types of yarn, so you are not wrong if you are different.

## SPINNING STYLES

A beginner should try for versatility as early as possible, for it is easier to learn a variety of styles before you have become completely accustomed to one. Some styles evolve from one to the other. For spinning different fiber lengths, wool breed types, and different size yarns, you will need to vary your style of spinning.

There is a decided advantage in keeping both hands equally trained in the primary spinning process (drawing out) by reversing the position and function of your hands. This way, either is trained in the drafting process. If you get a great wheel or suffer from bursitis, you will be able to spin with either hand, and do not have to stop and learn all over again with the other hand.

## THE INCHWORM

There is one style, which I will call here the *inchworm*, that is often used to teach a first spinning lesson. It is a natural way to start out if you have first learned with a spindle, and it is a "safe" style for beginners since the wool is less apt to get away from them. This style involves working quite close to the orifice, and using the hand closest to the wheel to cautiously inch out the wool from the stationary hand that holds the fiber supply and is farthest from the orifice.

While the advantage is that it is a surer way of handling your wool so that it holds together, it is a method that can never be speeded up very much. It remains nearly as slow as in the beginning, even after you get good at controlling the size and texture of your yarn, and it can quickly become a habit that is hard to break. Once you have the feel of your equipment and materials and are confident to move your hands more, you should try *drawing out* your wool by moving the hand that is farthest from the orifice and holding the fiber supply.

## THE FEEL OF SPINNING

To get the real feel of spinning as soon as possible, try to let the twisting of the wheel help pull out the necessary wool fibers. The hand closest to the wheel should *not* be used to draw out toward the orifice. You can use that hand to pinch off the twist until you have drawn out enough wool to cope with the twist, and you can use it to pick out seeds and second cuts that protrude from the twisting yarn. Its primary function, however, is to provide firm traction against which the other hand can pull as necessary to draw out the twisting wool.

You also use the hand closest to the orifice to smooth out fuzzy places as the fibers are twisting. This smoothing action should be done before the twist is complete in order to effectively catch in any unruly wisps. Since the wheel is still adding twist to your yarn as it is being drawn in, smoothing at this point has the effect of catching unruly hairs into the twist.

## OVERTWIST

To avoid overtwist, do *not* keep the hand farthest from the orifice in one place, just allowing the fibers to twist. You must always keep it moving, either drawing back as the twist enters the yarn or moving forward to allow the yarn to wind onto the

**85.** *The inchworm*

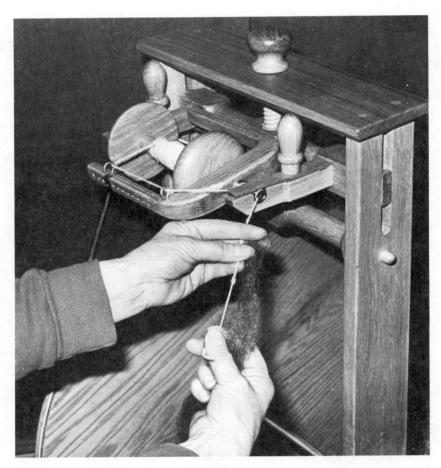

**86.** *Joining fiber supply onto leader yarn. Note the knot in the leader.*

bobbin.

With any great amount of overtwist, the yarn just kinks up and will not go through the orifice. When this happens, you must stop treadling (which adds more twist) and draw out your wool supply in such a way as to allow that extra twist to travel into the unspun wool to unkink the already spun yarn. It may then be easier to wind that portion of the yarn into the bobbin by hand.

When your feet are moving, you are adding twist, so the slower your feet move, the less twist is added, which gives your hands time to learn to handle the wool. (For more information, see "Conquering Overtwist" chapter.)

## SHORT DRAW STYLE

A better way to start than the inchworm, which causes a bad habit, is the *short draw*. With this, as with other styles, the hand farthest from the orifice holds the carded fibers. The hand nearest the orifice should be about six inches from it and controls the amount of twist that is allowed into the carded fibers.

To begin, you need a length of *leader* yarn (your fibers can more easily cling to *wool* yarn) attached to the core of the bobbin, up over the hooks, through the exit hole, and out the front of the orifice. A fine hair pin that is straightened out and has a sharp hook bent into one end is a good hook to use to pull the yarn through the orifice. Bend the other end of the hair pin into a loop to which you can tie a piece of string. Let your leader yarn hang out of the orifice about twelve inches, and tie a knot in the end of it so you can join on more easily and so the fibers cannot slip off as the leader yarn pulls onto the bobbin. Grasp the leader by the hand nearest the orifice, and you are ready to start spinning.

Have a few wisps of wool drawn outward from your handful of carded fibers, and place that against the last few inches of your leader yarn, which always remains on the spinning wheel in order to get you started the next time. Treadle very slowly, and let a bit of the twist through the fingers of the hand that is pinching the leader. If your bit of carded fiber is against the leader, the twist will catch into it and start forming yarn. Spinning that first yard of yarn is tricky, for you want it to cling to the leader while you draw back on your fiber supply, thinning it to yarn size, before too much twist gets into it.

Drawing your wool out thinner is easy only when you have a very small amount of twist in it. Treadle *slowly*, let a very little bit of twist into the fibers, draw them out into yarn, and then release the remaining twist that is building up behind the hand nearest the orifice so that twist runs into your loosely twisted yarn. Ideally, this will be no more than is needed for soft yarn. At this point, you must advance the hand that holds the wool supply, allowing the spun portion to be drawn onto the bobbin. At this stage, do not be concerned about what size yarn you are spinning; just draw out fibers, let the twist into them, and wind the yarn onto the bobbin. The hand holding the fiber supply should not stop moving — it should either be drawing out yarn or moving that yarn toward the bobbin. If it stops, your feet must also stop.

## USING THE HOOKS

As you spin and the yarn winds onto the bobbin, you should change the position of the yarn passing over the hooks on the flyer arm so that the yarn winds on evenly. The hooks determine where the yarn winds onto the bobbin. If it remains over the same hook too long, it builds up into a high ridge and some of the yarn slips off the edge of that ridge, making it difficult to wind off into a skein as well as somewhat limiting the amount of yarn you can get on your bobbin.

## OVERTWIST IN THE SHORT DRAW

If you are getting your yarn overtwisted and kinky using this short draw, then you are treadling faster than your hands are forming the yarn. You may need to actually stop your feet occasionally to allow your hands to catch up. Try to treadle as

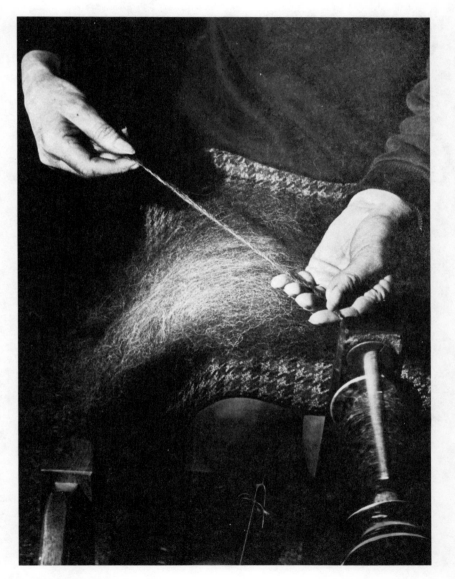

**87.** *Short draw style*

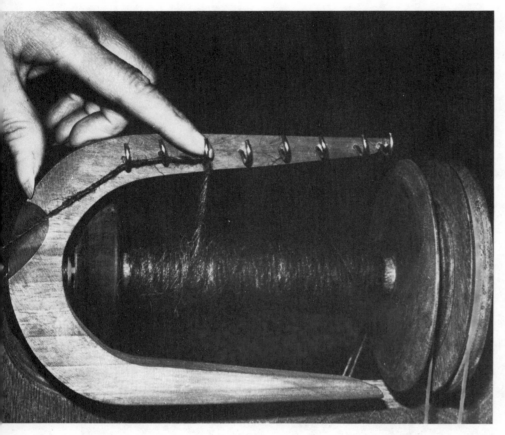

**88.** *The hooks are used to determine where the yarn winds onto the bobbin.*

slowly as possible while still keeping the wheel in motion.

To repeat the method, pinch off the twist as it comes from the wheel with the hand nearest the orifice. Do not treadle too fast, for you will build up more twist than your drawn out fibers can absorb when you let the twist run into them. Draw back on the hand with the wool supply, let a small amount of twist into the fibers between your hands so the fibers do not come apart as you draw them out into yarn, then allow the rest of the twist to come past your pinching fingers into the lightly twisted yarn. At this moment, the yarn must be headed toward the spinning wheel, winding onto the bobbin. If there is too much twist for that amount of drawn out wool, you have treadled too much in the time it took your hands to draw it out.

The pull exerted by the correct adjustment of the drive belt tension, plus the ratio between the flyer pulley and the bobbin pulley, are the factors involved in the way the bobbin draws in the yarn. (This is described in detail in "Spinning Wheel Operation" chapter.) Your part is to let it draw in *before* it gets too much twist.

## ADJUSTING TENSION MID-BOBBIN

When you have your bobbin about half full, the weight of the yarn on the bobbin, plus the difference that yarn makes in the diameter of the bobbin core as it winds in the yarn (drawing in more yarn with each turn of the bobbin than it did when empty) causes you to notice less of a pull from the wheel. This can be adjusted by a little tighter tension on your drive belt. When you have wound off your yarn into a skein and have started spinning again with an empty spool, you will need to adjust again to the previous tension.

## WINDING OFF YOUR YARN

When you have a fairly full bobbin, move the drive belt off the bobbin pulley onto the smaller groove of the fork pulley. This releases the tension and allows the bobbin to move freely. If your wheel has only one fork pulley and one bobbin pulley, place both belts onto the bobbin pulley. Since it is the smaller of the two pulleys, this should allow the bobbin to move freely. Wind off your yarn into a skein on a niddy-noddy, a skeiner stick, or just around your hand and bent elbow, leaving the leader yarn attached to the bobbin. The yarn usually comes apart at the point where it is attached to the leader. Tie this skein loosely in several places to prepare it for washing.

## SKEINER (OR SKEINING) STICK

This is simpler to use than a traditional niddy-noddy and a little easier to make, too. You can make one that is one yard in circumference (eighteen inches long) for measuring skeins, or one that is one and one-half yards around (twenty-seven inches long) that is a convenient length for use on the homemade swift (fig. 157). (Actually, to end up with preshrunk yarn of one yard or one and one-half yards as measured on the stick, you should add two inches to the one yard stick's size and three inches to the distance around the one and one-half yard stick.)

An interesting comparison between this stick and an actual niddy-noddy is that while the skeiner stick is easier to use than an actual niddy-noddy, it does something that a niddy-noddy does not do. It *adds* one twist per turn around the stick, if you have spun a Z twist (by turning your wheel clockwise) and then wound the yarn off on the stick in the normal manner (overhand *away* from you). One twist per one and one-half yards is not enough to be noticeable, but it is interesting. On the other hand, the stick *subtracts* one twist from each round of S-twist yarn or it subtracts one twist from Z twist if you wind overhand *toward* you.

## LONG DRAW STYLE

This is just an extension of your short draw, except that you stretch and draw out the fibers *as the twist comes into them*. It is the logical progression from the short draw, and must be done a little

faster to be smooth and efficient. The hand next to the orifice does not do as much pinching off of the twist; it provides only a firm grip on the yarn so that the other hand has something to draw against, as necessary, to even out any thicker places in the yarn. Once a sufficient amount of twist is in your length of yarn and it can be drawn out no thinner, you should immediately allow the bobbin to pull it in. If it is too kinky, you are treadling too fast, not feeding it onto the bobbin soon enough, or hesitating before you allow it to move toward the bobbin. The tendency is to hesitate between the drawing out motion and the pulling in motion.

With practice and reasonably good wool, this method lends itself to greater speed than the short draw.

**89.** *Winding yarn from filled bobbin onto a skeiner stick*

## UNSUPPORTED LONG DRAW (DOUBLE DRAFTING)

This is used more with medium-heavy yarns than with finer yarns and is a long drawing out of an unsupported wool mass. Its attenuation is evenly spread over the long draw as the twist is moving into it. The pull is exerted on it from *both* directions, some from the twisting of the wheel (and the hand nearest it) and some from the pull of the hand farthest from the orifice that is doing the actual drawing out of the wool. The hand closest to the orifice will not be used much in pinching off the twist, but is used often to pull against to even out yarn size and texture.

This is not an easy style for beginners, for it is jerky and uneven if not done at a good speed. It can also result in a lot of accidental slubs and bumps if the wool has not been oiled and well carded since it depends on an even slippage of the fibers. You control the twist and yarn size by drawing it out as it is twisting.

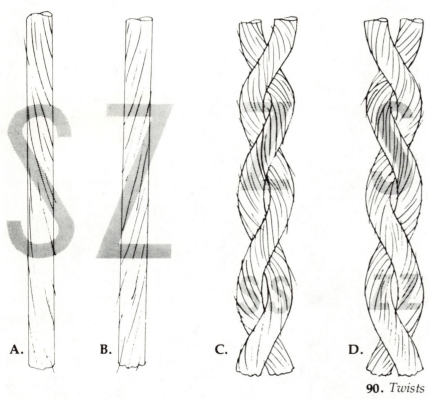

**90.** *Twists*

**A.** *Turn your drive wheel counterclockwise to spin this S twist.*

**B.** *Turn your drive wheel clockwise to spin this Z twist (the most common twist for singles).*

**C.** *Here two S-twist singles are plied together in a Z twist.*

**D.** *Here two Z-twist singles are plied together in an S twist.*

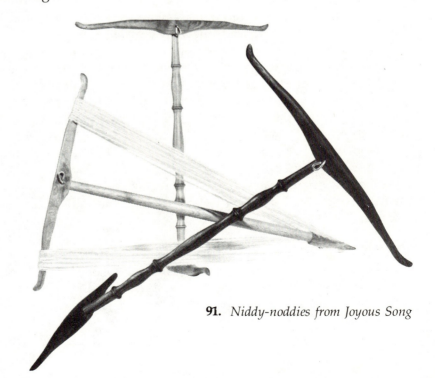

**91.** *Niddy-noddies from Joyous Song*

 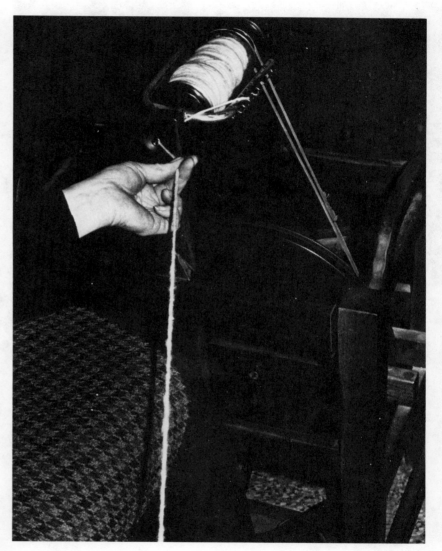

**92.** *Long draw style*
**A.** *The wool is being attenuated (note the moderate twist).*

**B.** *The yarn is fully attenuated, with the correct twist, and is ready to be wound onto the bobbin.*

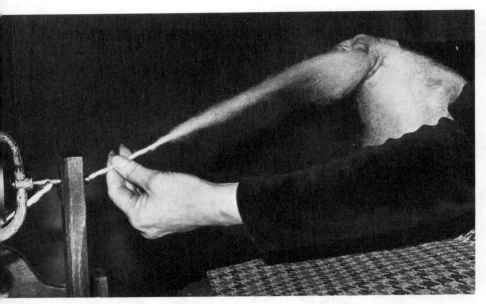

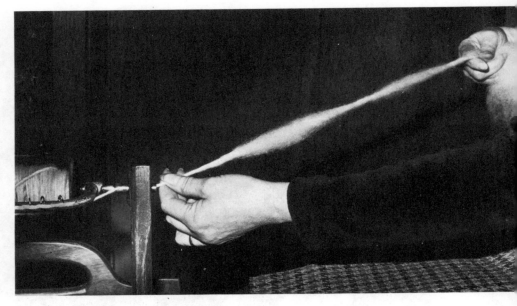

**93.** *Unsupported long draw*
*Step 1. This is the start of the unsupported long draw.*

*Step 2. Now a small amount of twist is in the wool, and it is being drawn out.*

Because it is a fast way of spinning a medium-heavy yarn, it is valuable for that purpose. It differs from the long draw in that you release, from the hand holding the fiber supply, a handful of wool and draw it out as the twist is entering it. At first, it seems to be drawing out into a lot of alternating thick and thin places. As you continue to stretch it (not letting it get too twisted or it cannot be drawn), it evens out. The thin places have enough twist in them so they get no thinner, and the thicker places do not have so much twist in them that they cannot be drawn out more, once you get proficient at this method. Prior ability in general spinning is required for success at this, for it depends on skill and speed in order to be a smooth operation.

## WOOL SUPPLY

It is convenient to have your carded wool, rolags, combed tufts, or Z-shaped strips from the drum carder within your reach while spinning. A natural thing is to have some in your lap. If you are spinning wool that still has bits of seeds or other vegetable matter in it, however, do not keep wool in your lap because seeds and other undesirable matter will fall onto the wool in your lap. A table or bench next to you prevents this. The Z-shaped strips (see "Drum Carding" chapter) can be coiled in a basket for easy access.

## JOINING NEW FIBER SUPPLY

Do not spin right up to the very end of your carded fibers; leave a generous unspun area for easy joining on of the next wool. (With practice, fewer fibers are needed for joining.) It is then simple to fan out this untwisted mass, lay the end of your next supply of fibers against it, and treadle. Drawing out as

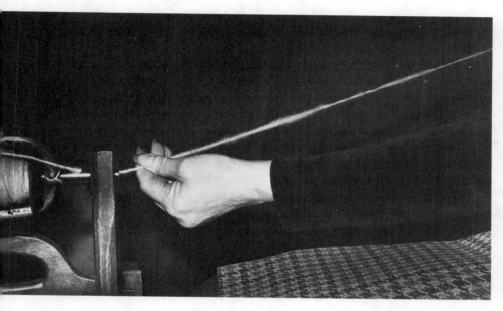

*Step 3. There is continued
drawing to even out the yarn.*

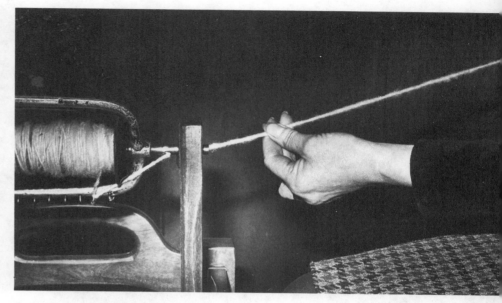

*Step 4. Completed draw. Having uniform size
and correct twist, the yarn is now ready to wind onto the bobbin.*

the twist enters causes them to spiral together. The yarn then remains a continuous twisting of fibers as though there was no joining.

In one-ply yarn, the joining must be done well or you will have a weak place in the yarn, which will pull apart when it is being wound off the bobbin or fray and come apart if it is used as weaving warp. Conscious attention to joining is necessary only during the learning process. In practicing the joining on of a new wool supply, you will at first have to interrupt your spinning process in order to accomplish it, but you should aim for the skill to join on without stopping or even slowing down (see "Speed Spinning" chapter and fig. 117). This will eventually become as automatic as steady treadling.

My husband learned to spin after I did and I expected him to have the usual beginner's problems in joining. But instead of fanning out the last of his unspun fibers to join on a new supply, he divided them into two unspun portions, lapped the end of the new fiber supply between them, and drafted them out together quite easily. This sounds like a slow process, but he still does it this way, with no interruption of rhythm or speed, and spins an exceptionally strong warp for his afghans, jackets, and vests.

As you develop your own spinning style, you can work with other ways of feathering together the merging fibers by manipulating them with your fingers to achieve the desired result. Do not hesitate to experiment. (For more on joining technique, refer to "Speed Spinning" chapter.)

## UNIFORMITY OF YARN SIZE

When you have learned to spin and are planning a proj-

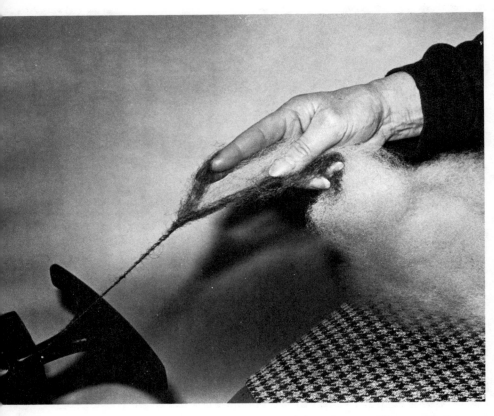

**94.** *Joining the new fiber supply between the divided unspun portion of the last fibers.*

skeins to see if you have spun a constant size for your intended project.

This does not mean that you should always spin the same size, for part of the challenge of spinning is to develop the ability to spin whatever size you want. You will want to be able not only to spin the size you want, but to have the size consistently the same over however many skeins you need.

The regular rhythm of hand and foot movement will greatly assist you, as well as the regulation of the drive belt tension to maintain an evenness in the size of your yarn. By this is not meant a yarn without irregularities, but a control over the *amount* of irregularity occurring within a given yarn size. What you are aiming for is a *basic* size, still allowing for texture variations.

## DESIGNATING YARN SIZE

If you are spinning several sizes of yarn to sell, you can use your own system of size indications, such as numbers, letters, or names for each yarn size. In the *cut system,* which designates the sizes of 1 to 100 for commercially spun wool yarns, the smaller the number, the larger the yarn size.

We started out by using size numbers 1, 2, 3, 4, and 5 for the sizes we were spinning to sell, but used the smaller number for the smaller yarn size. My first reasoning was to have them designate ounces per 100-yard skein:

Size #1 was one ounce per 100-yard skein.

Size #2 was two ounces per 100-yard skein.

Size #3 was three ounces per 100-yard skein, etc.

But in practice, it soon became clear that such a fine gradation of sizes was not necessary, and a wider range of yarn sizes would be more salable, so it evolved shortly into more difference between sizes:

Size #1, which we now spin only for our own use, is one and one-half ounces per 100-yard skein.

Size #2, which we use for warp and for crocheted berets, is two and one-half to three ounces per 100-yard skein.

ect using your handspun, it will be necessary to have several skeins of yarn that are spun the same size for either weaving or knitting.

It is helpful if you get in the habit of always measuring off all your skeins in some standard length, such as fifty or one hundred yards. By using the one yard or the one and one-half yard skeiner stick, this will be simple. Knowing they are all the same quantity of yarn by length, you can check the weight of the

Size #3, which we now sell to knitters and weavers, is four to six ounces per 100-yard skein.

Size #4, spun to order now, is seven to nine ounces per 100-yard skein.

In actual practice, the weight of a given size varies depending on the type of wool used and on the firmness (amount of twist) of the yarn. The important thing is to keep the skeins uniform for each project or each sale.

## WASHING AND PRESHRINKING YARN

After winding your yarn off the spinning wheel bobbin onto your niddy-noddy or skeiner stick, tie it loosely in several places. This prevents the skein from snarling during washing.

To assure minimal shrinkage after the yarn is used for either knitting or weaving, wash the yarn gently in warm water with either soap or detergent. If you have spun it in the grease without washing the fleece, it is obvious that it needs washing. But even clean wool yarn needs the other effects obtained by washing — a relaxing and *setting* of the twist that has been put into it. If unwashed, a short length of yarn taken from the skein would unwind and lose its twist if you did not hold onto both ends of it.

Use warm water, not too hot for your own comfort, with either soap or a mild detergent dissolved in it. The advantage of detergent is that it rinses out more easily. We have found no need to buy special wool washing preparations. In the wash water, however, Borax can help eliminate such odors as the distinctive smell sometimes found in ram fleeces, the mustiness of a fleece that has been too long in storage, or the noticeable odor of some spinning oils.

Hand wash the yarn, because a felting action will occur if the yarn goes through the gyrations of a washing machine. Then rinse it in water of about the same temperature as the wash water. A washing machine with a spin cycle that you can operate separately provides an ideal way to remove the wash and

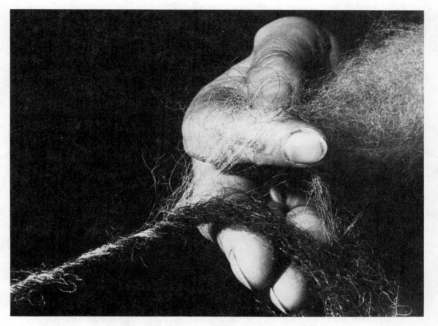

**95.** *Joining by feathering of the new fiber supply, merging it with the unspun portion of the last fibers.*

rinse water. This is kinder to the fibers than wringing by hand, and also removes more of the water.

## BLOCKING

Following the relaxing action of the warm water, blocking finishes the setting of the twist, under moderate tension, by allowing the yarn to dry that way. Put your damp yarn on a swift, remove the ties, and wind it onto a warping reel or over the back of a kitchen chair (one that will not be damaged by damp yarn), or build the yarn blocker described at the end of this chapter.

Hanging your damp skein with a weight at the bottom does not block all parts of the skein with equal tension and leaves some parts more kinked up than others. This is particularly true when you have any amount of overtwist. A proper blocking can minimize some of the overtwisted look and feel.

You could accomplish some of the "unkinking" action of blocking by just winding your yarn directly from the bobbin onto a skeiner stick or niddy-noddy and leaving it there for a week or so. However, this would not relax the twisted fibers (that takes moisture and warmth) in such a way as to make the yarn feel softer than when it was first spun, and it would do nothing to preshrink it for further use.

You could also wet the yarn when it is on an unfinished wood skeiner stick and allow it to dry there. While this is an improvement over leaving dry yarn on the stick for a time to counteract kinkiness, it accomplishes no preshrinking.

**96.** *Washed yarn wound on a blocker so it will dry while held at an even tension.*

When the yarn has dried on the blocker, remove the skein and it is ready for use in knitting, crocheting, or as weaving weft. (For warp treatment, see "Weaving with Handspun: The Warp" chapter.)

## PLYING OR DOUBLING

If you are going to ply your yarn, the customary way is to spin one bobbin of yarn, remove that bobbin from the fork, and replace it with an empty bobbin. Spin the second bobbin full, remove it also, and ply the yarn from both these bobbins onto a third bobbin.

To do this, both full bobbins should be put onto a *Lazy Kate*, which is a rod supported by a holder on each end. Some spinning wheels have their own built-in Lazy Kate to simplify plying. Knot the yarn end from both of these full bobbins to the leader on your empty bobbin. For plying them together, treadle to turn the drive wheel in the *opposite* direction from the way used for spinning the yarn. Two singles of Z twist spun with the drive wheel turning clockwise will be plied together in an S-twist yarn with your drive wheel turning counterclockwise. (If you ply them together in the *same* direction as they were spun, this is called *cabling*, which adds to the original twist of the singles. Cabled yarn is difficult to work with unless it is tightly blocked after washing.)

Hold both strands of plying yarn in the same hand, but with a finger between them so that they do not snarl or kink and can be held at equal tension. Treadling must be done evenly or it will cause an uneven twist in the plying.

For a beginner, plying together two strands can help minimize the overly thick and thin places in both strands and help to offset some of the overtwist. An overtwisted single-ply yarn, when used in knitting, can lean to the bias.

Some spinners prefer to always spin the same size yarn, as is done in some foreign countries, and do a two-ply or a three-ply to obtain larger size yarn. This system is easier to learn, and it is easier to become proficient in spinning a dependable yarn of even weight. It does, however, take a lot more time than spinning a one-ply to the exact size desired — fine, medium, or heavy.

There have been claims that single-ply handspun is not suitable for use as weaving warp, that it needs the strength of plying. A two-ply yarn is always stronger than either of the singles that comprise it, but this does not mean that singles cannot be used. Since warp yarn is only as strong as its weakest place, the object in spinning warp yarn is to make sure that it is evenly spun with no weak places. We have found no need to ply our warp yarns, and use our handspun for all our warps, even on the 100-inch wide blanket loom. (See "Weaving with Handspun: The Warp" chapter.)

Yarn spun on the great wheel or walking wheel (see "Learning on the Great Wheel" chapter) can be spun much softer than on a flyer wheel because there is no pull on the yarn from the wheel. A most unusual effect can be obtained by plying very soft, fine yarn from the great wheel. The Sarah Great Wheel has skeiners that mount on the axle of the wheel when needed to wind yarn off the spindle. When two skeiners are filled, they are both put on the axle, and the yarn from them is easily plied.

Another occasion for plying is when using a spinning wheel that does not have a sufficient bobbin-fork pulley ratio to do a good job of spinning yarn as heavy as you want. Here, nicely spun singles can be made and plied to make a yarn of a size that could not be spun as readily on that wheel. For this, use a tight drive belt tension when plying in order to make up for the small pulley ratio.

## SPECIAL EFFECTS

Many special effects can be done by plying. Using two singles of different colors is the simplest of them.

Yarn with boucle-type snarls, which can be produced at regular or irregular distances, requires holding one of the singles

**97.** *Plying on the Sarah Great Wheel, using two skeiners on the hub and the plying loop on the bench*

in each hand. The *boucle snarl* is made by lessening the tension on one of the singles, and flipping it back and forth quickly. If it is the ply with the most twist, it performs the snarl more easily. When done in two colors, these textural snarls can be in alternating colors, or in only one of the colors.

*Wrapping* is another type of plying. To do this, one of the singles yarns to be plied is held taut (usually in the left hand) while the other yarn is held more loosely in the right hand. The loosely held yarn wraps around the other strand during plying. The twist is considerably reduced in the strand that is being wrapped (the taut yarn) so wrapping is one way of using up a badly overspun skein of yarn. In fact, the twist is reduced so much that the wrapped strand is weakened if it is not over-twisted. Some spinners resort to plying a commercial thread along with the singles that is being wrapped in order to give the yarn strength. The wrapping technique may be varied in many ways to produce other unusual effects.

Many other novelty yarns can be achieved by plying, including a *cat's whisker tuft* made by inserting short, snipped wool between the plies at desired intervals.

## BLOCKING

Plied yarn, like singles, is much easier to use after it has been washed and blocked. There are some exceptions to the blocking rule, such as two thick-and-thin yarns plied together, where blocking slightly reduces the loose, fluffy appearance of the slubs.

## YARN BLOCKER PLANS

### List of Materials

| Item | Name | Quantity | Material | Length |
|------|------|----------|----------|--------|
| 1 | Reel end | 2 | ¾-in. plywood, 14 in. wide | 15⅛ in. |
| 2 | Reel spacer | 2 | ¼-in. plywood, 6-in. diameter | |
| 3 | Reel stretcher | 6 | 1 × 1½ in., fir or pine | 25 in. |
| 4 | Reel hub | 2 | 1¼ × 4 in., fir or pine | 6 in. |
| 5 | Reel crank | 1 | 1¼ × 3 in., maple | 7½ in. |
| 6 | Reel handle | 1 | ¾-in. dowel, maple | 4½ in. |
| 7 | Reel shaft | 1 | 1-in. steel conduit | 29¼ in. |
| 8 | Reel bolts | 3 | ¼-in. steel, with washers | 3½ in. |
| 9 | Reel screws | 12 | #8 steel sheet metal | 2 in. |
| 10 | Base frame | assembly | 1¼ × 4 in., fir or pine | |
| 11 | Base blocks | 2 | 2½ × 2½ in., fir or pine | 3½ in. |

*Note: To use this as a warping reel for a short warp, make the base 3 in. higher, make dowel holes on each end of the reel, and insert 3-in. dowels.*

**98.** *Yarn blocker*

Note: Dimensions are in inches except where marked.

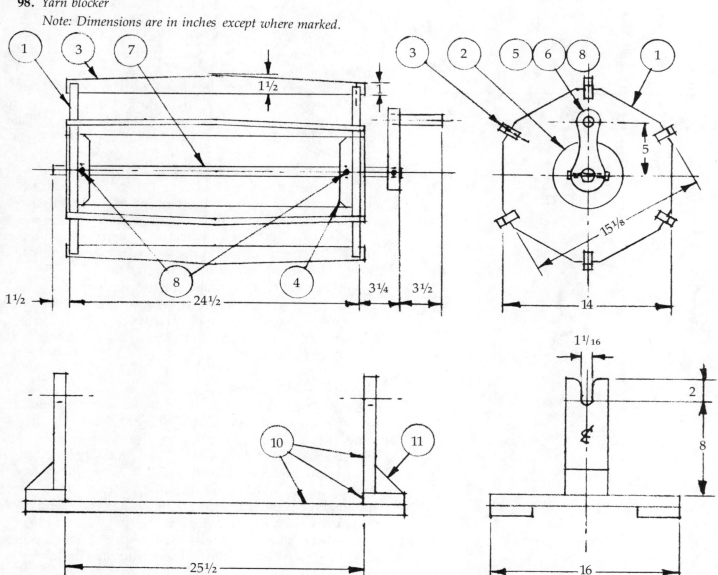

# 8

# Learning
# on the
# Great Wheel

**99.** *Spinster at the great wheel*

The great wheel or wool wheel was developed after spindles and before the spinning wheel having a flyer and treadle. Spinners now are more likely to learn on the treadle wheel, which is more available, but there has been a growing interest in great wheels.

The earlier versions of the great wheel had what is known as *direct drive* — that is, the belt from the large drive wheel turns the pulley fastened to the spindle. Some of this kind are still used in the Appalachian and Kentucky mountain regions of this country. Plans for making a very simple direct drive wheel are found in the "Building a Spinning Wheel" chapter.

The *Minor's head*, named after its inventor and patented about 1810, was an improvement added to the great wheel that made greater speed possible with less effort. It had an accelerating wheel between the drive wheel and the spindle, and became so popular that the whole Minor's head was made in factories and sold in country stores from around 1860 to 1875.

With either the direct drive or the accelerating wheel, the spinning process on the great wheel is the same. When you are just learning, however, using direct drive can be an advantage. It is difficult to slow down the accelerating head and still maintain any rhythm and coordination.

## SPINNING WITH DIRECT DRIVE

To spin with direct drive, put the large drive band around the drive wheel and around the pulley that directly drives the spindle. If you have a Minor's head, the short belt between the accelerating wheel and the spindle can probably be disengaged and the main drive belt transferred to the spindle pulley.

For a *leader*, tape or tie one end of a two-foot length of commercial yarn or handspun to the base of the spindle. Holding this yarn at a forty-five degree angle to the spindle, slowly turn the drive wheel clockwise. The leader spirals around the spindle, and twist is inserted as the leader flips off the tip of the spindle.

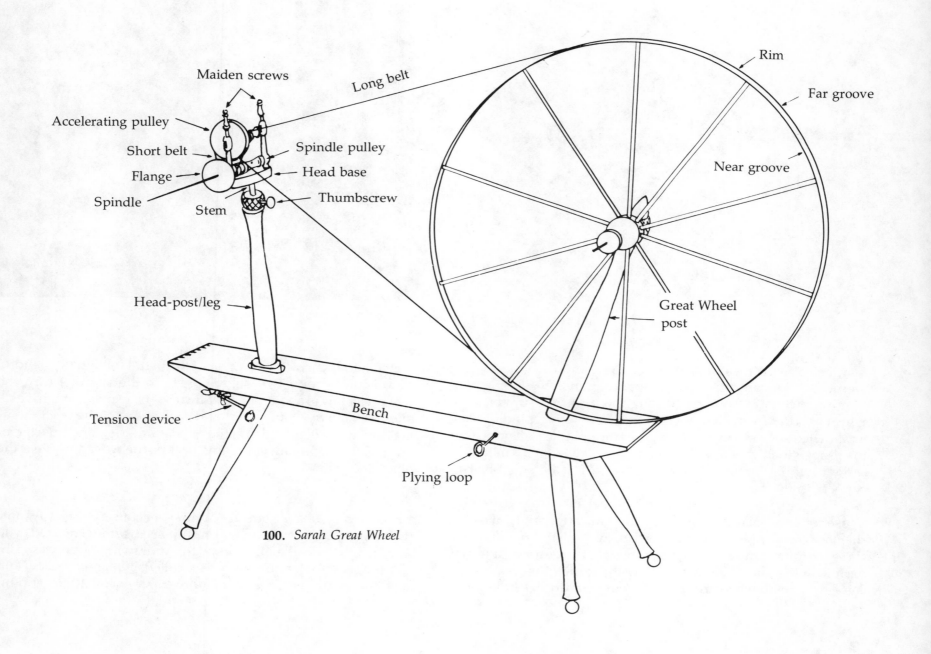

Maiden screws

Long belt

Rim

Far groove

Accelerating pulley

Spindle pulley

Near groove

Short belt

Flange

Head base

Spindle

Thumbscrew

Stem

Head-post/leg

Great Wheel post

Tension device

Bench

Plying loop

**100.** *Sarah Great Wheel*

**101.** *Bat head direct drive*    **102.** *Minor's head*

If the belt comes off the drive wheel and the wheel is not warped, this means that it is just not in alignment. Alignment of the drive wheel is done by turning the post that supports the wheel in order to line it up with the pulley on the spindle. Most great wheels have several grooves on the spindle pulley, so that the groove that lines up with the drive wheel would not necessarily be the groove that would be used for the small belt to connect to the accelerating wheel.

The makers of the Sarah Great Wheel encourage beginners to use commercial roving or top to start out, as learning is faster if the fiber is well prepared and easy to spin. With roving, pull off a three- to four-inch section of fiber and fold it around your leader yarn with the fibers at a *right angle* to the leader. You can do this same thing with well-carded wool from your drum carder, pull-

ing off a four-inch cross section of the batt. Holding the handful of fibers at a forty-five degree angle to the spindle, turn the wheel clockwise about one-half turn so the leader starts to catch and twist fibers. Draw your hand back ahead of the twist, holding the wool *lightly*. Turn the wheel another one-quarter or one-half turn, pulling your hand back as the twist draws out the fibers into yarn.

TWIST

When you have spun about three feet of yarn this way, note the amount of twist in that yarn. If it seems undertwisted, you can turn the wheel a bit more without drawing out more yarn. Adding twist to the yarn this way is called *spinning at the head* and is not necessary when you are more experienced in the amount

**103.** *Direct drive on antique wheel with Minor's head*

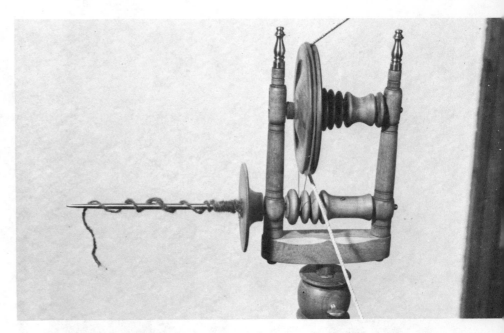

**104.** *On the Sarah Great Wheel, you can change to direct drive without having to dismantle the Minor's head in order to put the drive belt down on the spindle pulley. Since it has twin pulley grooves of the large diameter on the accelerating wheel, you just loosen the large drive belt and place it around the large pulley, right next to the large pulley holding the short belt that connects to the spindle.*

of twist needed. If the yarn seems overtwisted, reverse the wheel a small amount to take out some of the twist in the yarn, or just draw out a few more inches of the fibers to let some of the extra twist run into them.

## WINDING ON

The yarn you have spun should now be ready to wind onto the spindle. Reverse the wheel just enough to take the yarn off the spindle point. With direct drive, reversing the wheel to clear the point moves the wheel a little more than you have to move it when you use the accelerating head.

With the yarn clear of the point, move your hand close to the hub of the drive wheel (with the yarn at a right angle to the spindle) and wind the yarn onto the spindle by turning the

**105.** *Spinning yarn at a forty-five degree angle to the spindle*

wheel clockwise again. Yarn should be wound on close to the flange, gradually building up a cone shape with the widest end against the flange. Leave enough yarn unwound to spiral to the tip and about six inches past it. The hand holding the wool returns to its position at a forty-five degree angle to the spindle, and draws out fibers into yarn as you slowly turn the wheel clockwise. This will all be one continuous motion once you have learned the process.

When you have spun nearly all the fibers in your hand, fold another cross section of batt or roving around the unspun fibers remaining, and continue.

The great wheel does require better fiber preparation than is necessary with a treadle wheel. This is partly because you use only one hand to control the drawing out of the yarn, and also because you cannot draw *against* the spindle. Yarn must be drafted so lightly that you are not pulling against the tip of the spindle.

## SPINNING WITH THE MINOR'S ACCELERATING HEAD

To use this, put the long drive belt around one of the small pulley grooves on the shaft of the accelerating wheel, and the small belt around the large pulley of the accelerating wheel and the spindle pulley below it. The main difference between this and the direct drive is that the spindle turns about five times as many turns to each revolution of the drive wheel. (The exact speed ratio varies with different wheels.) This means that you have to turn the wheel more slowly than with direct drive, unless you are able to draw out your yarn much faster.

Just as with direct drive, you turn the drive wheel clockwise, drawing out your yarn at a forty-five degree angle to the spindle. (If the whole Minor's head is placed at a little more than a right angle to the drive wheel, you can work within a slightly wider angle.) To wind on the yarn, reverse the wheel just barely enough to unspiral the yarn from the tip of the spindle so that it can easily be wound onto the base of the spindle.

If you learned to operate the wheel when using the direct drive, your only difficulty now may be in reversing the drive wheel to clear the point of the spindle. I practiced only one day with direct drive, and it took me quite some time to curb the tendency to turn the drive wheel too far in reversing the wheel when I changed to using the accelerating wheel. It was easy enough to speed up my draw to keep up with the faster spindle, but I still had a heavy hand when reversing the wheel, trying to go much farther than the two or three inches necessary.

With the speed and efficiency of the Minor's head, you can spin fine yarn (needing more twists per inch) more easily than with the direct drive. Most people do not realize that, for fine yarn, a proficient spinner on a great wheel with the accelerating head can easily equal the production of a good spinner using a treadle wheel. The quality of the yarn spun still depends on the condition of the fleece and its preparation.

**106.** *Winding yarn on. Your hand is close to the hub, and the yarn is at a right angle to the spindle.*

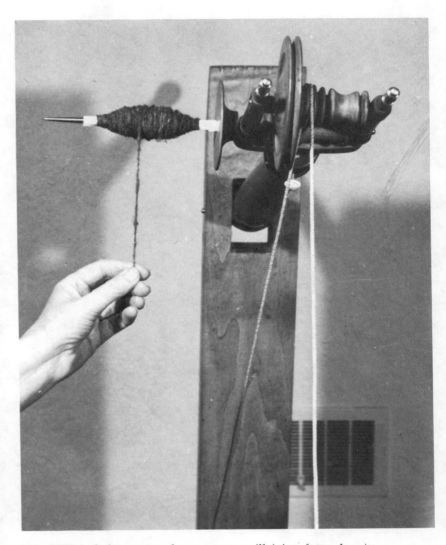

**107.** *Elliptical shape wound on a paper quill (view from above). This can be used as a bobbin for weaving or as a way to store yarn, and is a good idea with direct drive wheels having no flange.*

**108.** *Start of cone shape buildup of yarn wound onto the spindle*

## WOOL PREPARATION

Short fleece, oiled and either mill carded or double carded on the drum carder, spins nicely into fine yarn. Short or medium fleece that is in very good condition, washed gently, oiled, and opened with the flick carder, can also be spun into fine-weight yarn. The best portions of any silky, open fleece can usually be spun in the grease if desired, the tips opened with the flick carder if necessary. Unusually long wool must be *extremely* well prepared in order to use it on the great wheel.

If you are using hand cards, a well-rolled and compacted rolag does not spin as nicely as a loose, airy one, nor as well as wool peeled from cards in a flat layer. Using a lifting motion with the cards as you card, working with small amounts of wool at a time, and not rolling these carded fluffs of wool is even better. This is known as *fluffy cloud* carding (see ''Hand Carding'' chapter).

The evenness or uniformity of the size and twist of your yarn depends on the coordination between the speed that you turn the wheel and the speed that you draw out the yarn, as well as on how far you turn the drive wheel in relation to how far you draw out a given amount of fiber. With practice, you develop a rhythm that helps you coordinate the turning of the wheel with the length of the draw, moving two or three steps backward in spinning and two or three steps forward in winding on. I have noticed that I usually keep my hand on the same spoke all the time, although I am not sure if this is a common habit in operating the great wheel.

For most people, a fairly lightweight yarn is the easiest size to learn to spin. It is also the easiest to spin with most spinning wheels. Replicas of antique wheels are particularly suited to fine yarn, and wheels that are not sturdy enough for heavier yarn or do not have a good drive belt tensioner can still be used for fine yarn.

Many wheels do not have an adequate pulley ratio for heavy yarn, but I have not known of any wheels that did not have a sufficient ratio for spinning fine yarn. You want a low pulley ratio in order to have a gentle action with fine yarn, especially fine yarn with short fibers.

## POINT-OF-CONTACT TECHNIQUE

In spinning fine yarn, one technique that is valuable from the standpoint of speed, and also because it helps eliminate overtwist, is what I call the *point-of-contact* style, a variation of the long draw. For this, the fiber supply must be held lightly in the hand farthest from the spinning wheel. This can be practically one-handed spinning, with the other hand used to reach for more carded wool or used if a lump or slub momentarily requires more tension for an extended draw.

With this style, you allow the twist from the wheel to draw the wool from the hand-held fiber supply, pulling your hand back from the orifice just ahead of the twist traveling up the fibers. This twist runs up almost to the tip of the fingers holding the carded fibers to be spun. The pull is all in one direction, with the fibers pulled toward the spinning wheel as your hand draws back just ahead of the twist, not really pulling on the yarn.

The resulting yarn is almost completely spun as it emerges from the fiber supply and should ideally need no further elongation. It has somewhat less elasticity when spun this way. In theory at least, it is not quite as suitable for warp as yarn spun with a simultaneous twisting and drawing, having its pull at both ends of the fibers being drawn out.

It is possible as a pure technique only with short or medium

# 9
## Spinning Fine Yarn

wools. Even with medium wool, you may occasionally find it necessary to use a modified drawing out, using both hands. Pinch the yarn with the hand closest to the wheel to allow drawing of the yarn to the desired size, against the solid resistance of that hand.

A hand position that can help you in this style is holding the fibers with your palm upward and your forefinger actually pointed toward the twisting fibers. The twist should extend

**109.** *Spinning fine yarn*

from the orifice almost to the *tip* of your forefinger. If you are drafting the fibers and the twist does not come that close, the fibers may part from undertwist and get away from you. If the twist passes that fingertip and goes into your palm-held fibers, you will not be able to draw and will have to slow up your treadling and move your hand back quickly to try to get ahead of the twist once more.

A common problem is that as you speed up the process (and it does lend itself to speed), you may be allowing the yarn to get progressively finer. When you note this happening, slow down a little and tighten the drive belt tension slightly. The pressure of your hand on the lightly held fiber supply, the speed of the treadling, and the drive band tension are the main control elements. Experiment with these and you will be able to keep a constant size and twist, as desired.

### FINE YARN ON THE GREAT WHEEL

Point-of-contact spinning is good preparation for using the colonial great wheel or walking wheel (see "Learning on the Great Wheel" chapter), in which one hand turns the wheel while the other does the spinning. With the flyer wheel, there is no harm done if you slip out of the style and draw against the pull of the wheel's twisting, but you need an even lighter touch with the great wheel, always keeping just *ahead* of the twist on that long draw in order not to pull against the spindle tip.

Although it is possible to spin almost any size yarn on the great wheel, it seems most suited to spinning fine yarn because the light touch needed is used to best advantage with fine yarn. The speed of the accelerating head quickly inserts the necessary twist for fine yarn, and the great wheel exerts no pull (unlike the flyer wheel) and so cannot put any strain on the most delicate of yarns.

### TWIST AND OVERTWIST

More twist is required to obtain maximum strength with

short fiber wool than with long fibers, and more twist is plainly more necessary in fine yarn than in heavier yarn. This is often expressed as *t.p.i.* or *turns per inch*. Fine yarn not only has more turns or twists per inch, but it also has a much sharper *angle* of twist.

Any amount of overtwist (more than is necessary for maximum strength of the yarn) will progressively weaken the yarn by straining the fibers until actual breakage occurs. The fibers in overtwisted areas in fine yarn are not stronger than those with adequate twist because the very sharp angle of their twist makes them exceedingly brittle, as well as kinky and harsh.

### BELT TENSION

For soft-twist fine yarn on a double belt wheel, keep a looser belt tension than when spinning a hard-twist fine yarn such as you would use in weaving warp. If the belt is too tight, it will force you to put more twist in the yarn or have the yarn come apart from the hard pull caused by the belt tension.

A belt that is treated with wax or resin may have too much grip for a soft fine yarn. Many spinners do use wax for spinning medium or heavy yarns or for a hard-twist fine yarn. Waxing does help your belt last longer.

I use a very soft, heavy-cotton cord, like twenty-ply mailing cord, which gives the good traction of a waxed cord without gumming up the pulleys. It responds quickly in stopping and starting, maintains an even traction, gives the desired slippage on the bobbin, but also wears out rather quickly.

### DOUBLE BELT: PULLEY RATIO

Most double belt wheels have one or more pulleys on the bobbin and two or more pulley grooves on the fork whorl. For spinning heavy yarn, use the largest fork pulley with the smallest groove on the bobbin, but for spinning finer yarns, you can use less pulley ratio. With fine yarn, you want more twist and a more gentle drawing in action, so if you have a choice of several

bobbin and fork pulleys, experiment with different combinations of pulleys to see how you like the feel of the wheel action. The combination used, if you have more than one choice, may depend on how fast you want to spin.

For fast spinning of fine yarn, I find I prefer the largest pulley of the fork combined with the small groove on the bobbin (to give about a 2.0 ratio): the yarn pulls in quickly and does not slow down the process. I keep a much looser belt tension for the fine yarn, so that while the belt draws in fast, it is gentle.

### SINGLE BELT: TENSIONING

Coordination of drive belt tension and brake tension can be

**110.** *In the point-of-contact technique, the twist in the yarn extends almost to the tip of the forefinger. Note the triangle of fibers (within the hand) that is being drawn out by the twist.*

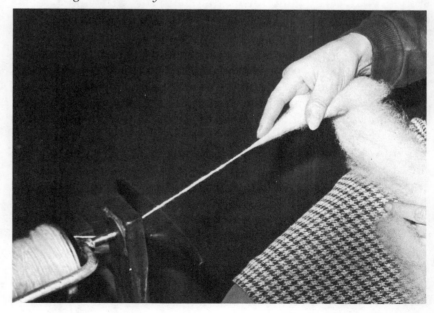

easily adjusted for spinning fine yarn if you start with both very slack. Adjust the drive belt tension first and then the brake, but use only a fraction-of-an-inch adjustment each time until the correct tension is reached to adequately pull in the yarn and twist it. In Indian-head tensioning, the brake is not always needed.

Actually, a single belt, bobbin lead system is not as suitable for a soft twist fine yarn. Even if the wheel is designed for speed, you do not have the subtle control that is needed for thin soft yarn.

## PREPARING LONG FIBERS FOR FINE YARN

Using long wool to spin fine yarn presents a different set of problems, depending on the way it is carded or combed in preparation for spinning. The least satisfactory preparation is to make rolags of it. If you card it on the hand cards, it is easier to spin if removed by hand rather than with the card — just peel it off and then spin from the corner of that fiber mass.

Strips of carded wool from a drum carding machine are easier to use. If the long wool is thoroughly teased before carding, it spins up into a woolen (in contrast to worsted) yarn, even though the carding straightens out quite a few of the long wool fibers. In worsted yarns, the majority of the fibers lie parallel to each other when carded or combed, and still parallel after spinning. In woolen yarn, the fibers are crisscrossed. For more of a worsted effect, wool that is not matted or tangled can be fed into the carding machine lengthwise, so that it does not get mixed up and so that it comes off the carding roller still in the parallel arrangement.

There are other ways of accomplishing this effect, such as by using the flick carder (described in "Hand Carding" chapter), or just by combing out locks of good quality grease wool with the worsted flicker and attenuating them into little strips, spinning directly from them. Combed locks can also be folded and spun out from the middle. You should experiment with various methods if you have an available supply of nice long wool.

Even with teased wool, carded woolen fashion, you still get a semiworsted effect by skillful attenuation of your carded long wool, maneuvering a high percentage of the fibers into a parallel position with no equipment other than your hands. This requires working with your hands far apart to accomplish a long attenuation of fibers.

## SPINNING LONG WOOL INTO FINE YARN

With long wools, an extended draw gives you a gratifying control of size and texture. Too much twist must not be inserted before the wool has been drawn to near its finished size, as this sets the size of the yarn so that it cannot be drawn out any thinner. With long wool, you cannot depend on it being drafted just by the pull of the twist that is exerted by the spinning wheel. You need to pinch off the twist often by the hand closest to the orifice, and pull against the firm position of that hand in order to stretch the partly spun fibers into an extended length of yarn of the size desired. Overtwist is also controlled by pinching off the twist, so the twist that has already entered the fiber supply can be drawn out farther, spread out over more yarn length, and thus be equalized.

Here your spinning style is governed by the fiber length as well as the desired yarn. Be sure to spin with your hands far apart or the unspun fiber area will not draw out well. Working with your hands too close together can mean that you may often be pulling on both ends of single long fibers and cannot draw out.

Wool should be well oiled in advance of carding and spinning, so that the carding is thorough and the fiber slippage is more easily controlled without the disturbing jerkiness caused by uneven friction. Water-soluble oil facilitates drawing out and controlling excess irregularities and heavy areas when you desire an especially evenly spun yarn, as for fine weaving warp.

Spinning thicker yarn depends, first of all, on the spinning wheel. You need a sturdy one because the tight belt required can be a strain on a fragile wheel. With a lightweight spinning wheel, placing it on a rubber mat will absorb some of the thrust of heavy treadling and prevent the wheel from edging away from you as you work. The bobbin must, of course, be oiled and should turn freely on the shaft of the spinning fork. Otherwise, the fork adds too much twist and the bobbin does not pull in the yarn well.

BELT

A soft, heavy-cotton drive belt gets good traction and responds quickly. Depending on the size of the pulley grooves, you might try twelve- to twenty-ply mailing cord, which is found where twines and cordage are sold. (See "Spinning Wheel Operation" chapter for lapping, splicing, and installing belts.)

If your spinning wheel accommodates a belt length between nine feet two inches and eleven feet, you might try a high-speed dental motor belt, which has a slightly harder finish, but still gives good control and lasts almost a lifetime (we have worn out one with constant use). It comes in several sizes and is especially good for heavy yarn and long fibers. However, being a *continuous* belt, it cannot be installed on a spinning wheel that does not come apart.

A wool belt is not practical because it is so sensitive to changes in temperature and humidity.

ORIFICE

The orifice must be large enough to pass the yarn. A common size opening is three-eighths inch, which accommodates quite bulky yarn (approximately fifteen yards to the ounce or even less) *if* it does not have excessive twist. It is not always the *size* of the yarn that will not go through, but the kinks. For general spinning of heavier yarns, though, an orifice opening of

# 10
# Spinning
# Heavy Yarn

one-half to five-eighths inch is more suitable.

## DOUBLE BELT: PULLEY RATIO

If the wheel does not pull in well for heavy yarn, even with the drive belt tension tight, then the ratio between the fork pulley and the bobbin pulley may be too small. The greater the ratio between these pulley diameters, the greater pull the bobbin exercises to draw in the yarn. If your drive belt is already on the largest pulley of the fork and the smallest pulley of the bobbin, the spinning wheel may not be well suited for spinning heavy yarn. I have found the best ratio for thicker yarns is 2.0 or more (which means the fork pulley is twice the diameter of the bobbin pulley) to allow for less twist and more draw-in. For extremely bulky yarn, a greater ratio is even better.

With a spinning wheel having more than one size pulley groove on the bobbin, you might want a woodworker to make the smallest groove even smaller, so that combined with the largest flyer pulley, you accomplish the two-to-one ratio.

## DRIVE WHEEL

Some of the spinning wheels that have the small pulley ratios also have a very large drive wheel for a high drive ratio. If the orifice size and pulley ratio are right and you are still having trouble, it is probably due to a large drive wheel that has a drive ratio a little fast for general use with heavy yarn, unless the wool is very well prepared. A twenty-inch drive wheel would need a bobbin whorl size of about two inches to be suitable for a medium-heavy yarn.

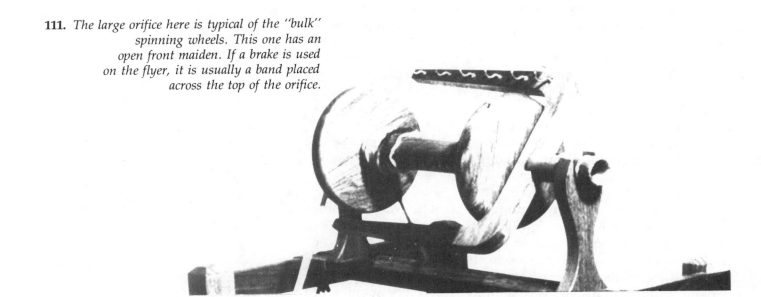

**111.** *The large orifice here is typical of the ''bulk'' spinning wheels. This one has an open front maiden. If a brake is used on the flyer, it is usually a band placed across the top of the orifice.*

Wheels designed specifically for very heavy yarn have drive ratios as low as 4:1 or 6:1.

## SINGLE BELT: BULK SPINNERS

There are a number of spinning wheels that are specially designed for spinning heavy (bulky) yarn, and some of these are shown in the "Spinning Wheel Operation" chapter. They all have a large orifice, but this factor alone does not make them perfect for heavy yarn. They also have a large flyer/bobbin capacity, and the drive wheel is usually about twelve to fourteen inches for a low drive ratio. Most are single belt, bobbin lead (Indian-head tension with brake on the flyer), which is actually more suited to the heavy (really bulky) yarn than a double belt arrangement. Several makes of spinning wheels have jumbo or bulk head spinner attachments available to use instead of the standard flyer when spinning heavy yarn.

## ADDITIONAL TWIST

Unlike a great wheel where no twist is added during the winding on of the yarn, with the flyer spinning wheel, the action of the spinning fork is still twisting the yarn as it is being drawn through the orifice. Since heavy yarn needs fewer twists per inch than fine yarn, you must learn to allow for this addition of twist. Otherwise, a yarn that seems to have the desired amount of twist during its drawing out will end up with more twist than you want by the time it gets wound onto the bobbin. In order to obtain a softly spun, heavy yarn, it must head for the bobbin *before* it gets the amount of twist that you want in the finished yarn.

## WOOL BULK

In handling your carded wool, take up enough bulk of wool to be drawn out and still make bulky, well-spun yarn. You cannot get yarn that is larger in diameter than the diameter of the drawn out, twisted wool fibers. This sounds obvious, but it is the problem in many cases. It takes wool bulk to draw out and still have yarn bulk, so start with an ample wool mass. It is easy to have a bulky strip of wool from the drum carder or from a mill carded batt. With hand carded rolags, try working with two of them at a time if necessary.

## DRAWING OUT

With a large-head bulk spinner, it is tempting to take a long strip of carded wool and just feed it in, letting the spinning wheel add twist and pull it in. While this can produce yarn with a useful effect, it is slightly less than real "handspun." Spinning is defined as making yarn from fibers by drawing out *and* twisting. The twisting and pulling in action are from the spinning fork and bobbin, but you must do the actual drawing out of the fibers. Spinning heavy yarn without drawing out gives you no control over the texture.

## TEASING AND CARDING

The ease of spinning and the amount of control you have over yarn size and texture, especially with heavy yarn, depend on your carded fiber.

Beginners have trouble with accidental slubs and nubs, and it is not all due to lack of spinning ability. Seeds in the wool are one of the causes of unplanned slubs, so removing them during the initial teasing is a good precaution. You should also try to prevent the neps (tiny snarls) that result from hasty or insufficient carding and carding done without previous oiling or teasing of the wool. "If you don't have time to do it right, how will you ever have time to do it over?" is what my mother used to say.

## STYLE

To achieve a good bulky yarn, you can use the short draw technique or the unsupported long draw (both described in "Learning on a Spinning Wheel" chapter). What I have referred

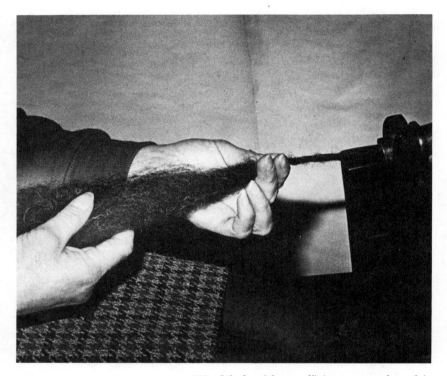

**112.** *Work with a sufficient mass of wool in order to allow drawing out and still produce heavy yarn.*

to as the point-of-contact style, where you draw your fiber supply back just ahead of the twist from the flyer, works best when spinning a relatively fine yarn.

## TREADLING

Slow treadling is needed more with heavy yarn than with fine because it requires less twist per inch and less twist per yard. Because tighter drive belt tension is needed, you can expect treadling to take more effort. Less effort is required with bulk spinners than is needed to spin heavy yarn on an all-purpose wheel.

Beginning spinners often ask how to avoid overtwist. One of the easiest ways is to understand its causes.

## SPINNING WHEEL

The spinning wheel frequently contributes to the problem by adding too much twist while it draws in the yarn. This can be remedied in one of several ways:

1. Tighten the drive belt tension to cause a stronger pull on the yarn. (Heavy yarn needs a much tighter belt than fine yarn.)
2. With a double belt wheel, having a *larger* ratio between the pulley groove on the bobbin and the pulley diameter on the fork will make the yarn pull in faster. If you have a choice of pulleys, use the largest one on the fork and the smallest one on the bobbin for greater drawing in.
3. Tighten the tension device on Scotch tension or Indian-head tension.
4. Make sure the bobbin turns freely on its shaft, because it will not draw in properly for spinning if it does not.

## SPINNER

Even if the spinning wheel operates perfectly, the beginner can expect to have some problems with overtwisting. Problems are caused mainly when:

1. The spinner treadles too fast and gets more twist than can be handled when forming the yarn. In the excitement of learning, slow and deliberate treadling is not easy.
2. The hands allow too much twist into the yarn before it is sufficiently attenuated and then try to draw it out in spite of the twist while even more twist is accumulating.
3. The hand holding the wool does not allow the yarn to draw into the bobbin soon enough or hesitates be-

# 11
# Conquering Overtwist

tween the drawing out action and the feeding of the yarn onto the bobbin.

4. The speed of winding on is too slow, not because of lack of drawing in by the wheel, but because the spinner does not allow it. If the spun yarn is held back instead of letting it wind on freely, the drive belt will be slipping on the bobbin pulley and no winding will take place until this pressure is released.

## TREADLING

Because it is so much easier to treadle than to make yarn, the tendency is to do too much treadling. One way to determine how much of your overtwisting can be attributed to over-treadling is to operate the drive wheel by hand for the following experiment, without using your feet at all. With your yarn supply still attached to the last bit of yarn you have spun, pinch the yarn with the hand nearest the orifice, allowing the fiber supply to dangle there. Keeping the twist pinched off, give the drive wheel one full turn, using the hand that ordinarily holds the fiber supply.

Now, take up your unspun wool with that hand, and draw out the fibers to a thin sliver (six inches long for fine yarn and up to eight inches long for heavier yarn). Then release the pinched-off twist to run into this length of fibers. It should be a nice soft yarn. There is not likely to be too much twist in it, even with a large drive wheel.

If the yarn needs a little more twist to make it strong enough for pulling onto the bobbin, give the drive wheel another half turn, this time with the hand that was pinching off the twist. This should be about enough, unless you have a rather small drive wheel. Add another half turn if needed, let it go slack, and look at the yarn. If it twists back softly on itself, making only coiled twists, it is a medium twist. If it kinks in too many places, this indicates overtwist.

Now give the wheel one more full turn, allowing the yarn to

pull onto the bobbin *as you turn the wheel*. If the drive belt tension and the pulley ratio are sufficient, one turn should be enough to wind that amount of yarn onto the bobbin.

See how little treadling is needed to spin that much yarn?

## HAND ACTION TO CORRECT OVERTWIST

If you get too much twist in the yarn before it is drawn out as thin as you want it, this can be corrected. Stop treadling and draw out more fibers, allowing the twist to run up into them, thus "absorbing" some of that extra twist from the spun part of your yarn. With the twist lessened, you should be able to draw out the whole length of yarn to the size you want by pulling against the hand next to the orifice, which holds the yarn firmly for this purpose.

If the yarn is close enough to the right size but just over-spun, this equalizing of the twist into the extra length of fibers reduces the overtwist so that it can all be wound onto the bobbin. You may have a few lumps that prevent it from winding on easily, so just rotate the bobbin by hand to wind in the yarn and do not worry about texture this time. With a little practice, you will be able to equalize the twist like this without stopping and will have overcome the whole problem.

## SOFT YARN

To not only avoid obvious overtwist, but also to achieve a really soft yarn, you should release the yarn to wind onto the bobbin *before* you get the maximum twist, meaning the amount of twist that allows no further attenuating of the yarn, even when drawing against the firm grip of your other hand. Otherwise, the additional small amount of twist added by the flyer as the yarn is being drawn in will make it less than a soft yarn by the time it is on the bobbin. Accomplishing this is just a matter of timing. The yarn must be fed onto the bobbin *before* you get what you may think is the right amount of twist.

Remember that before fiber slippage is eliminated in the

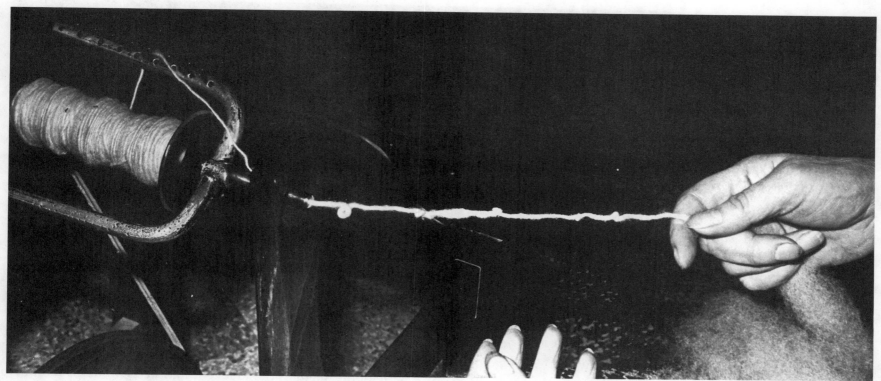

**113.** *Overtwist.* **A.** *This kinky yarn is badly overtwisted.*

drawing out process, you may be edging toward real overtwist, depending on how much more twist is added in winding of the yarn onto the bobbin. It is doubly important to watch this if your wheel has a little less than ideal ratio between bobbin pulley and fork pulley.

### SPINNING WITH ONE HAND

One effective way to eliminate overtwist is to cultivate the one-handed, point-of-contact spinning style, which is described in the "Spinning Fine Yarn" and "Speed Spinning" chapters. The hand holding the fiber supply draws back just ahead of the twist that is being inserted as you treadle. The hand nearest the orifice, which usually pinches off the twist as needed, is used as little as possible. The fibers are drawn out by the twisting and pulling action of the spinning wheel; you must keep *ahead* of that twist at all times, not letting the twist reach your hand. Allow the spun yarn to be pulled onto the bobbin as each length is spun. Although this is the fastest spinning technique, practice it *very* slowly, disregarding yarn size and texture, until you get the feel of the fibers being drawn out of your hand. By keeping ahead of the twist, you completely prevent overtwist. If the twist does catch up with you, it closes off fiber slippage and stops the spinning process. With practice, your hand will get very sensitive to the slippage of fibers and you will be able to eliminate

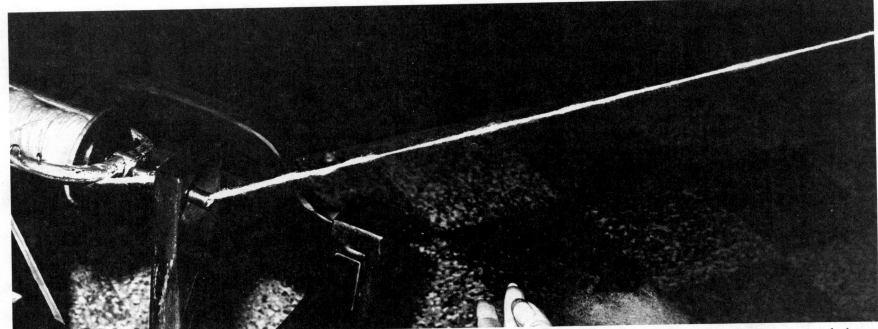

**B.** *By drawing out more fibers and letting the twist run into them, the twist is spread out over a longer strand of yarn.*

overtwist in other spinning techniques as well.

### UNIFORM SIZE/TWIST

A smoothly, evenly spun yarn does not show overtwist as much as a yarn that is spun with more size variations. In an uneven yarn, the excess twist naturally settles in the thinner spots, kinking them rather badly, and the amount of twist in the yarn is not spread into the thicker areas at all. The same amount of twist, if spread evenly over the whole length of yarn, might be a little overspun, but would not produce those tightly kinked places. It would still show up a handspun texture when off the wheel.

### WASHING AND BLOCKING

Do not pass final judgment on your yarn until it is washed and blocked. The washing relaxes the twist, and the blocking or drying of the skein under an even, light tension helps minimize the disadvantages of any remaining overtwist, making it easier to use the yarn in either knitting or weaving. Just drying the skein with a weight hanging from it does not give an equal amount of tension to all parts of the yarn (see "Blocking" and blocker plans in "Learning on a Spinning Wheel" chapter).

### PLYING

Plying, which is done at the opposite twist from the spinning of the single strands used, helps minimize overtwist (see "Controlling Irregularities" chapter). If your overtwist is in fine yarn, you may want to try plying as a way of making it more usable.

Irregularity can refer to unintentional slubs, lumps, and neps, or to a deliberate variation in size, texture, and color — a subtle nonuniformity. Since more spinners complain of excess irregularity than lack of it, its causes should be examined. They do not all originate in actual spinning techniques, but can be traced back to earlier stages in processing. While studying the causes, keep in mind that it is not the complete absence of irregularity that is desirable, but controlled irregularity.

## LUMPS WITH A CORE

These are often formed around weed seeds or burrs, bits of straw or large neps, and second cuts that remain in the carded wool. Cleaner wool of course overcomes some of the difficulty. This does not mean that *all* seeds and vegetable matter produce flaws, and removing all of them is not possible anyway. Many very small seeds fly out of clean wool as it is spun, especially in fast spinning of fine yarn. Some bits of straw will cling to the surface of the yarn and can be dislodged with a fingernail as yarn is drawn into the bobbin.

## FLAWS FROM TECHNIQUE

Other causes of lumps include faulty joining of rolags or carded strips, which makes a lump that may pull apart if the yarn is used for warp. Too short a draw when spinning, not allowing room for the complete drafting out of the fibers, leads to turned-back fibers and unsightly snarl-lumps that cannot be drawn out any farther. Another cause of flaws is an inadvertent pushing back of the wool supply rather than a drawing out, something done sometimes by beginners. This has an effect similar to ratting or back-combing in hair styling, and the remaining pushed-back fiber supply becomes increasingly tangled and hard to spin smoothly.

## SLUBS

These are little bunches of more or less parallel compacted

# 12

# Controlling Irregularities

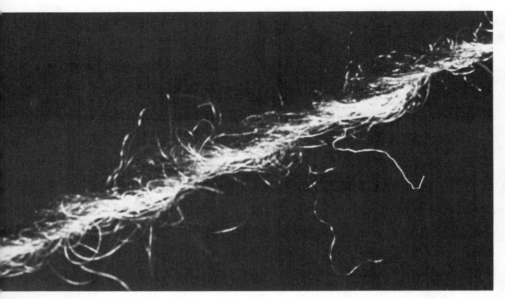

**114.** *Hairiness.* **A.** *Excess hairiness*

**B.** *When momentarily held, the fibers are caught into the twist.*

fibers, some of which have remained intact throughout the carding process. Others are caused by uneven attenuation or by allowing the twist to run into the fiber supply in such a way that it cannot be drawn. Additional factors that contribute to slub formation can be an excessive variation of staple lengths, not well blended, and oil or moisture that is not sufficiently distributed.

In dyed wool, localized felting may occur during the dyeing process and can show up as parallel fiber tufts that draw together during spinning.

Long or tapered slubs can be formed around foreign fibers. Ravelings from burlap sacks used to bag the wool; hemp, jute, or plastic fibers from twine used to tie the fleeces (which properly should be tied with paper twine made for that purpose); or long bits of straw are common offenders for they prevent normal slippage of fibers.

Slub yarn, used as an ornamental or textural effect and having soft, untwisted areas of varying diameters, is a good weft yarn. (Its spinning is described later in this chapter.)

## NEPS

These are tiny snarls of entangled fibers. Although produced during carding, they are caused by the entanglement of the wool when it is fed into the carder or hand cards. The washed wool itself (or the unwashed wool) has no real neps as such. After carding, they are easily visible if a thin web of carded wool is held up to the light. The neps appear as small dense areas or spots when compared with the surrounding fibers. When the wool is attenuated, they are like small whorls of fibers with a pronounced core. Individual nep fibers, if untangled and measured individually, are always much shorter than the average length of fibers being carded. This does not mean that the naturally shorter fibers of a fleece are more prone to snarling, but

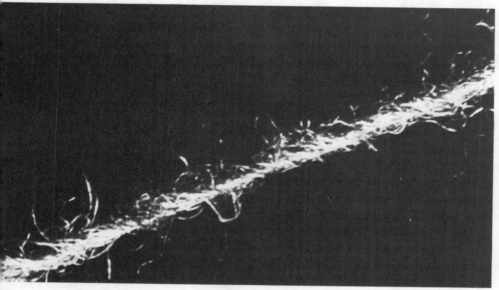

**C.** *This eliminates the overly hairy place in the yarn.*

## HAIRINESS

This is a desired quality for some purposes, and can be encouraged by brushing the finished fabric. However, protruding fibers can cause a stickiness of warp and interfere with a good shed, so they are seldom desired in *warp* yarn.

One cause of hairiness or fuzziness is spinning of carded wool without any attenuation before or during spinning, which amounts to just twisting it. This does not catch in nearly as many fiber ends as if it were both drawn out and twisted. Bulk spinning wheels encourage this kind of twisting-spinning, so make an extra effort at drawing out when using them.

There is a smoothing motion, which should be an automatic part of spinning, that coaxes loose fiber ends into the twist. This motion is especially important in fast spinning in order to produce a good yarn. As the yarn is pulled into the spinning wheel and wound onto the bobbin, there is a bit more twist going into the yarn. It is this twist that can easily catch in protruding fibers if the yarn is smoothed lightly, with the hand closest to the orifice, as it is being wound in. The fingers run along the yarn, smoothing in the hairs that can hardly be seen while the yarn is in motion, picking off any bits of vegetation that are hanging onto its surface, and catching onto any large, visible bits of wool that stick out from the yarn surface. This brief pinching of the fiber tuft detains it sufficiently to twirl it around the yarn being drawn in and catch it partly into the twist.

that they have suffered breakage after snarling when forcibly pulled apart in carding.

Neps can be prevented in part by:
1. Carefully washing fleeces — not rubbing or unduly wringing and gyrating.
2. Not running water directly onto the wool.
3. Carefully, thoroughly teasing the fleeces prior to carding.
4. Adding both oil and moisture (combined) prior to carding, causing increased elasticity and less breakage. This also lubricates some of the existing tangles so they pull free, and makes individual fibers more flexible.
5. Allowing a resting period between washing, teasing, and carding. Even flax fibers benefit from periods of rest.

## TWITS OR THIN AREAS

These excessively thin places, especially in fine yarn, can break easily under the strain of overtwist, which localizes in the thinnest places. They most often occur as two twits with a short, thick slub in between. Up to twenty percent of the fibers pass clear through the slub, being tightly twisted into both thin portions. These few fibers carry all the tension supported by a thick place and cannot slip; thus the slub is locked into place. The short slub in many instances has a nucleus of impurity, such as a burr or large nep. If the foreign material is spotted during the drawing stage, long enough before the maximum twist is in the yarn, you can pick it out.

## SIZE DEVIATION

Deviations in yarn size are sometimes called irregularity. In spinning a certain number of skeins of yarn alike, whether for warp or weft or for knitting, what is needed is an *average* diameter that remains fairly constant in all the skeins. This allows for deviation from the average, either larger or smaller, of an amount that is appropriate for the intended use.

While the textile industry is equipped with electric regular-meters to check yarn size, the handspinner can work for uniform *weight* in each skein. If each skein is measured off in a predetermined yardage, such as fifty to one hundred yards, and each is carefully weighed, the *average* size can be checked from skein to skein. For fine yarn, a gram scale is more precise and shows up smaller differences in skein weight.

## PLYING

Plying can compensate for irregularity by averaging out the thick and thin places, as well as by reinforcing weak places in single-ply yarns that might otherwise not be usable for some purposes.

The direction of the twist when plying two singles is ordinarily opposite to the direction in which the singles were twisted. This is done by having the drive wheel turning in the opposite direction. When plied this way, the surface fibers lie almost parallel to the axis of the yarn, running in about the same direction as the yarn.

If they are plied in the *same* direction, the fibers lie at almost right angles to the axis of the yarn. This plying in the same direction as the original twist, called *cabling*, produces hard, high-twist effects and great elasticity, and actually augments the twist of the original singles. If you need this type of yarn, as for making rugs, it should be blocked after washing and allowed to dry under moderate tension so that it does not have as much tendency to kink, snarl, or untwist (see ''Blocking'' in ''Learning on a Spinning Wheel'' chapter).

## OVERTWIST AND IRREGULARITY

The nonuniform nature of handspun makes the angle of twist a more important concept than the turns per inch. This angle of twist varies along a strand of yarn — less of an angle in thicker places and greater in thinner places. In general, thin yarns require more twist to hold together and thick yarns require less twist. This generally applies also to an unevenly spun yarn — the thin places will *be* the ones with the most twist.

Uneven yarn can be corrected before you draw it onto the bobbin. When a more even yarn is desired, the thick places can still be drawn thinner if you stop treadling and allow the twist to run farther into the untwisted but attenuated fiber supply. In other words, if the original drawing out has too much variation in size, this can be overcome by distribution of the twist over a longer area. The yarn can then be stretched and drafted, giving the spinner another chance to achieve the desired effect. For this elongation and equalization, the hand nearest the orifice provides the firm support against which the stretch of the drawing out can be accomplished.

Overtwist is a relative thing, and the amount of yarn twist that is ideal or desirable varies according to the intended use. Warp requires enough twist to withstand the stress and friction of weaving and provide elasticity. On the other hand, weft yarn, which takes little wear during the weaving process, can be about as soft as is suitable for the feel of the finished fabric. Rug yarn can have a lot of twist for durability or medium twist for softer surface texture. Knitting yarn can have soft twist for sweaters worn next to the skin, harder twist for outdoor sweaters, medium twist for good wearing qualities, or slightly softer for more comfort.

## UNDESIRED SMOOTHNESS

Wool top and wool roving are sometimes purchased when good, clean fleeces are hard to find. Dissatisfaction with lack of irregularity and too smooth a yarn is often voiced by spinners using combed wool top. You can minimize this smoothness by pulling apart the strips of top, and mixing them and teasing them. Or you can use a winnowing motion, beating the pulled-apart top with a flexible switch. This helps give a more lofty feel as well as textural irregularity when spun. Recarding with other wool is the easiest way to undo the slick machine look where nonuniformity is wanted.

While combed wool top is the most homogenous form of processed fiber, bleached wool roving will also lack some of the recognizable qualities of handspun yarn unless it is given special handling. You can alter its appearance considerably by dyeing and teasing or recarding before spinning, or alter it to a lesser degree by dyeing it after spinning.

## DELIBERATE IRREGULAR EFFECTS

For a planned slubbiness, there is a rather devious way to produce an effect known as *wobbled yarn,* one of the tricks of the old-time spinners. This requires nothing more than a knotted joining in the spinning wheel drive belt, the larger the knot the better for this purpose. It exerts a sudden pull on the fibers for every revolution it makes around the bobbin pulley, and affects the evenness of the spun yarn.

For the greatest degree of texture, a well-teased but *uncarded* wool can be used. The faster it is spun, the more irregular it becomes. This is effective in natural color or vegetable-dyed fleeces, where the variations in color combine with the naturally random spinning in a way that looks both intentional and attractive.

The carding together of two different wool types makes a mixture that is prone to slubbing, and is easily manipulated to do so during spinning. It makes it, however, a little harder to

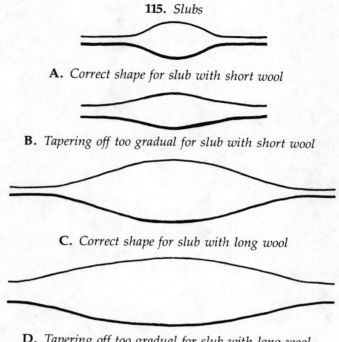

**115.** *Slubs*

**A.** *Correct shape for slub with short wool*

**B.** *Tapering off too gradual for slub with short wool*

**C.** *Correct shape for slub with long wool*

**D.** *Tapering off too gradual for slub with long wool*

control the exact placement of the slubs.

## DELIBERATE THICK-AND-THIN SLUB YARN

A blobby, thick-and-thin yarn is a useful weft for weaving scarves, stoles, pillows, coat materials, and other fabrics needing an interesting texture. You need a spinning wheel with a rather large orifice (about three-fourths inch) in order to accommodate a large, fluffy slub. Medium-length fleece is the best type to use for this yarn. A short staple wool can be made into only very short slubs, with fine yarn in between; otherwise, the slub pulls apart. Very long staple can be made into only a very

**116.** *Slubs. Step 1. A flat blob of yarn is held by
the hand nearest the orifice while wool beyond it is drawn to a thin sliver.*

*Step 2. The twist has jumped into the
thin sliver of wool, making the yarn between the slubs.*

long slub, and is rather hard to work with even then.

The challenge is not just to produce a thick-and-thin yarn, but to make soft slubs, connected by nicely spun yarn without overtwist. This should not be lumps and bumps that happen by accident, but a contrived texture, with the size and placement of the slubs completely controlled by the spinner. I would suggest that you not try this yarn until you are already able to spin without overtwist because the slubs are not very attractive with overspun, kinky yarn between them. The final washing process, in this case, will do nothing to minimize the kinks, and this yarn is not usually blocked.

Here is one type of yarn that requires the hand nearest the orifice to be doing a real share of the work. It firmly grasps a section of the fiber supply just past the last spun part of the yarn and does not allow any twist to go into the portion that it holds. Let a little bit of twist build up behind it while the other hand (the one holding the wool supply that you are spinning) draws out the untwisted fibers (the ones right next to the wool that is held) into a thin ribbon of untwisted fibers. The twist is then released by the hand near the orifice, and runs *past* the slub (really "jumps" the slub) and into the thinly pulled place, leaving an untwisted slub with thin yarn on both sides of it. The size of the strip (or rolag) of wool that you are working with will determine the maximum diameter of the slub just as the wool staple limits its length.

As you release the twist, run your fingers lightly across the slub, following the angle of the loose twist in it, to prevent excessive fuzziness. Then, spin the additional amount of yarn you want between the slubs. Repeat the whole process, making another slub, another area of thin spun yarn, and so on.

## SLUB SIZE AND SHAPE

Do not let your slub taper off too gradually. Decrease abruptly so that the slub will be strong enough to hold together. The shorter the fibers, the more abrupt the start and end of the

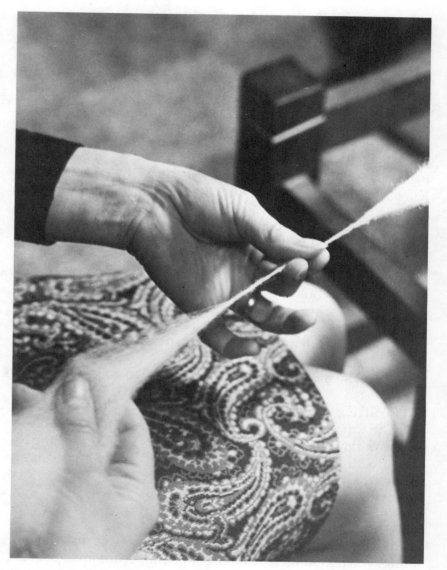

*Step 3. The yarn between the slubs can be spun as desired until you want to insert another slub.*

slub needs to be. The larger the portion of wool that is grasped and "frozen," the larger the slub can be, depending on the type of wool used. With a little practice, you will be able to control both the size of the slub and the size and length of the yarn between slubs.

## TWIST

Experiment a little to determine the minimum amount of twist needed to keep the yarn between the slubs twisted enough to be strong and yet not so much as to "kinkle." This differs from wool to wool. No added amount of extra twist will make the *slubs* any stronger; the twist will all settle between slubs.

## UNSLUBBING SLUBS

If your deliberate slub pulls out and spins into a smooth yarn, one of the following is the cause:
1. The wool was just too short to make slub yarn.
2. There was a combination of having almost-too-short wool and drive belt tension that was too tight.
3. You did not draw the yarn next to the slub fine enough, soon enough.
4. The slub was too long and/or tapered off too gradually.

## PREPARING WOOL

The batt from the drum carding machine is more suitable for slub yarn than are rolags from hand cards. When separating the batt into strips to prepare it for spinning, you will need fairly thick strips in order to obtain fat slubs. You can use thinner strips for smaller slubs.

## HAND TECHNIQUE

If you are spinning a large amount of slub yarn at one sitting, you may want to change your hand technique, not using the normal way of pinching with your thumb and the next two fingers, but grasping the wool mass with your whole hand, palm upward, instead. I admit it is not quite as handy and looks funny, too, but it prevents you from having a sore thumb after a few hours of using it to make the slubs. This is especially important if you are using wool that is longer than medium length and therefore harder to pull into slubs.

## WASHING

When you wind your completed slub yarn from the bobbin into skeins, tie each skein loosely in five or six places. In some ways, it is a shame to have to wash this yarn because it looks so good before it is washed. But unless this is done, you have no real assurance of the outcome when you have to wash whatever you make. Also, it is easier to work with after washing, and the free ends are less prone to untwist when you are working with the yarn.

Wash and rinse the skeins gently. If the fleece was fairly well washed, you can shorten the process by eliminating the washing, and just rinsing the skeins. Avoid wringing them out. If you use the separate spin cycle in a washing machine, this removes the water gently. (A more fun way is to twirl them over your head in a mesh bag.) Then, hang them up to dry *without* weighting or blocking the skeins in any way. This brings out the fluffiness of the slub.

When you feel you have mastered the spinning process, you will want to speed it up and turn out more yarn in less time. Like overtwist, the slowness of the spinning process is not always the fault of the spinner.

## WOOL SUPPLY

Good quality wool is important for speed. It should not be too weathered or sheared so late in the season that it is gummy. Nor should it have too much vegetable matter in it, for this results in unwanted slubs and nubs and often prevents the fibers from drawing out evenly.

Proper preparation is necessary. A good fleece poorly carded is often no better than a poor fleece that has been oiled and well carded. Using carding oil can help in the easy slippage of fibers during the drawing out process. Thorough and uniform carding is also necessary if the drawing of the wool is to be a smooth and uninterrupted process.

With any fleece, there is usually one size in which it can be spun more easily. If a specific yarn size is immaterial, then spin each fleece in the size that spins the easiest for this will also be the fastest. The right size for easy and fast spinning of a particular wool becomes apparent with a little experimenting.

## SPINNING WHEEL SPEED

Fast spinning also has a lot to do with your equipment. Some wheels are suitable for fast spinning of fine yarn, a few are good for fast spinning of medium-weight yarn, fewer are for both, and some are not designed for speed at all. If speed is important, your wheel should have the following:

1. Good balance. It will otherwise shimmy or wobble, which wears out parts and puts stress on parts not designed well. Vibration of an unbalanced flyer can hinder speed and eventually damage the shaft.
2. A heavy drive wheel. This is helpful for momentum.
3. A well-balanced drive wheel with durable bearings. An unbalanced drive wheel allows the belt to slacken

once for each revolution.

4. A large drive wheel and/or high drive ratio. The drive ratio determines how fast you must treadle to accomplish your fast spinning. (*Drive ratio* is wheel diameter divided by bobbin pulley diameter for *bobbin lead*, or by flyer pulley diameter for *flyer lead*.) Speed with fine yarn requires a higher drive ratio than fast spinning of medium-heavy yarn. Keep in mind that most beginners cannot handle a wheel with a high drive ratio.

5. Sufficient pulley ratio. If one of the fork pulleys is about twice as large as the bobbin pulley diameter, you can use it to get a good strong pulling action for wool. While you might generally want to use one of the lesser pulley ratios when spinning fine yarn, you could try a looser belt and a greater ratio (up to 2.0) for speed, which is usually my choice.

6. Large yarn capacity. A long bobbin and wide fork mean that you need not stop so often to wind off skeins.

7. Lubrication. Follow the maker's instructions for oiling the bearings, leathers, and gears. To avoid unnecessary wear, clean off old oil before adding new oil in order to remove dirt that has collected. As a general rule, use lighter oil for fast-moving parts and heavier oil or cup-and-axle grease for slow-moving parts. Vaseline is also excellent for slow-moving wood parts.

## JOINING

The joining on of the new fiber supply is one place where you can get slowed down. If this process is always practiced in motion, rather than as a stopping-joining-starting sequence, it will become faster. At first, a beginner will need to use both hands and a sizable lapping of unspun wool.

Speed not only requires greater dexterity, but some small changes in technique. In joining, for instance, the feathering of the fibers together (the last of the previous fibers with the first of the new fibers) will be done with one hand and controlled more from *within* the hand than from in front of it. The thumb, index, and middle fingers control the wool supply to be joined, while the ring and little fingers control the remaining unspun portion to which you are joining. This is the same hand position used to hold chopsticks. (If it is easier for you, the ring and little fingers may control the wool supply to be joined and the other three fingers may control the unspun portion.) Allow the fibers to filter together over several inches of yarn, the distance depending on the size of yarn and the length of the fibers.

A good joining is always of unspun fiber to unspun fiber. Note how easily your yarn comes apart at the place where it was attached to the leader yarn, when you are winding off a skein. This is an example of what happens when you join unspun fiber to spun fiber.

## CHANGING HOOKS

Changing the yarn from hook to hook in maintaining an evenly filled bobbin can also interrupt your speed. While learning, do not change hooks at the same time you join on, for this counteracts your attempts to learn to join quickly. Change hooks when you have to stop or slow down to remove seeds from your wool, so that your practice of the joining process is always done in motion.

There is a way to change hooks without using your hands, if you start out with your yarn through all the hooks, filling the far end of the bobbin. You can slow down just slightly, allow a momentary reversal of the drive wheel (this is possible only with a double-action treadle) with some slack in your yarn, and it will slip off the farthest hook onto the next hook. As it does, take up the slack in your yarn so it does not continue to come off hooks. Too much reversal of the drive wheel or too much slack in the yarn lets the yarn fall off *all* the hooks, so work on

**117.** *Held in one hand, the new fiber supply and the last of the unspun fibers are feathered together in a perfect joining, which will be undetectable and as strong as the rest of the yarn skein.*

**118.** *Yarn is over the back of the flyer arm to prevent it from becoming airborne at fast speed.*

this at slow speed until you can do it perfectly every time. Then try doing it faster.

Keep your wool supply within easy reach so you do not lose speed and momentum when you reach for it. A table or bench beside you, or a basket for rolags or coiled Z strips from the drum carder, enables you to spin a whole skein without losing speed because of an inconvenient wool supply.

## AIRBORNE YARN

A problem like this is not possible on a spindle wheel, but with a flyer wheel there is a certain high speed when the yarn tends to become airborne, hooping up out of the hooks on the flyer arm as it is drawn in. This can cause the yarn to come down on the hooks and snag on one, or settle down over some hooks and under others. This can sometimes be counteracted by bending the first hook, nearest the eye of the fork, into a more closed loop.

On wheels with a thin flyer arm, such as the metal fork of the Columbine (or the Made Well sold in Canada), you can place your yarn so it goes through the orifice and up over the *back* of the flyer arm, coming down through only one hook at the place where you want it to wind onto the bobbin. This is possible only when the side exit hole, between the orifice and the arm, is close to the arm or in line with it.

There are wheels, such as the Pirtle spinner, that have a sliding, closed yarn guide, so there is no problem of the yarn raising out of the hooks. On a custom-made wheel that has a slender and rounded flyer arm, such as Ernest Mason's wheel, you can request that the exit hole be made in line with the flyer arm for using this speed practice.

## FINE YARN TECHNIQUE

It helps to adjust your style to accommodate both the raw materials and the yarn size you want. This is the advantage of versatility in spinning techniques.

What I have called the point-of-contact style, described in the chapter on fine yarns, is the fastest way to spin fine yarn. The hands and the feet are both accelerated, but must stay coordinated so that the twist extends almost up to the fiber supply at all times. This is just not possible with any overtwist for you cannot "stay ahead" of overtwist, and staying just ahead of the twist is the key to this technique.

You occasionally use the hand closest to the orifice to provide a momentary firmness against which the yarn can be pulled if a further attenuation is needed, as in the drawing out

of slubs. This is important, for you will be working with a belt tension that is not firm enough to pull against, especially with medium-length wools when this is sometimes necessary. This style works best with shorter wools.

For fine yarns with medium wools, it is easier to use the long draw in which the hand nearest the orifice more often provides the basis for drawing out the fibers. It gives a firmness to pull against in putting the finishing stretch on each length of yarn. The fibers are handled lightly in all but this last moment of each draw (see "Spinning Fine Yarn" chapter).

## HEAVY YARN TECHNIQUE

For fast spinning of heavy yarn, use the long draw or the unsupported long draw, the latter usually being faster if your wool is well prepared (see "Learning on a Spinning Wheel" chapter).

In the unsupported long draw, where the drafting out of the mass of fibers depends on having enough twist entering them to form yarn, but not so much as to prevent the drawing out of the thicker places to match the thinner places, foot movement most be closely keyed to the formation of your yarn. The faster you go, the more trouble you will have if there is either undertwist or overtwist.

The short draw, requiring a pinching off of the twist, releasing it into the drafted fibers, etc., uses too many extra hand movements to be fast.

For more information, see the "Spinning Heavy Yarn" chapter.

## FLOOR REEL

Another way to speed up is in the way you wind off your yarn. Here is a simple floor reel you can make to wind off your skeins much more quickly than by hand. A skilled woodworker can improve on this basic plan.

**119.** *Floor reel*

2 × 4 × 24

1-in. hole for axle

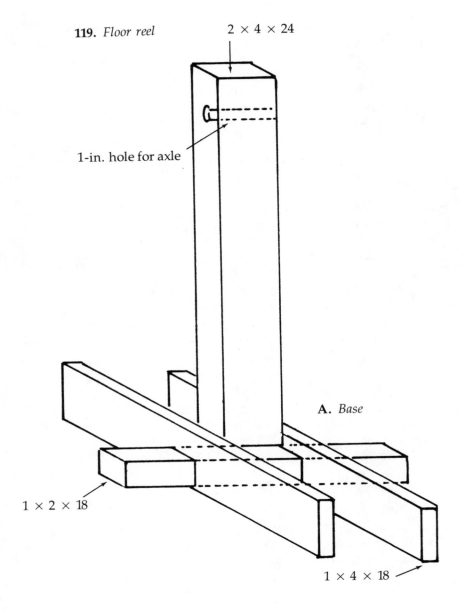

A. *Base*

1 × 2 × 18

1 × 4 × 18

FLOOR REEL FOR 2-YARD SKEINS

List of Materials

Arms: 2 pieces of molding — 1½ × ½ in., 26 in. long
4 pieces of dowel — 1-in. diameter, 5 in. long (crosspieces)
7 pieces of wood — ¼ × 1¼ × 1¼ in. (caps for crosspieces)
(For 1½-yd. skeins, make arms 20 in. long)
Hub: 1 piece of wood — 2 × 2 × 4 in.
Axle: 1 piece of dowel — 1-in. diameter, 8 in. long
Base: 1 piece of wood — 2 × 4 × 24 in.
2 pieces of wood — 1 × 4 × 18 in.
1 piece of wood — 1 × 2 × 18 in.

*Note: Dimensions are in inches except where marked.*

**B.** *Hub*

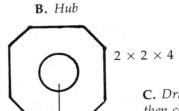

2 × 2 × 4

1-in. hole

**C.** *Drill several ½-in. holes, then chisel out a slot for the arm to go through. Make a similar slot for the other arm to go through at right angles.*

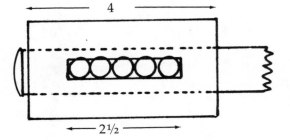

4

2½

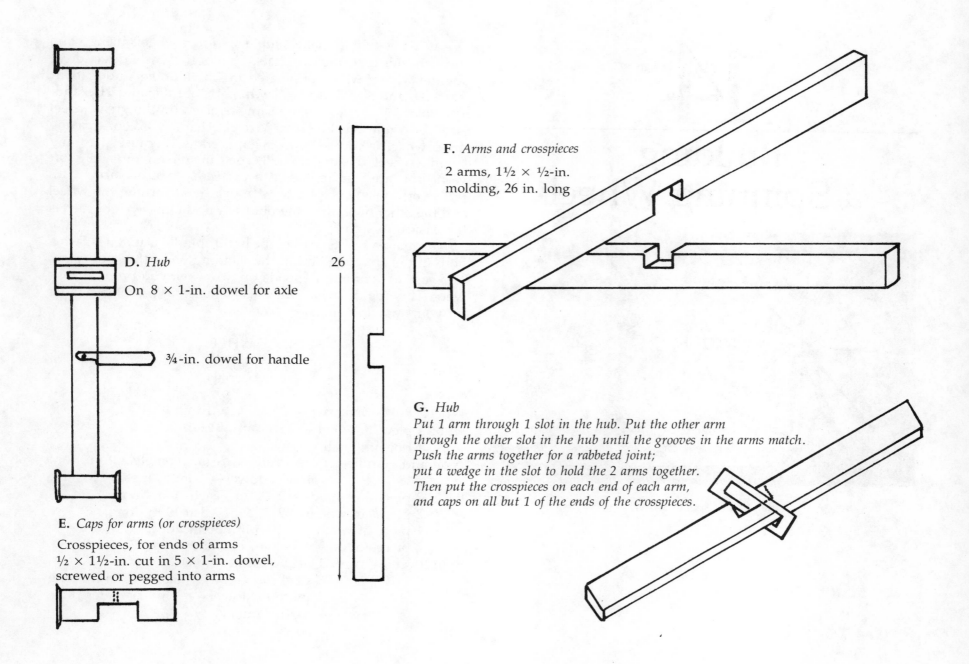

**D.** *Hub*

On 8 × 1-in. dowel for axle

¾-in. dowel for handle

**E.** *Caps for arms (or crosspieces)*

Crosspieces, for ends of arms
½ × 1½-in. cut in 5 × 1-in. dowel,
screwed or pegged into arms

26

**F.** *Arms and crosspieces*

2 arms, 1½ × ½-in.
molding, 26 in. long

**G.** *Hub*

*Put 1 arm through 1 slot in the hub. Put the other arm
through the other slot in the hub until the grooves in the arms match.
Push the arms together for a rabbeted joint;
put a wedge in the slot to hold the 2 arms together.
Then put the crosspieces on each end of each arm,
and caps on all but 1 of the ends of the crosspieces.*

# 14

## Building
## a Spinning Wheel

**120.** *Simple spindle wheel*

It is possible to make simple spinning wheels using hand tools and inexpensive materials. One of these is a direct drive spindle wheel, which originated in China and/or India about 500 A.D. and is still used today in parts of India and Thailand. The spinning method is the same as used on the great wheel (see "Learning on the Great Wheel" chapter) except that the drive wheel is turned with a hand crank. Because, like any spindle wheel, it exerts no pull, you can spin an unusually soft yarn. You are not limited to a particular size of yarn by an orifice or hooks, except that with one hand turning the wheel and the other hand drawing out the yarn, a fine-weight yarn is the easiest to spin.

Its main advantage over the hand spindle is that it is faster, both in the spinning and in the winding on of the spun yarn. The ease of spinning depends on how well you prepare your wool. This spindle wheel may also be used as a bobbin winder for your weaving quills.

### SPINDLE WHEEL

#### List of Materials

Wheel: 8 wooden slats — 24 × ¾ × 1 in.
Hub: 1 piece of wood — 4 × 4 in., 3½ in. long
    1 finishing nail — 3 in.
Axle and Handles: 1 steel rod — ⅜-in. diameter, 18 in. long
    1 piece of dowel — 1-in. diameter, 2 in. long
Base: 2 pieces of wood — 2 × 2 in., each 17 in. long
    2 pieces of wood — 2 × 2 in., each 10 in. long
    1 piece of wood — 1 × 3 in., 30 in. long
    2 pieces of dowel — 1-in. diameter, each 12 in. long
Spindle and Pulley: 1 heavy leather shoelace
    1 steel rod — ¼-in. diameter, 18 in. long
    1 piece of dowel — 1-in. diameter, 1 in. long (for pulley)

1 piece of dowel — 1-in. diameter, 1 in. long (for button on end of spindle)
1 wooden, cupboard door knob — 2-in. size (for flange on spindle)

### Wheel

Make 8 slats — 24 in. long, ¾ in. thick, 1 in. wide. Drill a ¼-in. hole ¾ in. from the end of each slat. Both ends can be tapered for a better appearance, but it is not necessary.

Clamp all the pieces together. Find the exact center, end to end and side to side, and bore a ⅜-in. hole through the whole pile at the center.

Put a ⅜-in. metal rod through 2 of them, place the slats at right angles to each other, and mark them where they cross on both sticks. Saw a cut about ¼ in. deep at the marks on 2 pairs of slats. With a knife or chisel, cut the wood out between the cuts to make a rabbet joint.

On the next 2 pairs of slats, make the cut ½ in. deep instead of ¼ in. deep. Chisel out between the cuts as before.

**121.** *Spindle wheel*
  *Note: Dimensions are in inches except where marked.*

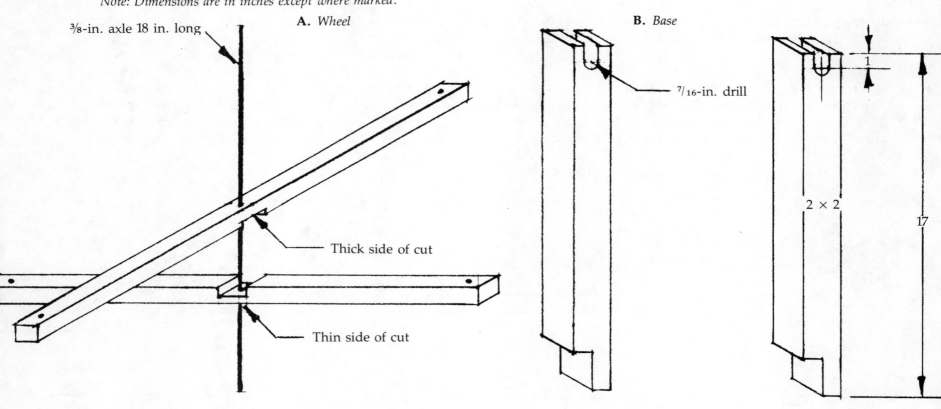

⅜-in. axle 18 in. long

**A.** *Wheel*

Thick side of cut

Thin side of cut

**B.** *Base*

⁷/₁₆-in. drill

2 × 2

1

17

Then glue (using Elmer's Glue-All is fine) 1 of the ¼-in. cuts to 1 of the ½-in. cuts for each pair. Put the slats on the rod to do the gluing so the hole is always centered, but do not glue them to the rod.

When they are dry, put 2 pairs of crossed slats together, having the thick sides of the cuts next to each other and still on the rod in order to keep the holes centered.

Position slats so that the 2 nearest each other are midway between each of them rather than aligned exactly opposite each other. Mark each side of each pair of crosses to get a Maltese-cross kind of marking on the sticks, and make a cut, ¼ in. deep, between the markings. Chip out between the cuts, as before, and join 2 crosses together, creating 2 separate wheels, each having 8 spokes.

## Hub

Take a 4 × 4-in. piece of wood, 3½ in. long. Find the center of the end grain side by drawing a cross from corner to corner. Drill a ⅜-in. hole straight through, being sure your drill is vertical to the top surface (a drill press is more accurate for this).

You can slice off the corners so you have an 8-sided hub for the wheels.

## Handle

At this point, remove the ⅜-in. rod and bend it to make the handle. Make a right angle bend 11 in. from 1 end. Make another right angle bend about 4 in. farther along. The 3 in. left over is where you install your wooden handle. The handle is a piece of 1-in. dowel that is 2 in. long and has a hole bored from end to end (about a ⁷⁄₁₆-in. hole). Keep the handle in place with a washer and cotter pin.

## Base for Spindle Wheel

Take the 2 × 2-in. pieces of wood that are 10 in. long and put them together, side-by-side. Make marks in the center of them, the width of the 1 × 3-in. board, so you can center it across them (at right angles).

Make 2 cuts the depth of your 1 × 3-in. board on each 10-in. piece. Chisel out between the marks on both boards.

All the way through *1* of the 10-in. pieces of board and within an equal distance from either side of the 3-in. cut, drill 1-in. holes 5 in. apart. Place 1 end of the 1 × 3 × 30-in. piece in the 3-in. cut with the end even with the edge of the cut edge.

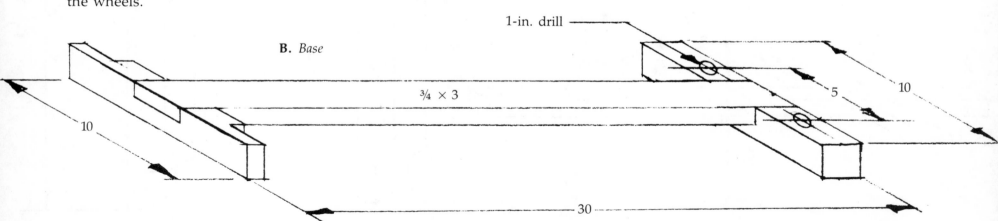

**B.** *Base*

¾ × 3

1-in. drill

10  10  5  10  30

Glue, peg, or screw it in place.

Before you put the other end of the 1 × 3 × 30-in. board in place, you should make the cuts to assemble the uprights that hold the wheel. Make cuts (as shown in fig. 121B) in 1 end of each of the 2 × 2-in. boards, 17 in. long, which are the uprights. In order to fit the joints together, make cuts in each end of 1 of the 2 × 2 × 10-in. pieces (*not* the one with the 1-in. holes bored in it).

Before assembling the uprights, make a slit in them in which the wheel can ride. Bore a $\frac{7}{16}$-in. hole through the width of both of the uprights at once (these are the 2× 2 × 10-in. pieces) about 1½ in. down from the top. (This is the opposite end from the cuts used to join them to the base.) Cut out a $\frac{3}{8}$-in.

wide slit down to the hole in each board so the axle can be put in place.

Where cuts enable them to fit together, assemble the 17-in. pieces with the base. Glue, peg, or screw them in place. The 3-in. board (30 in. long) fits into the cut slot that is 3 in. wide. Secure this into place, also.

### Spindle Holder

Make the spindle holder from the 10-in. long dowels. Bore two ¼-in. holes, 1 in. apart and 1½ in. from the top of both 10-in. dowels. Put the other end of the dowels into the 1-in. holes in the base, with the holes in the upper end of them facing the long axis of the base.

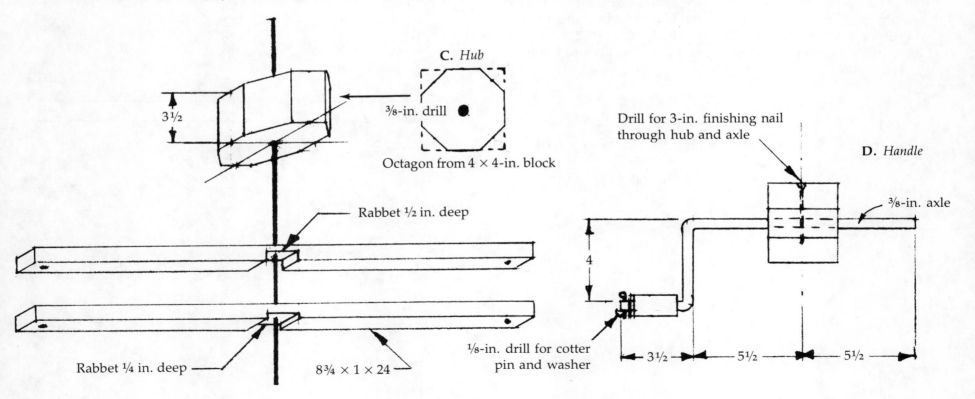

**C.** *Hub*

$\frac{3}{8}$-in. drill

Octagon from 4 × 4-in. block

3½

Rabbet ½ in. deep

Rabbet ¼ in. deep

8¾ × 1 × 24

⅛-in. drill for cotter pin and washer

Drill for 3-in. finishing nail through hub and axle

**D.** *Handle*

$\frac{3}{8}$-in. axle

4

3½       5½       5½

## Assemble the Wheel

Put the wheel together temporarily, with spokes and hub on the axle. Drop the axle into the cuts of the 2 uprights. There should be about ½ in. between the wheel and the uprights on each side. With a file, mark the position on the axle (you can slide the spokes away to do this).

Remove the spokes and axle from the cuts in the upright. Then remove the spokes from the axle and return the hub to the marked position on the axle. Then bore a small hole, the size of a 3-in. finishing nail, straight through the hub and the axle, but no farther (not into the other side of the hub). This is not easy unless you have a drill press, but ours was done with a hand drill.

Then put it all back on the axle again. Drive the finishing nail through the hole in the hub and axle, and into the hub on the other side of the axle. It helps if you first take a smaller piece of wire, about 4 in. long, that you can drop into the hole in the hub. Use it as a feeler to locate the position of the hole in the axle before you try to drive in the nail.

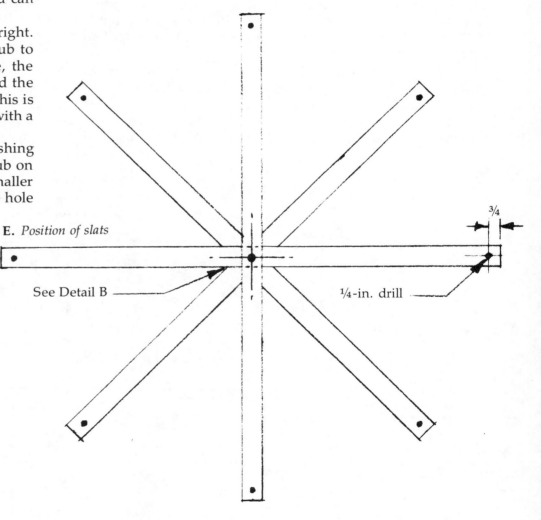

E. *Position of slats*

See Detail B

¼-in. drill

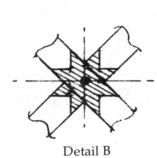

Detail B

## Spindle

Take your 18 × ¼-in. iron rod and file or grind the end to a smooth point.

## Pulley

Cut a groove ½ in. from the end of a 1-in. dowel all the way around it. File or grind it about ⅛ in. deep and as evenly deep as you can. (It is easier if you use a longer piece of dowel, then cut off the 1 in. needed for the pulley.) Take the 1-in. long dowel and drill with a ¼-in. drill through the center of the end grain. Tap gently onto the blunt end of the spindle, and down 4 in. Add a button of dowel to this end.

## Spindle Flange

Take a 2-in. wooden cupboard door knob, bore a ¼-in. hole through the center, and tap this onto the tapered end of the spindle, 9 in. from the end.

## Maidens

Get a leather shoelace and thread it through the 2 holes in the 12 × 1-in. dowels (fig. 121F). Tie the spindle in place and trim the knots. The point of the spindle should be on the same side as the crank for the wheel. (This can be for using the left hand on the crank and the right hand for spinning, or it can be reversed.)

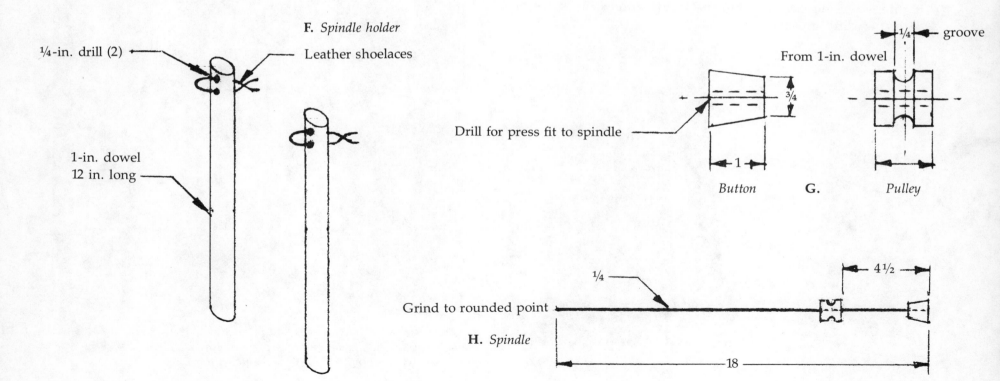

**F.** *Spindle holder*

¼-in. drill (2)

Leather shoelaces

1-in. dowel
12 in. long

¼ → groove

From 1-in. dowel

Drill for press fit to spindle

¾

1

*Button*     **G.**     *Pulley*

Grind to rounded point     ¼     4½

**H.** *Spindle*

18

## Lacing Wheel for Pulley Track

Take a 20-strand cotton string and put it between the spokes of the wheel over the axle, crisscrossing from one 8-spoke wheel to the other. With a crochet hook, pull a loop of string through the hole to the outside and turn the loop back over the spoke. Cross over to the other set of spokes and repeat. Continue in this way to make a zigzag lacing, pulled snug but not tight. Tie the ends together.

## Drive Belt

Using the same kind of string, make a belt going around the wheel and around the pulley on the spindle. Tie fairly tight, at least tight enough to make the spindle revolve. This can be tightened as necessary when the lacing and/or the drive belt stretches during usage.

**122.** *Maiden*

**123.** *Each spoked wheel is fastened to the hub with four 1½-in. #8 sheet metal screws. Additional gluing and/or mitering is optional. Note the method of lacing the wheel for the pulley track.*

**124.** *Bicycle wheel*

## BICYCLE WHEEL

Another possibility for a homemade spinning device is one in which you use a bicycle wheel for the drive wheel. Although it is shown here with a double belt propelling a flyer and bobbin, it is even simpler to make if it turns a spindle because it then needs only a single belt. With flyer and double belt, keep in mind that the spinning fork (with hooks for yarn guides) is fixed to the spindle shaft and that the bobbin must turn freely on that shaft. The bobbin pulley groove must be smaller than the flyer pulley groove. About a 2:1 pulley ratio is good for medium-size yarn and about a 1.5:1 ratio for finer yarn.

Pulleys can be made by cutting 3 discs for each pulley out of plywood or masonite, and cementing them together. The center disc is smaller in order to form the pulley groove. These round discs can be cut with a drill, using "hole saw" attachments, which can be purchased to cut diameters from ¾ to 2½ in. The bobbin pulley can be made from 1-in. and 1½-in. sizes, and 2-in. and 2½-in. sizes can make the flyer pulley.

This wheel can also be made as a single belt, bobbin lead style, with a single belt propelling only the bobbin. The flyer can have an adjustable brake similar to those seen on several of the bulk spinners in the "Available Spinning Wheels" chapter. This brake can either go over a flyer pulley or over the front of the flyer shaft near the orifice. In either case, it exerts a drag on the flyer so that the yarn is wrapped around the bobbin.

Note the wing nut and slot in figure 125. This gives a large range of adjustment for tightening or loosening the drive belt. The flyer is mounted with a hinge, and a wedge is used under the flyer to tighten the belt for a finer adjustment, such as midway in the filling of the bobbin, when just a little more tension is needed.

**125.** *Drive belt tension can be adjusted by turning the wing nut that moves the flyer assembly.*

**126.** *The hinge on the flyer assembly allows additional small adjustment of drive belt tension by use of a wedge.*

I have arranged these terms in the general order that you will need them to understand the weaving chapters that follow.

# 15
# Weaving Terms

## WARP

The warp is the series of longitudinal threads that you weave across, once they are placed on the loom. These long threads, parallel to the sides of the loom, each go through one heddle and through one dent in the reed (see "Reed" below). You decide the length of the warp before you start, and then wind the threads to that exact length on a warping frame or a warping reel (see "Building a Floor Loom and Reel" chapter). The length of the warp determines the amount of fabric that can be woven.

## REED

This is a comblike piece that is set in the beater. It is used for spacing the warp threads and beating in each weft thread. The *dents* are the spaces between its vertical wires, and the *dents per inch* are the number of those spaces in an inch. They must relate to the number of threads you want per inch in your warp. Ordinarily, you use one thread in each dent, at least when using #4, #5, #6, or #7 reeds. When you use up to eight, ten, or twelve handspun warp threads per inch in finer yarn, you could put two threads to each dent, using a #4, #5, or #6 reed. This would then allow more space to pass any slubs or nubs in your warp yarn.

## REED HOOK

This is a thin metal or plastic hook used for drawing threads through the reed when threading a loom. You can make one out of a short metal or plastic ruler by cutting it to shape and smoothing the edges. Keep it within reach, hanging on the loom, for you will need it if you have to replace a broken thread.

**127.** *Author weaving thirty-inch skirt material*

SHED

This is the space between two layers of warp threads, made when the heddle frames are raised and lowered by the treadles. Your shuttle is thrown across through that space to insert a weft thread.

WEFT

The weft is the transverse thread in the cloth, the thread woven across the warp to form the fabric. The old term is *woof*.

To insert one weft thread, depress treadles to open up one of your two tabby sheds. This will be treadles 1 and 3 on the counterbalanced loom that has four treadles. Pass the shuttle carrying the yarn through this open shed. Bring the beater forward to press it into place.

As the beater presses this weft thread into place, change your shed (this will mean depressing treadles 2 and 4). There are reasons for changing the opening of one shed to the opening of the other shed, just at this particular time:

1. It holds the weft in place right where you have beaten it in.
2. It allows the beater to clear the new shed of any en-

tangled fibers of handspun as it goes back into position.

3. It permits a double beat of the weft if necessary, after the shed is changed, without the beater wearing on the warp. The second time, the beater needs to move only a few inches.

The weft must be beaten evenly, and a rhythm of action helps you accomplish this. Any lack of uniformity of spacing in weft threads shows up as streaks across your cloth, particularly in solid colors.

BEATER

The beater is a swing frame that holds the reed. It is moved against the cloth to beat each weft into place. Hold the beater in the center to avoid an uneven pressure against the fabric. Always grasping the beater to the right side of the center would cause your fabric to be beaten in more closely on the right side.

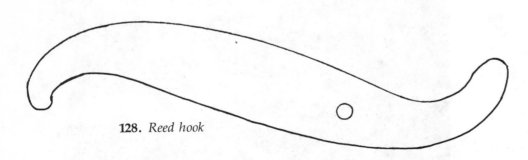

**128.** *Reed hook*

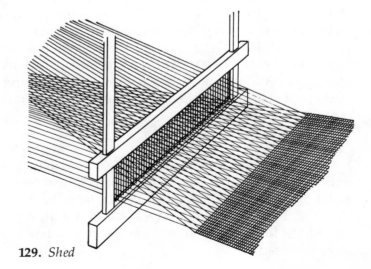

**129.** *Shed*

## HEDDLES

The heddles are lengths of string or wire, with an eye in the center, through which one thread of warp passes. They hang in heddle frames or harnesses between the reed and the back of the loom, and are raised and lowered by the treadles. The threading of individual warp threads through heddles on different harnesses determines what kind of pattern can be woven.

String heddles are better than metal ones when using a handspun warp because they cause less wear. Seine twine or four-ply carpet warp can be used to tie your own heddles. If you are replacing metal heddles on a loom that has a rigid heddle frame, the string heddles will have to be made the exact length of the heddles that you are replacing.

## HEDDLE TYING

A heddle-tying jig can be made from dowels mounted on a shaped board (fig. 130). The measurements are for the loom shown in the "Building a Floor Loom and Reel" chapter. To make replacement heddles for metal heddles of a different size, these dimensions can be altered.

To cut your string for making a large number of heddles on this type of jig, you can measure it around the base. Wind your twine around and around the base lengthwise, and cut through it at one end with a razor blade. Tie each heddle with three square knots, as shown. A dozen or more can be tied at a time. Slip them all off the heddle jig at once onto two pieces of dowel, which will keep the heddles from getting twisted before you put them onto the harnesses.

There is a heddle and harness maker shown in the following chapter.

## TREADLES

These are the foot pedals used to depress the harnesses of

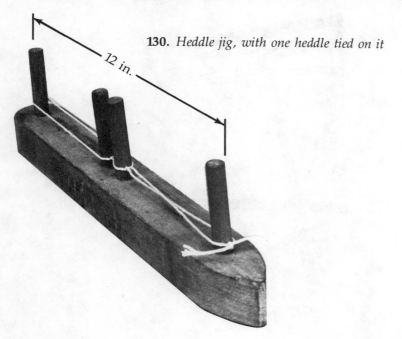

**130.** *Heddle jig, with one heddle tied on it*

12 in.

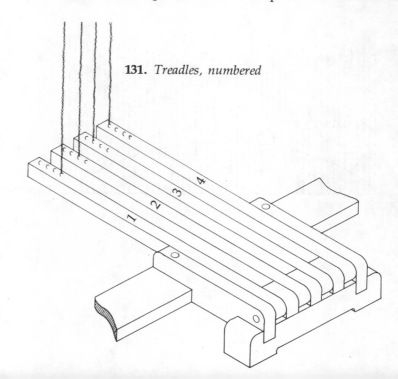

**131.** *Treadles, numbered*

a floor loom, which open up a shed through which you pass your shuttle. The floor loom plans in this book show a four-harness counterbalanced loom with four treadles, each connected to one harness, for using both feet at once.

Treadles 1 and 3 are both pressed down to open up one shed for one weft thread. Then treadles 2 and 4 are pressed, opening the other shed for the next weft. By alternating these, you weave a plain *tabby* weave. By treadling a sequence of treadles 1 and 2, 2 and 3, 3 and 4, 4 and 1, you would be making a *twill* weave.

To coordinate the actions of your hands and feet when weaving tabby, there is a standard way of throwing your shuttle to tie in with the treadle action. Your shuttle starts at the left when you depress treadles 1 and 3, and your shuttle comes from the right when you depress treadles 2 and 4. While this has no effect at all on your woven article, it does help you

remember where you are. If the shuttle is ready to be inserted from the right, you will know that the treadles to press are 2 and 4.

A tie-up with six treadles, which is a little more common, has two treadles for the tabby or plain weave, each controlling two harnesses. The other four treadles tie up to a combination of harnesses to weave twill or whatever pattern for which the warp is threaded. On a loom tie-up such as this, which uses *one* treadle for each of the two tabby sheds, the shuttle enters from the left when the left treadle is used and from the right when using the right tabby treadle.

LAMS

These are levers that operate the heddle frames. The lams are connected to the treadles and the heddle harnesses midway between the two. This makes it possible to connect each treadle

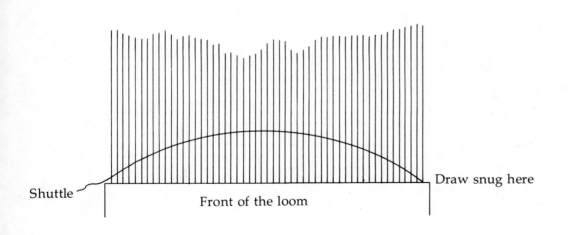

Shuttle · Front of the loom · Draw snug here

**132.** *Selvedges*

**133.** *Warping frame*

to the center of the harness or harnesses that it operates.

## SELVEDGES

The threads along the edge of your fabric, as it is woven, are the selvedges. Neatness of selvedges is one of the marks of a proficient weaver. Too much drawing in of the edge will make the reed wear on the selvedges so they fray and break. On the other hand, a loose weft thread will leave loops at the edge, making the selvedges sloppy. To hit a happy medium that makes nice selvedges, pass your weft yarn across, draw it snug at the selvedge edge where the throw of the shuttle originated, and then adjust it in the center of the distance from edge to edge, to lie in a generous arc.

## CROSS

This is an interlacing figure eight formed at one end of your warp as you wind it. The cross is tied in place to keep the threads in order for placing them on the loom.

## WARPING FRAME

This is a frame or board with dowel pegs on it for winding the warp threads to the proper length and keeping them in sequence. It is easier to construct than the warping reel, but is not as fast and efficient to use. The main features of a warping frame are the pegs for zigzagging the warp to obtain the desired length of warp, and the pegs that form the *cross* at one end of the warp. Forming and maintaining this cross is important for it prevents snarled threads when you put your warp on the loom.

**134.** *Warping reel*

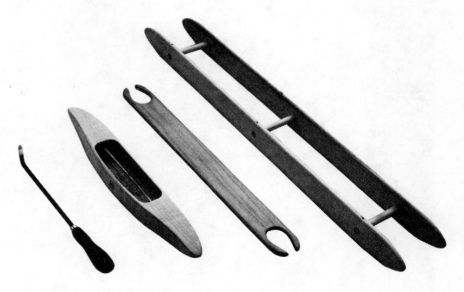

**135.** *Left to right: reed hook, boat shuttle, flat shuttle, ski shuttle*

**136.** *Three strips of header (before actual weaving begins)*

## MAKESHIFT WARPING ARRANGEMENT
## (FOR SHORT WARPS)

The heddle jig can be used to form a warping setup if you do not have a warping frame made. Just clamp the heddle jig to a convenient table or bench and measure off from it the distance that you want for the length of your warp. You need some kind of a post or chair arm to use for the far end of the warp. The warp starts at that point, goes to the heddle jig, where you wind it around the dowel in a figure eight each time to make the cross that is so necessary, and goes back to the starting point. Each warp chain should not be more than twenty or twenty-four threads wide, making it easier to size the warp and easier to tie it on the permanent warp.

## DUMMY OR PERMANENT WARP

This is a short warp (about two yards long) made of cotton carpet warp and threaded on the loom, to which the handspun warp is tied. It eliminates the need to thread each subsequent warp through the heddles and the reed. By tying onto it, the handspun warp is drawn through the heddles and the reed as it is rolled onto the back beam. The waste of handspun is minimized as it allows you to weave up to the end of each warp.

For convenience in counting and checking warp threads when tying on, especially for a wide warp, a two-color system can be used, such as twenty threads black and twenty threads white. Then the handspun warp can be made in chains of twenty to correspond with the divisions of the permanent warp. This way, you will know that you have missed a thread if you do not come out even with each group of twenty.

## HEADER

The header or filler is a narrow strip of heavy cloth. It is woven in at the beginning to even out the tied warp before starting your weaving with yarn. Usually two or more narrow strips are used, wool ones being the most satisfactory. They are removed after the weaving is taken off the loom.

## APRON

The apron is made of heavy canvas or duck, one end attached to the front cloth beam and the other end holding a wooden or metal rod to which warp ends are tied after the loom is threaded. Another rod is sometimes attached to the apron rod by loops for easier tying on, and sometimes laced to the apron.

The back warp beam can have an apron, but more often has just strips of webbing holding a wooden or metal rod to which the warp connects. For more information, refer to the loom plans (fig. 164).

## RATCHET

Some kind of ratchet, or cog or tension device, is necessary to hold the back warp beam and the front cloth beam firmly in place. As you weave, the ratchet at the back is loosened to allow you to wind the warp forward by tightening the ratchet at the front. You need a sturdy tensioning arrangement for weaving with handspun warp because of its unusual elasticity.

When you are not weaving, the tension on the warp should be slackened by loosening the tension on the front beam. Another practice that is helpful when your weaving has been interrupted for several days is to take out the last two threads of your weft and reinsert them. Beat each of them into place and continue with your weaving. This prevents any discernable line at the place where you stopped.

## TABBY

The plainest weave is tabby. Weft threads go over and under consecutive threads, as in darning. Its original meaning also specified that warp and weft yarn be of equal size and woven off in a "balanced" manner, with neither warp nor weft

**137.** *Tabby weave with handspun yarn*

being prominent. It has now come to mean any combination of yarn sizes just woven off in a plain weave.

## TWILL

Twill is another simple weave, but the weft threads form a diagonal pattern, going over and under two warp threads at a time. This is made possible by a *twill* threading of the warp (the same threading that produces tabby, described in the following chapter) plus the manner in which the treadling is done (see "Treadles").

While alternating weft strips of tabby and twill weave can create an attractive texture, it must be done carefully. Since twill pulls in much more than tabby, a wider arc must be left in each weft thread of the twill stripe.

SHUTTLE
　　The device for carrying the weft yarn across the warp.

BOBBIN
　　The tube or quill used in a boat shuttle, carrying your weft yarn. Quills are wound on a bobbin winder.

END
　　End is a term used to designate one warp thread.

SWIFT
　　This is an adjustable frame for holding a skein of yarn to wind it into balls or quills for weaving or knitting. (Another type of swift, which can be easily made, is shown at the end of "Weaving with Handspun: The Weft" chapter.)

**138.** *Bobbin winder. The quill is partly wound on the paper core.*

**139.** *Umbrella swift clamped to table*

**140.** *Squirrel cage swift (skein winder)*

Handspun yarn that is to be used as warp will need to be spun more carefully than weft yarn. Faulty joinings are apt to come apart during weaving (warp sizing helps prevent this) and large slubs or bumps can hang up on the heddles or cause yarn to be broken by the reed.

## YOUR FIRST PROJECT

Since fewer problems are encountered in a short warp, your safest first project should be short and not too wide. It could be a pillow, using your first few skeins of bumpy yarn as textured weft, or it could be a scarf. With this short warp, you gain experience and confidence in the use of handspun and learn what problems to anticipate (and avoid).

## WARP LENGTH

Because of the natural elasticity of handspun yarn, the amount of take-up in the weaving process, the relaxing of the warp length when it is not stretched, and the amount of shrinkage when you wash your woven article, you should figure generously in excess of the desired finished length. You can allow as much as twenty percent of the original warp length, at the time it is wound firmly on the warping board or reel, for loss in shrinkage, take-up, and so on. For warp yarn that is overtwisted, allow closer to twenty-five percent. You gain a few inches more, per same number of sections on the warping reel, if you warp from center-pull balls instead of from skeins on a swift. The yarn from balls is not being stretched as it is warped, so you do not lose as much in immediate relaxing of the yarn as you take it from the reel. If you record the warped length carefully and compare it with the finished amount of weaving, then you will know how much to allow in future warps.

Figure at least six inches of your warp for tying onto the front apron before you start weaving, and for weaving in your header strips. Also allow this much at the end of the weaving.

# 16
# Weaving with Handspun: The Warp

**141.** *Author tying handspun warp onto front apron rod*

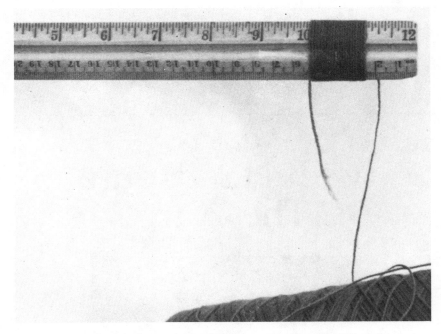

**142.** *Winding yarn around a ruler helps the weaver estimate the number of warp threads to use per inch of weaving.*

There is less waste at the end when using a dummy warp, which I will describe later. If you are weaving a scarf, this beginning and ending yarn is the fringe.

## WARP WIDTH

The number of threads in your warp will be the number of threads per inch times the number of inches across the width of your proposed warp. A simple way for a beginner to estimate the number of threads to use per inch in handspun is to take a piece of the yarn that will be used for warp, and wind it closely around a ruler. *Do not use that many threads per inch* in your warp

or the threads will cling to each other from being too close, and you will not be able to weave. Use only *half* that number of threads per inch or even one thread less than half. This number of threads should then be the number of dents per inch in the reed you use, if you use one warp thread per dent (see ''Reeds'' in previous chapter).

In using handspun, it is important not to set your warp too close and cause sticking or fuzzing. Warp sizing can counteract this somewhat, but you are safer to have too few threads per inch than too many. You can use a slightly heavier or even a much heavier yarn for weft so that your finished cloth is not too loose. Because of take-up and shrinkage in both the warp and the weft, the fabric is tighter when finished than it appears to be while it is being woven.

## STRING HEDDLES

If you are going to be using handspun yarn consistently for warp, string heddles are advised for they are much easier on your yarn. They can replace the metal heddles that are already on a loom. (See heddle-tying jig, fig. 130, or the heddle and harness maker shown here.)

## DUMMY OR PERMANENT WARP

The *dummy warp* is a short warp of strong cotton (usually carpet warp) about one and one-half to two yards long, threaded correctly through the heddles and the reed, with the right number of threads per inch for your particular project. Although it has been facetiously called a ''dummy's'' warp, do not discount its value when working with handspun. Compared with other ways of warping, there are several advantages of using a dummy or permanent warp:

1. It eliminates waste of handspun warp yarn.
2. It simplifies the warping of handspun.
3. It eliminates the need to rethread the heddles and the reed for each subsequent warp of the same threading.
4. It makes you more inclined to start another project,

knowing the tedious threading procedure need not be repeated.

After sizing and drying, your chains of handspun warp will tie onto this dummy warp, which projects out of the front of the reed after it is threaded on. From there, your handspun warp is wound through the reed and heddles onto the warp beam, leaving enough of it in front of the reed to tie onto the front apron of the loom.

## WINDING A DUMMY OR PERMANENT WARP

The number of threads you use in a dummy warp is the same number of threads you want in the width of your handspun warp, but each thread of this permanent warp should be only about two yards long. With this short length, in a cotton warp, the cross is not as important as it is in a longer wool warp, but making the cross is good practice, and it will be used to position your leash sticks.

If you are using a warping reel, measure approximately two yards from the far end of the dowel that forms the cross and back around the reel, to a point at the other end where a peg can be placed to mark off your distance.

On a warping board, you would measure the distance from the far end of the cross, then back and forth across the pegs to one that is at a proper distance to give you the length you want. It helps to wind a brightly colored string along this distance to follow with the warp chain.

You start your warp at the peg to which you measured at the opposite end from the cross. Wind from there to the dowels, where you form your cross with a figure eight movement of the warp yarn, always winding this "8" in the same direction, and back to the start. Go back and forth for the number of threads you need for your warp. If it does not seem that you can easily get that number of threads on your board or reel, divide your dummy warp into two chains.

The last time you get back to the starting point, cut off your

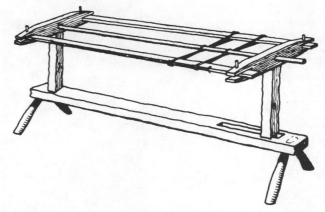

**143.** *Heddle and harness maker. Here, the heddles are tied onto the sticks, which are the bottom and top rods of the harnesses. The center rod is removed and the heddles remain on the other sticks, which fit on the loom. Reprinted by permission from Marion L. Channing's* The Textile Tools of Colonial Homes *(Marion, Massachusetts: The Channings, 1969).*

string, leaving a few extra inches. Tie that end to the end you used to start, and you have completed your dummy warp.

## TYING THE CROSS

Before you take the warp off the frame or reel, the important thing to do is to tie the cross in place (fig. 146). This keeps those threads in the order they were wound, and prevents the tangling that would occur in a longer warp or a wool warp if they were not kept in sequence.

Make a tie also at the opposite end, tying the warp threads together close to the dowel where you started. Remove that dowel (this is at the opposite end from the cross) and snip through the loop where the warp went around the peg.

**144.** *These leash sticks are holding the cross in the warp, between the heddle frames and the back of the loom.*

If this were a longer warp, you would start *chaining* it at that end — making a loose loop of warp, reaching through it to draw the warp through in another loop, and then drawing another loop through that, and so on. In a long warp, this shortens it temporarily to where it can be easily handled. (It is called a *chain* even if you do not chain it.)

### PUTTING PERMANENT WARP ON THE LOOM

When you have the number of threads wound that you need for your dummy warp, in one chain or more, you are ready to start putting it on the loom. If the back apron or back beam of your loom has a rod for attaching your warp, that rod can be slipped through the end loop of the tied cross on your dummy warp chain or chains. This will hold all the warp threads to the back warp beam.

To keep the permanent warp threads in sequence for easy threading through the heddles, which is the next step, use leash sticks, one slipped through on each side of that cross formed by the figure eight that you tied. Once the leash sticks have been placed through the warp chain(s) to hold the cross, the ties can be removed because the cross is secure. The loops of the chain should be centered on the rod and spread out to approximately the width of what you are going to weave.

The leash sticks are held in place by being tied together at each end through a hole bored in each end of each stick. They are then slid forward on the warp until they are just over the top of the back of the loom, a position they should keep while you are weaving. When your dummy warp, and also your wool warp tied to the dummy warp, are being wound onto the back beam, these leash sticks should be slid *forward* each time the warp is wound farther back. While you are weaving, each time you wind your warp forward for a new weaving position, these sticks should be slid to the *back* of the loom again so they do not restrict your shed. They keep your warp threads well separated as they come forward toward the heddles and facilitate the weaving of handspun.

### DUMMY WARP THROUGH THE HEDDLES

To thread your four-harness loom for a tabby or plain weave, consecutive dummy warp threads are taken (starting at the right) and threaded through the heddles — one thread through a heddle on the back harness, the next thread through one of the next forward harness, the next thread on the next forward harness, the next thread through a heddle on the front harness. This sequence is followed across the complete width of the warp. With an overhead beater, the whole beater assembly could be removed to give more working space for threading heddles, and then replaced for drawing the warp through the reed.

**145.** *Tie-ups*

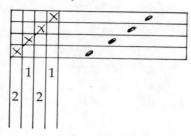

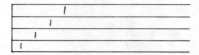

**D.** *The dots used to indicate threading are sometimes written as lines.*

**A.** *Tie-up for four treadles. Press down both number "1" treadles for first tabby shed and press down two number "2" treadles for the second tabby shed. Repeat. (This applies to the counterbalanced loom where you use both feet at once.)*

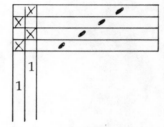

**E.** *This tie-up is written for a two-harness tabby, using two treadles alternately.*

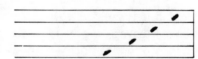

**B.** *These dots between the lines are to show in what sequence the warp threads are drawn through the heddles on the four harnesses.*

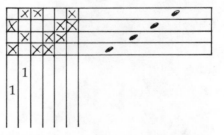

**F.** *Tie-up for six treadles. The left two treadles are tied up for tabby (the other four could be used to make twill combinations). Press down alternately on the two left treadles (for tabby sheds).*

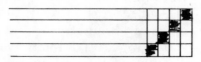

**C.** *The dots are sometimes shown as dark squares.*

**146.** *A cross is tied in the warp on the warping
reel before the warp is chained and removed from the reel.*

To thread heddles easily, leave one heddle at the very right
end of each heddle frame or set of heddle sticks to hold the
frame in place. Push the others back to the left, where it is
simple to take one heddle at a time and move it into position at
the right for pulling one warp thread through it. This way,
you are not likely to get any heddles crossed and threaded out
of sequence.

You are able to take the dummy warp threads in sequence
by noting how they come through the leash sticks. To pull the
threads through the heddles, use a wooden-handled, rug crochet hook or a long reed hook (fig. 135).

The above threading is for tabby, but can also be treadled
to produce a twill or a broken twill pattern. With a four-harness
loom, you can warp up for a great variety of patterns just by the
way you draw your warp ends through the heddles on different harnesses. Another way to get a pattern effect, even on a
two-harness loom, is to do it with change of color and texture
in your warp and weft yarns.

## DUMMY WARP THROUGH THE REED

When all your dummy warp threads are through the heddles, you are ready to draw them through the reed. A flat reed
hook works well for this (fig. 135).

With an overhead beater, like the one on our equipment
plan loom, have it at its very front position to give you more
working room for this process. Your warp should be centered
in your reed, so measure and determine the center and mark it
by tying a bright thread there. You will use this mark each time
you change to a different width of warp. Measure to the right a
distance of half the width of your warp, and start drawing
threads through at this point.

Starting at the right side, take consecutive warp threads as they come through the heddles, and draw each thread through one dent of the reed. Be careful not to miss any threads or take them out of sequence, and do not skip any dents in the reed. Any mistake in threading the heddles or the reed must be corrected or the error will be woven for the full length of your warp.

When your dummy warp is all drawn through the heddles and the reed, the hardest work of weaving is done, and you are ready to tie your sized handspun warp onto it and reel it onto the loom. Wind your dummy warp back onto the back warp beam until there is about ten inches of it projecting from the front of the reed. Tie it in bunches so it is held securely until you are ready to tie on your wool warp.

## WINDING YOUR HANDSPUN WARP

Wind your handspun yarn into a warp of the same number of threads as your dummy warp, but of whatever length you have decided. Warp it longer than you think you need for your project, remembering the loss of length due to elasticity, take-up, shrinkage, and so on.

Divide your number of warp threads to determine chains of equal size. We wind our chains in twenty or twenty-four thread widths so they are easy to handle and easy to size. The yarn should already have been washed and blocked, so it is both preshrunk and easier to handle.

Measure off the distance on the board or reel for your warp, as you did with the dummy warp. Tie the cross in each chain, and make a tie also at the peg at the far end of the cross, tying around the warp threads.

At the peg where your warp begins (the opposite end from the cross), tie both sides of the warp chain together, just in front of that peg. As you slip the warp off that end, slip the scissors in where the peg was and cut the warp ends. This leaves you cut ends at that end of the warp, but they are tied together.

To chain your warp, make a loose loop at that end, reach through it and grasp the warp, bring it through that loop in a loop, reach through it with your other hand and bring it through another loop, and continue to chain like that until you get up near the cross. Do not pull the cross through the loop; just tie the last loop loosely against the rest of the warp, below the cross, with a light piece of string. You will break that string when you want to unchain.

Chain each section of warp lengths, as you make them, until you have the required number to make up the whole warp. I would suggest that you warp a few extra threads, so that you have a replacement for any thread that may break. Size these extras, too. As you get better at spinning warp, breakage will not be a problem.

## SIZING YOUR WARP CHAINS

To protect your handspun yarn from the wearing action of the heddles and reed, and to strengthen any weak places, you should use a warp sizing on your chains before they go on the loom. Warp dressing, a product applied to the warp after it is on the loom, is not as much help as is sizing, which is applied to the warp prior to tying it on the loom.

The sizing product we have used for many years is a natural hide glue that comes in dry granules. (At one time, it was manufactured for many industrial uses, and came in many different grades with differing jell strength and viscosity. It was also used for sizing canvases for oil paintings.) The outward appearance of various granular glues differs only as to the mesh (fineness of grind), which is no indication of strength, so if using ground glue of an unknown strength, test it to determine a workable dilution. (For glue sizing, see "Sources" chapter.)

To use the sizing granules, soak them first in cold water, and then dissolve them by adding boiling water and stirring. The ratio of our sizing is three tablespoons of granules to one cup cold water. This quantity is liquefied by adding one cup

**147.** *Chaining the warp.* **A.** *One loop is drawn through the first loop in the warp to make a chain.*

**B.** *Alternating hands to avoid twisting the warp, pull another loop through the last loop.*

boiling water when the glue is well soaked and has absorbed the cold water. Multiply this ratio by the amount of liquid sizing you want to make. One quart of liquid is about enough for a narrow warp that makes one or two scarves. Any leftover liquid sizing can be saved for the next use.

Dip your warp chains completely in this hot sizing (it absorbs better when hot) and wring them out. The best way is with an old washing machine wringer (see "Sources" chapter for clamp-on hand wringer). Without a wringer, remove glue by stripping your hand tightly along the length of the chain, rather than by twisting it. Remember to wash off the wringer and the utensils you use with very hot water.

Now hang up the sized chains to dry. Remove the ties that hold the last loop to each chain. Then unchain them so they will dry more easily and have no kinks in them when dry. If you have a basement or attic with low rafters, you can put nails in the rafters at a convenient distance apart to suspend the stretched warp for drying. Or on a nice day, dry them out-doors, draped over a clothesline or a fence. These chains must be *completely* dry before you tie them onto your dummy warp ends. When dry, the warp yarn is quite stiff because of the sizing, but the sizing washes out easily after your article is woven.

Any leftover sizing keeps in a cool place for several weeks, or in a covered jar in the back of your refrigerator for an indefinite time. Warm it to liquefy it for the next use.

### TYING HANDSPUN WARP ONTO DUMMY WARP

The cross that you tied at the end of each warp chain is used now. It keeps your handspun warp threads in perfect sequence while you tie them onto the dummy warp. Start at the right side of the loom and tie one thread of handspun onto one thread of dummy warp, all the way across.

There are reasons for using a weaver's knot for tying on the warp. It is a fairly flat knot so it slips through reed and heddles well. It can be untied quickly by pulling hard on one of the ends

**148.** *How to tie a weaver's knot*

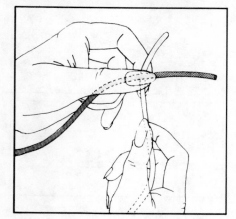

*Step 1. Left over right*

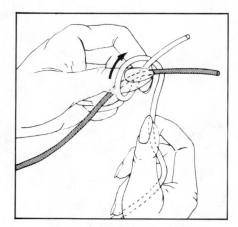

*Step 2. Circle both ends*

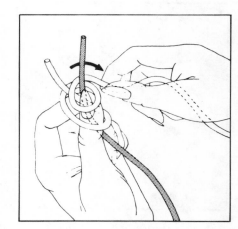

*Step 3. Circle left end*

to straighten it out (best to pull on the cotton warp end), and then just slipping the other yarn off. If tied properly, it does not slip or come undone while it is in use on the loom.

One way to hold the cross in your handspun warp while you tie it on is to use two short pieces of dowel. They should be about ten inches long and sanded until smooth. Slip one through on each side of the cross, and hold the dowels together at each end with a heavy rubber band crossed around them. This holds them firmly, but is easily adjustable. After the dowels are inserted in the cross of a warp chain, cut the yarn loops at the tied end of the cross to give you ends to start tying onto the dummy warp. Also remove the ties that held the cross.

It is easy to see which thread to tie, taking them out of the cross held by the dowels, one by one, and tying each thread onto one dummy warp thread. The sequence of the dummy warp ends can be seen where they emerge from the reed.

When you are good at tying on, and are sure you will not be interrupted you can discard these dowels and just insert the fingers of one hand into the openings of the cross, taking the threads out one by one for tying.

When all the chains are tied on across the width of the dummy warp, you are ready to wind the handspun warp onto the loom.

## WINDING ON THE HANDSPUN WARP

Gently pull each knot back through the reed, then wind up some of the dummy warp onto the back beam until the knots are against the heddles, behind the reed. Slide your leash sticks forward each time you wind your warp to the back, to prevent them from slipping over the back of the loom.

To make sure the warp is untangled and will not be broken by the reed, comb it out with your fingers to straighten and untangle it. Then work your knots through the heddles, all the way across the width of the warp. When all the knots are pulled back through the heddles, wind up some more of the warp onto your back beam. Before proceeding, make sure that no knots were faulty and have come untied and that no threads

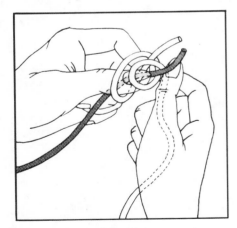

*Step 4. Slip thumb under left end*

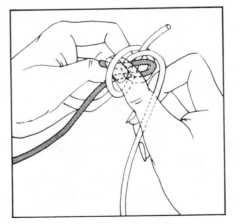

*Step 5. Push left end in and through first loop*

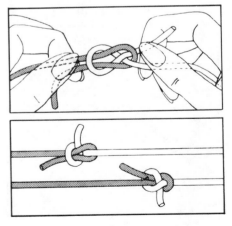

*Step 6. Grasp left end (or both ends) and pull tight*

have broken.

To ensure that the warp will lie smoothly as it winds onto the back warp beam, and that one layer of warp threads will not cut down into the layer below, you will need to insert something between these layers. You can use smooth, flat sticks made from screen door stripping. Cut them to lengths that are wider than your warp, but not wider than the back beam, and sand them until they are smooth. Some weavers use folded newspapers, but they can be messy. I would recommend pieces of light-weight cardboard or very heavy-weight wrapping paper cut to a length a little wider than your warp and a width of eight, ten, or twelve inches. The nice thing about using these is that after they have been used a few times, they take on the curve of the beam and are easy to insert after that.

The rest of the warping should be done under tension, which is easiest to do with one person in front of the loom to hold the warp chains, and one person at the back, turning the back warp beam to wind on. The woman who sold me my first loom had a sign on the wall that said, "Weavers live two by two." While it is possible to warp a loom alone, it goes faster with two people.

The person who is holding the warp chains combs them out with his fingers to remove any tangles, then holds half the width of the warp in one hand and half in the other hand (fig. 151) with gentle tension, while the other person winds it onto the back beam. This is an intermittent process since you must stop to comb out tangles as each straightened section goes through the reed. Keep an even tension on all the threads of the warp because loose threads will show up in your weaving.

**149.** *Dowels holding the cross in the dry sized warp. The top loop will be cut, and those ends will be taken consecutively and tied onto the dummy warp.*

**150.** *Warp tied on, ready to roll onto the loom*

When your warp is wound on until the ends of it are about even with the front edge of the loom, you are "warped."

## TYING WARP ENDS TO CLOTH APRON

Be sure both back beam and front beam ratchets are engaged before you start to tie the warp onto the front apron. Otherwise, one or the other will keep slipping as you tighten your warp knots. Bring the cloth apron up over the front beam of the loom to where the ends of the warp can be tied onto the stick attached to the apron. To tie on, first make one tie at each end and one in the middle. These have to be adjusted later, but they will hold the apron in place where you can work with it.

Starting at the right side of the warp, take two sets of four adjoining warp threads, four threads in each hand. (This is where a second rod, attached to the rod in the apron, is more convenient than a single rod within a notched hem of the apron.) They go over the top of the rod, around under it, and tie across themselves in a single knot. Do not use a double knot because it will need tightening after you have tied the whole width of warp, eight threads at a time. When you have them all tied on, go back across, tightening each knot to obtain an even tension on all the warp threads. Be sure that the end knot on each side is not loose because these contain your selvedge threads.

Now you are ready to start weaving!

**151.** *Winding the warp onto the loom*

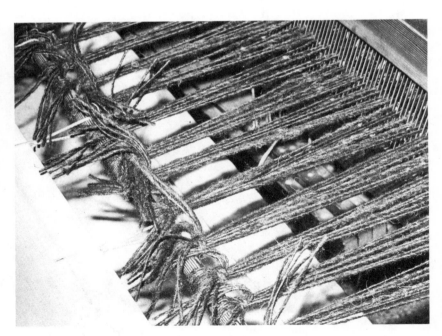

**152.** *Warp on the loom. The ends are tied onto the rod, which is attached to the front apron.*

## FILLER

Before you start with your handspun weft, you need a couple of rows of filler (header) to even up the warp threads, which bunch together where they are tied to the apron or rod in front. This can be done with two strips of heavy fabric, such as that used for carpet rags, about three-fourths inch wide and longer than the width of your warp. Beat them in close to the knots. If you are not using the beginning of the warp for fringe on your completed article and want to skimp on the waste, the strips can be as narrow as one-fourth inch if they are woolen, because the yarn clings to woolen strips.

## ADJUSTING TENSION

By taking in the ratchet arrangement at the front, adjust the tension on your warp so it is fairly tight. A tight warp tension offsets some of the uneven twist of a beginner's warp and also makes it possible to beat in the weft without getting it too firm. The looser the tension, the tighter the weft tends to beat in, even with an intentionally soft touch. With any areas of overtwist in your weft, the material feels more harsh if woven off too firmly. With a scarf, stole, or pillow as your first project, a soft beat is more suitable. If you are weaving a small rug, then hard beating of the weft is entirely in order, and you can put overtwisted yarn to good use.

## TREADLING TO OPEN SHED: FOUR TREADLES

If you are using the four-harness counterbalanced loom tied up to four treadles, you use both feet at once to depress the treadles that make your tabby or plain-weave sheds. With treadles numbered 1 to 4, from left to right, this means that you depress treadles 2 and 4 for one shed, throw your shuttle of yarn across, and then depress treadles 1 and 3 for the other shed. Repeat these two actions for a plain-weave fabric.

The first loom I bought was tied up this way, one treadle to each of the four harnesses, and I have always preferred this

# 17
# Weaving with Handspun: The Weft

**153.** *The white filler strips, also called headers, even off the warp. Note the arc of weft yarn that is not yet beaten in.*

rather than a tie-up to six treadles. Maybe it seems more like dancing, using both feet at once.

## TREADLING TO OPEN SHED: SIX TREADLES

Actually, the more common tie-up is that of using six treadles, two of them for the tabby shed (two harnesses tied to each tabby treadle) and the other four tied up for pattern (in this case twill or broken twill) by each being tied to two harnesses. For this six treadle tie-up, you use only one foot at a time. Depress one of the "tabby" treadles for one shed, depress the other one for the alternate shed, and repeat, for plain weave. ("Weaving Terms" chapter also deals with the treadling sequence.)

## ARC OF WEFT YARN

One of the problems of weaving with handspun is allowing the edges to get pulled in by not having sufficient arc in each weft thread. After you throw each pick of weft yarn, rather than having it go straight across, adjust it to form an arc before beating it in. This arc of each thread is formed after firming up the selvedge by drawing the weft snug at the very edge. The arc allows both for the elasticity of the yarn and for the normal take-up as the weft threads go over and under the warp threads. For example, on a thirty-six inch width of weaving, the weft can arc about four inches at the center before it is beaten in. On a forty-four inch width of weaving, the weft can arc about six inches at the center. When weaving with materials other than handspun, you need not allow as much arc.

As you start out, the first two or three rows need little or no arc. There will be a certain amount of normal drawing in once you get past the first inch or so, and you want the beginning to be no wider than the rest of the weaving.

A weaving width of thirty-six inches should not pull in more than one and one-half inches at the most. Each time you relax the tension to wind the warp forward, check with a tape measure. If it is pulling in more, then you should allow more arc in the weft. "Bubble" it, if necessary, by making several small arcs across the width to make an even longer weft thread.

## GAINING WIDTH WITH UNBLOCKED WEFT

Ordinarily, you will find it much easier to work with weft yarn that has been washed and blocked. But, if there is an advantage to gaining a few more inches of fabric width, it helps to use unblocked weft. The unblocked yarn lies in a more irregular line in the arc, and amounts to extra inches of weft in each arc. When you wash the finished fabric and lay it out to dry, you can block it out that much wider, smoothing it out with your hands. The unblocked yarn also achieves a less uniform textural effect.

There is one disadvantage to this method. If you try to pack too much extra yarn into the arc, or if your yarn is over-twisted, it can end up with a tabby weave in which warp and weft are not always lying at right angles to each other. The crinkled weft pushes the warp threads out of line, creating an effect that is sometimes described as "chicken scratches," which will be more noticeable after washing.

## SHUTTLES

The most efficient type of shuttle for any width over ten or twelve inches is some type of boat shuttle that carries the bobbin of yarn across the whole width of warp. A good shuttle should be very smooth on all sides, and especially smooth and polished on the bottom so that it does not catch on your warp.

On the common boat shuttle, the side toward the reed (away from the opening) should be flatter than the front side so that it stays close to the reed as you throw it through the shed. The opening is in the opposite side and is easier to use if it is a rather long slit instead of a small round hole. It is not only easier to thread the yarn through the longer slit, but there is also a more even feeding of the yarn as it unwinds off the elongated bobbin shape. (There is also a mill-type shuttle that feeds off the end, but the beginner is not likely to use it.)

For very heavy yarn, a boat shuttle is not practical because it does not hold enough yarn. When working with heavy yarn, you could use a stick shuttle, which is easy to make, satisfactory for narrow widths, and can accommodate heavier yarn.

## WINDING SHUTTLE BOBBINS

With handspun, allow for its lack of uniformity — yarn size, texture, and color vary. To get a more unified effect, have all the necessary weft yarn spun and wound into bobbins before you start weaving. Then mix up the quills to ensure a more even distribution of irregularities. If this is not possible, at least work from two skeins of yarn at a time, winding both into quills and alternating their use.

Plastic or wooden quills can be purchased, but plain brown paper makes good homemade quills. Cut out four- or five-inch squares of paper (the size depends on your shuttle size) and round off all the corners so the yarn does not catch on them. Bobbins can be wound on a bobbin winder or on the spindle wheel, for which plans are shown in the "Building a Spinning Wheel" chapter. Or, a hand drill with a tapered metal rod instead of a drill can be clamped to a table and then turned like a bobbin winder.

Wrap one edge of your paper quill tightly around the shaft, catching the beginning of your weft yarn under the outer edge of the paper. Hold it there as you begin winding. Make an elliptical shape, winding back and forth, gradually building up higher in the center. Zigzagging occasionally keeps the yarn from slipping off the ends.

When making bobbins, the skein is held on a swift of which there are several kinds. (See plans for making your own swift at the end of this chapter.) Swifts, hand winders, and

**154.** *Yarn wound onto a paper quill is inserted in a boat shuttle.*

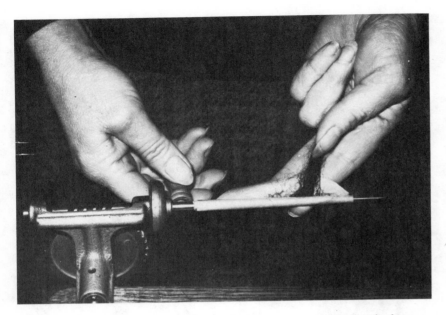

**155.** *Winding a paper quill. Catch the yarn under the edge of the paper in order to begin.*

electric winders are available at spinning-weaving supply shops or can be ordered from catalogs (see "Sources" chapter).

## CHANGING BOBBINS

When you have used up one bobbin, start weaving with the next by overlapping the two ends. A one-inch overlap is usually sufficient and need not be done at the selvedge. If these are not cut ends, they will be undetectable. (A cut end will pop out to one side or the other.) Yarn can be broken by untwisting it before pulling it apart, leaving tapered ends.

## MOVING HEDDLE FRAMES

When you wind your warp forward to get more weaving space, handspun tends to carry the heddle frames forward with the warp. Each time, before tightening the warp completely, move each heddle frame back to its original position. If there is a slub or heavy place hung up in a heddle eye, it can be noticed and pulled through individually, without damage to the warp yarn.

Check your heddle eyes to make sure the warp, when it is at rest, is in a straight line from the front of the loom to the back. This is always a good policy, but more so with handspun. If the heddle eyes are above or below this line, the tie-up on the heddle frames should be adjusted.

## MENDING WARP THREADS

If a warp thread breaks during weaving, you can replace it with one of the extra threads that you warped and sized. Pin one end of the extra thread to the woven material a few inches back from the edge of your weaving, run it through the reed and through the heddle that had the broken thread in it, and hang it over the back of the loom. It should be weighted to correspond as closely as possible to the tension of your warp. Continue with your weaving for a few inches. Then unpin the end that is pinned into your weaving, break off enough of the end to taper it and mend it into the cloth alongside the thread that it is replacing so that it does not show. Continue weaving, and when you have woven sufficiently to pull forward the broken end of the original warp thread, break off your substitute thread and attach your broken warp thread to the weaving with a pin, and continue. You can later mend it in, as well as the second end of your substitute thread. With the natural irregularities of handspun, these mended-in ends will not show.

The main thing to remember is never to cut an end. Always break it, even if you have to untwist it and pull it apart to make it break. A cut end pops out on one side or the other of the material, while a broken, frayed end is so tapered that it clings to where it is woven in, and stays there.

Any time you have to make a knot in your warp, remember to untie it and mend in both ends after weaving a few inches past the knot.

## SELVEDGES

On a narrow warp of sized yarn, selvedge problems should be minimal if you remember to throw a generous arc of weft. On a wider warp, especially if you have overtwist in your weft, it may tend to pull in despite your arc. If you cannot keep it from pulling in, you may want to make a *template*, which is a guide used to keep the material at the woven width. By attaching it to the selvedge about one inch behind your weaving position, the material will be held in at that width. The template should be moved about every three inches of weaving. (See template plans at the end of this chapter.)

## SELVEDGE PROTECTORS

There is another way to strengthen and protect selvedges of a wider warp, if you are having trouble with them, and it is convenient because it can be done after you have tried weaving and run into difficulty. Just add two additional selvedge threads to each side of the warp on the loom, using cotton carpet warp. Tie them onto the front cloth apron, run them back through the reed and heddles and weight them heavily, hanging the excess length at the back of the loom. (Added selvedges should be threaded onto alternate heddle frames in continuation of the sequence of your original tabby-twill threading.) Move the weights back as you weave, keeping them just above the floor. Be sure the threads are weighted to a bit tighter tension than your warp. Since these added threads are smooth, the tension of the finished selvedge can be adjusted to perfection after the cloth is off the loom and again after the cloth is washed, if necessary. These extra selvedge threads will slide from each end, and can be drawn to the best tension for your woolen material, just like adjusting the gathers on a basting thread. I had to do this on my first long handspun warp because I had not yet discovered the use of sizing to protect the warp. Experi-

**156.** *Weaving three scarves will necessitate six neat selvedges.*

ence in weaving with handspun and in spinning your warp and weft, combined with the habitual use of sizing, eliminate the troubles that might make this method necessary.

## WEAVING TOWARD THE END OF THE WARP

In weaving off a warp that has been tied to a dummy or permanent warp, you can weave easily right up to the point where the knots, of handspun onto permanent warp, are in a position just behind the heddles. For blankets, afghans, or scarves, where you may want a long triple-knotted fringe, this leaves just about the nine to ten inches you need for tying the fringe.

For fabrics, ponchos, or articles needing only a short fringe, you can wind the warp forward once more, bringing the knots very carefully through the heddles to just behind the reed, so you can weave a few more inches. With careful handling, you can even bring the knots through the reed and weave right up to them, but this takes more patience.

## CUTTING OFF

Before you remove your material from the loom, you need to do something to prevent loosening of the weft along the cut edge. If it is to be an edge without fringe, one that will be in a seam, it should be overcast with fine yarn and then machine stitched after it is cut off. If the edge is to have a knotted fringe, do not overcast it but just weave in two or three rows of filler, preferably wool, to hold it.

Wind the warp forward, bringing the knots to ten to twelve inches in front of the reed, before you cut. Cut just behind these knots so they are not left on your permanent warp where you will be tying on your next warp. It is simpler to trim knots off the fringe than it is to trim the warp. The permanent warp ends can be loosely knotted in groups in front of the reed, after cutting, to hold them safely until needed.

## USING CLAMPS

You will find that clamping two flat sticks, using small C clamps, across the permanent warp in front of the reed is a great help when you are ready to cut off. These sticks remain clamped onto it until you are ready to tie on again, and the ends will not have to be knotted in groups to keep them secure. To tie on, the warp ends are pulled out one at a time, in sequence.

After you have done this a few times, you will probably want to make a permanent piece of equipment — drill holes through both of the sticks in four places and use bolts and wing nuts to hold them together. This device is also useful with a longer warp when you want to cut off one article, still having enough warp on the loom to weave another one. Just put it on to hold the unwoven warp threads in place, and cut off as close to your woven article as desired. Then you can tie the remainder of the warp onto the front apron when you are ready to continue weaving.

## FINISHING THE FABRIC

Handspun material, just off the loom, can be a disappointment until it is washed. Washing is necessary not only to improve its appearance, but to remove the warp sizing and to fluff up the yarn. Also, it takes heat and moisture to relax the warp and weft yarns and make them fully accommodate each other.

Cut edges, intended for seams when the fabric is tailored, can be machine stitched, close to the previously overcast edge, before washing in order to prevent any raveling. Fringes also should be tied right after the material is removed from the loom.

As with washing fleeces, there are standard things to avoid: having radical changes in water temperature, leaving undissolved soap or detergent in the water, and running the wash or rinse water onto the material. You should also keep the process moving once you start — from soaking and rinsing to whatever drying procedure you choose. Do not allow the wet material to develop wrinkles between these processes.

We soak our material in hot detergent water, souse it up and down gently after soaking, and spin the water out. (We use a centrifugal extractor, but the separate spin cycle of a washing machine can be used to remove the water.) Promptly rinse the material, remove the rinse water with the extractor or machine, and lay the material out flat to dry.

We have found it most effective to lay the article or material out on a blanket-covered piece of hardboard or plywood. If you smooth the material carefully with your hands when you arrange it on the blanket, you will usually eliminate any need for pressing.

You can also roll material in large mattress pads to absorb the excess moisture, then lay it out flat on sheets or blankets to dry. Some weavers choose to use clothesline drying, fastening lots of clothespins close together to avoid rippled selvedges, or hang the fabric between two clotheslines. This type of drying does not allow smoothing of the damp fabric, and so it usually necessitates a good steam pressing of the fabric when it is dry.

Some materials need no pressing and others need a thorough pressing to give a professional appearance. The more inexperienced the spinning, the more benefit is gained from a hard pressing. The nap can be raised afterward, if desired, by brushing.

## HOMEMADE UMBRELLA SWIFT PLANS

The dimensions of this particular umbrella swift are perfect for a skein 1½ yd. around made on the 1½ yd. skeiner stick (fig. 90). It actually fits from a 3½-ft. to a 5-ft. skein.

To fit a 1-yd. skein, the top crosspieces should be about 1 in. shorter, and 2 in. should be added to all the vertical pieces in order to allow a more gradual taper.

Further instructions are not necessary because this swift is so easy to make.

## List of Materials

2 pieces of wood — each 1 × 3 in. and 20 in. long (base)
1 dowel — 1-in. diameter and 9 in. long
1 dowel — 1-in. diameter and 1 in. long (top of stem)
2 strips — 1 in. wide, ⅜ in. thick, 26½ in. long (base of umbrella); holes in 1 in. from end, sticks out beyond slanting slats
2 strips — 1 in. wide, ⅜ in. thick, 10 in. long, holes ½ in. from ends (top of umbrella)
8 strips — ¾ in. wide, ³⁄₁₆ to ¼ in. thick, 18 in. long; holes ½ in. from each end
1 steel rod — ⅜ in. thick, 30 in. long (imbedded only a few inches in dowel stand)

*Note: You may not need to use these exact dimensions.*

**157.** *This ''Christmas tree'' swift is a simple type of umbrella swift, and is easy to make with hand tools.*

TEMPLATE PLANS

The template length is adjusted to the proper fabric width. Then the sharp pins in the template ends are hooked into the selvedge edges (with the template open). The template is then flattened into the "closed" position in order to hold the fabric at the correct width. Move the template forward about every 3 in. of weaving.

**158.** *Template*

*Note: Dimensions are in inches except where marked.*

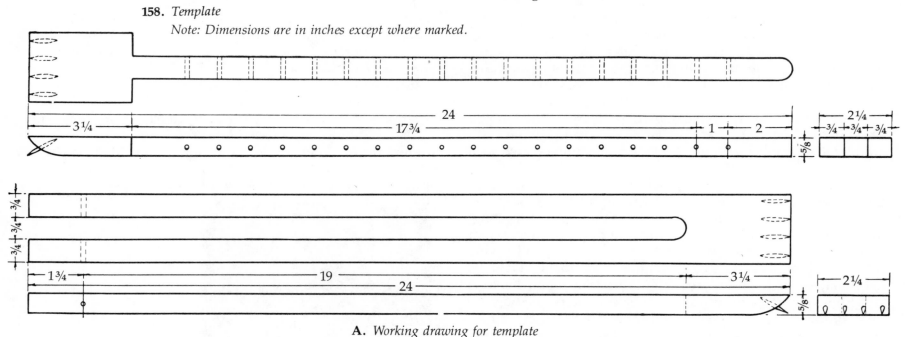

**A.** *Working drawing for template*

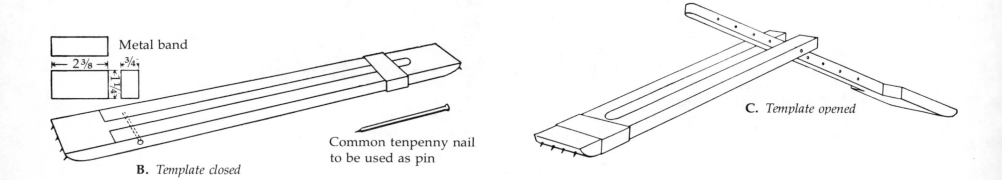

Metal band

Common tenpenny nail to be used as pin

**B.** *Template closed*

**C.** *Template opened*

In weaving with your own handspun yarn, you are limited by the materials you have and should develop your project around the yarn. A varied warp, although half hidden, adds a lot of interest to the final effect.

## COLOR IN THE WARP: STRIPES

If you warp up in stripes of irregular widths, you can weave them off with a plain weft to make vertical stripes or with a weft of corresponding stripes for a plaid.

For this kind of warp, the sequence and width of your stripes are usually determined as you wind the yarn on the warping reel. One disadvantage of this way is that it makes such a project of the planning. Also, after these striped warp chains are sized and dried, you still have to sort them out and tie them onto the permanent warp, trying to keep the stripes in the order you planned them when you wound them on the reel.

## COLOR IN THE WARP: RANDOM

A less systematic method of tying on allows you to design the warp on the loom and is a lot more fun. For this, warp an assortment of solid color chains, but do not tie them onto the loom as solid areas.

Keeping the threads in order with the cross, tie each chain on, scattering it across the width of the warp, and skipping over areas where that particular shade is not wanted. It can be tied on in a series of however many threads of this color are wanted in one place.

Then take another chain of sized handspun and tie it on in the same manner. The chains will overlap, but can be separated into several sections once they are tied on and draped across chairs or other convenient objects (clear across the room if it is a long warp). This is done only to make them easier to comb out and untangle when you start rolling them onto the loom.

While there is a little extra time required to organize these overlapping chains for winding them onto the loom, you have

# 18
# Weaving Projects with Handspun

**159.** *Random color and texture in handspun fabric*

already saved that much time by having made only solid color chains. It would have required changing colors too frequently if it had been planned on the warping reel.

To have the latitude of putting shades wherever you want them without running out of colors, it helps to have more chains than are needed. On the other hand, there is a certain challenge in having to make do with exactly what you have. In either case, it is the yarn you have that determines the effect you get. As we say at our house, "Take what you've got, and do what you can."

## TWO WEAVING PROJECTS

The following projects are written up in 2 different ways for 2 weaving widths. Either of these can be woven on the loom for which building plans are given in this book, but the first one (size 10 to 12 woman's vest, and the baby blanket) can be done on a loom as narrow as 38 in. Actually, the sizes will be determined by the width of your warp. In the second project, the 38-in. loom makes a baby blanket size, and the 44½-in. weaving width makes a larger square that can be used for either a baby blanket or a poncho. The 38-in. loom makes the small size vest while the 44½-in. width is needed for the large size.

Following the instructions, weave the vest first, then the blanket or poncho. This means that the last 10 in. of your warp, which is harder to weave, does not have to be woven since it will be utilized as fringe on the second project.

The blanket or poncho, which uses your warp yarn for fringe at the beginning and the end of the woven portion, can have knotted-on fringe added to the selvedges after you take it from the loom (before washing it). Some of the yarn to be knotted on at the sides of the blanket will be the unused underarm yarn from the loom-shaped vest and will be just about the right length for the fringe.

### Yarn Sizes

The size of handspun yarn to use in these projects is difficult to describe by either weight or by twists per inch because of too many variables, such as type of wool and amount of twist or overtwist, so I will compare it to familiar household items. The warp should be about the size of the middle section of a round wooden toothpick in order to use 5 threads per in. The weft should be heavier, at least as thick as a match-stick. It can be even larger for a firmer, more interesting texture.

## SMALL VEST AND BABY BLANKET

### Permanent or Dummy Warp

Make a permanent warp 1½ to 2 yd. long using carpet warp (you use up about 1 in. of it each time you cut off a warp). It takes 5 threads to the inch for a total of 190 threads (38-in. width). For easy handling, you can make 7 chains of 24 threads and 1 chain of 22 threads.

Warp this onto the loom for tabby-twill threading (see "Weaving with Handspun: The Warp" chapter) and use #5 reed for the 5-to-the-inch warp. Some weaving books express this as 5 e.p.i., which means 5 *ends per inch*.

### Handspun Warp

You need a total of about 3 yd. of handspun warp to weave both items. If your warping reel or warping board does not come out conveniently to exactly 3 yd., better to make it a few inches more rather than a few inches less. You can weave the baby blanket a little longer if you find you have extra warp. When you have wound your warp and chained it, be sure to treat it with the sizing described in the warp chapter. Let it dry thoroughly before you tie it onto your permanent warp.

Since the outer 7 in. of the warp (next to the selvedges) will be the fronts of the vest, keep these 2 sides fairly alike so the vest fronts will match.

The warp yarn (about the size of the middle section of a round wooden toothpick) can be a solid color, tweedy, or arranged in regular or random stripes.

## SMALL VEST

### The Weft

When your handspun warp is on the loom and tied to the front apron, weave in 2 or 3 narrow strips of wool filler. You should have used up about 10 in. of your warp in tying onto the apron and weaving the filler (header). When you take the vest off the loom and remove the header strips, this 10 in. will make a triple-knotted fringe.

After the filler, weave in tabby for about 14 to 15 in., allowing a good arc of weft (after you have woven the first inch of the vest, which needs very little arc). If you want a longer vest for a tall person, weave it 16 or even 17 in. long. When you reach the 14- to 17-in. length, you are up to the armhole. Stop with your shuttle at the right-hand selvedge.

Now start the loom shaping, which makes this garment much easier to tailor than if it were just a rectangle.

### Dividing Width for Shaping

For this part of the vest, you need 3 quills of yarn, the one attached to your weaving and 2 more. One can be in a shuttle (for the center portion), but for the narrower strips at each side (the front shoulders), it is usually easier to use quills and not be encumbered with shuttles.

Open up your tabby shed as if you were going to pass your shuttle clear across. Count off 18 of the *top shed* threads (this is actually 36 threads total) and bring your shuttle through that many only and up through the top. Let that shuttle rest on the woven material, and count off the other shoulder with your shed still open. Count off 18 *upper shed* threads (a total of 35 or 36 threads) from the left selvedge. There, insert the quill that will weave the left shoulder and bring it through the shed, emerging at the left selvedge. (Leave a few inches of yarn sticking out where the quill was inserted.) These 2 quills that are through the counted-off sections will weave the front shoulders.

Leaving the same shed open, count off for the center sec-tion, which will be the back of the vest. Count off 6 *upper shed* threads from the point where the shuttle or quill emerges from the right shoulder (this leaves a total of 13 threads for the under-arm) and insert your third quill or shuttle there, leaving about 2 in. of yarn sticking out. Bring it across through the shed to a point that is 6 *upper shed* threads from the left shoulder, and bring it out through the top of the shed.

Now, beat in these 3 sections and change your shed. Bring each of the 3 quills or shuttles back across its own section of the warp, emerging at the point where each was inserted. The center portion and the left-hand shoulder will each have a couple of inches of yarn to weave back into this same shed.

Now proceed to weave these 3 separate sections (with the unwoven underarm areas between them) for several inches. Here is one instance where you want to deliberately tighten in your selvedges! At the armhole edge, you should keep a very firm selvedge, and even narrow it in a little to make a proper fitting arm edge on the vest. This puts an extra strain on your warp, but you should have no trouble if you have used sizing.

When you have woven a few inches, your work will look like figure 160. Now is the time to weave a small tab at each underarm, which will give a firm underarm seam when you tailor the vest. This takes 2 small quills of a yarn about the weight of the warp (this should definitely be finer weight than the weft). A small tapestry beater or narrow width of wide-toothed dog comb is also needed to press these threads into place, as you cannot use the loom's beater when you weave these tabs.

### Tabs

Open up a tabby shed for quills coming from the right-hand side, and insert each of the finer-yarn quills through one of the 6 upper shed portions that were left unwoven for the underarm. Change sheds and weave back across this portion. Here you should tuck in the wisp of yarn that hangs out where you inserted the quill. Change sheds, then firmly push these 2

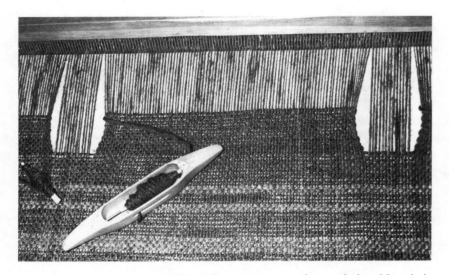

**160.** *Vest woven past the armholes. Now it is time to weave the underarm tabs.*

threads back against your weaving, using the small beater or comb. Weave back and forth on these narrow tabs, pressing the yarn in snug every 2 passes of the quill. When your tabs are about 3 in. long, stop with the quills at the right side of the tab. Break off your yarn, leaving about 6 in. for overcasting. Thread the yarn into a large yarn needle and overcast the end of each tab with the 6 in. left from its quill.

### Up to the Shoulders

Continue on with your 3 sections of weaving now that the tabs are done. Weave a total length of about 14 in. from the beginning of the armhole to the end of the weaving, which will be the shoulder seam. Stop with your quills all at the left selvedge and break off your yarn from each quill, leaving about 1 in. to tuck back into the next shed.

### Overcasting the Shoulders

Take 3 quills of finer yarn and insert them at the left selvedge, overlapping the ends that you just broke off. Weave across each width with a quill. Change sheds, beating the threads in firmly.

Break off each yarn from its quill, leaving about 10 in. from each of the edge quills for overcasting, and leave about 24 to 28 in. for sewing the center (wider) width.

Thread the sewing yarn from the right-hand quill into a large yarn needle and overcast the right shoulder edge. Do the same with the left shoulder edge and with the center.

### Cutting Off

Wind your warp forward until the overcast edges at the end of your vest are at the front of the loom so that you can cut off by using the breast beam to guide your cutting.

If you have a clamp arrangement, which was mentioned in the preceding chapter, this is a good time to use it. Clamp the 2 flat sticks across the warp threads about halfway between the reed and the overcast edges. Cut off about ½ in. from your overcasting, and also cut the unwoven portion of the warp that is at the underarms.

### Taking Vest off the Loom

Release the front ratchet and unwind the vest from the front cloth beam. Untie the knots that tie it to the apron. We find that the overcast edges stay in even better condition during washing if we now machine stitch close to the edge, right on top of the overcasting. Stitch the 3 edges — the 2 shoulders and the back. Also stitch the end of the tabs. Then trim off the unwoven yarn that is hanging from the tabs and save it to knot fringe on the selvedges of the blanket.

### Tying the Fringe

Remove all but 1 of your headers. Leave in the header next to the first pick of weft yarn, and take it out as you tie the knots. Take out about 6 in. of the header and count off 4 threads from the edge. Tie them in a single knot, drawn close against the edge of your weaving. Go on across the whole width of the fringe, taking out the header and tying threads 4 at a time.

If you have the exact number of threads called for in the project (190), this does not come out exactly in multiples of 4. By tying a couple of knots with 5 threads, you will still come out even.

When you have tied all the knots for the full width of the warp, taking out the header just before your knots, you are ready to check for any mistakes in your weaving. If you find any skipped threads, mend them before tying the rest of the knots. This can be done by taking back the warp thread to where the skip occurs. Weave it back in correctly, using a large yarn needle.

Proceed to do the second row of knots. Start with 2 threads for the first knot. Then 4 threads for the next knot, 2 from each of the knots in the previous row. Continue across, ending with another 2-thread knot. Do the last row the same way as you did the first row. With each knot, the 4 threads come from ½ of each of 2 knots below it.

The third row finishes your fringe, unless you have inadvertently left more than 10 in. for fringe and want to make a fourth row in order to use up more of your excess warp.

### Washing the Vest

Prepare a place to spread out the vest before you start to wash it. This can be a blanket-covered table or a freshly vacuumed carpet where the vest may remain until it is completely dry.

Fill a basin with hot water and dissolve detergent in it. Soak the vest for 10 to 15 min. Then souse it up and down in the wash water a few times and spin the water out of it in the spin cycle of your washer. Run rinse water about the same temperature as your wash water. Rinse the vest and then spin out the rinse water. If you do not have a machine with a separate spin cycle, then squeeze out the rinse water, rinse it again (it takes at

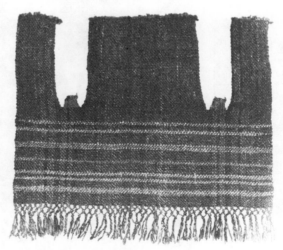

**161.** *Woven vest that has been washed and laid out to dry. The fringe was tied before washing.*

least 2 rinses without the spin), and squeeze out what water you can. Roll it in towels to absorb some of the excess water (this is not necessary after a spin cycle) and spread it out right away to dry.

### Hand Pressing

Your vest fabric will require little or no pressing if you press it out with your hands while it is damp, immediately after washing. Make sure you do not pull it unevenly in any direction and also straighten out the fringe so that it dries nicely. Leave the vest flat on the table until it is *completely* dry.

### Tailoring

All that the tailoring consists of is sewing down the tabs and sewing the shoulder seams.

To prepare for stitching the shoulders, trim off the excess yarn from each overcast edge, and trim the tabs. Turn down the tabs and stitch them with 2 rows of stitching, about ⅛ in. apart, at the overcast edge of the tab. The side to which you turned and stitched the tabs is now the inside of the vest.

With the vest inside out, pin the top of each front shoulder to the top edge of the back. Your first stitching lines will be A-B and C-D (dotted lines as shown in fig. 162B).

Turn the vest right side out. At the back neck edge there is about ½ in. in line with the stitching on each of the shoulders, that can be turned down and stitched against the fabric of the back, line B-C. This makes a firm neck edge, which is helpful when you go to put the edging around the whole front of the vest.

**162.** *Tailoring the vest*

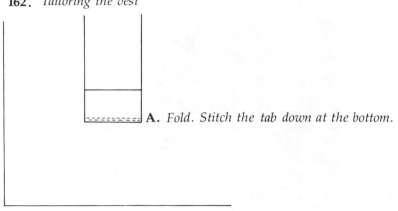

**A.** *Fold. Stitch the tab down at the bottom.*

**B.** *Stitch the shoulder seam.*

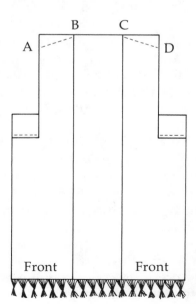

To prevent any raveling and to give the finishing touches to the shoulder seam, stitch down the triangles formed by the tapered shoulder seam. Stitching from the wrong side, follow the diagram in figure 162D. Starting at C, stitch to the right of the shoulder seam that is opened up, to point D, then back on the other side of the opened-up seam, to point C. Stitch C-E, then along the slanted front edge to F. From there to D-G and back to H. At H, the stitching ends at the place where you stitched down the back neck edge.

Repeat this stitching with the other shoulder and you have completed the tailoring. This triangular stitching gives a nice firm shoulder.

### Crocheting the Edging

The edging starts at the bottom of 1 front and goes up the front, around the neck, and down the other front edge, ending at the bottom of that front edge. We finish all our vests with 6 or 7 rows of single crochet, using yarn about the size of the warp yarn. It can be in a color that matches the vest, which we often use with our pale vests, or in a contrasting color, such as black on a vest woven in shades of dark wool.

Single crochet your first row carefully, trying not to pull up the front edge of the vest by crocheting too tightly. You can usually pick up 1 stitch in each front loop along the selvedge, the loops being where the weft yarn turns back into the shed each time.

Keep the beginning and end of each crochet row in line with the knots of the first row of fringe knots at the bottom of the vest. When you are finished, the crocheted band will look like an extension of the woven part of the vest, straight across the bottom. You can then cut 20-in. lengths of the yarn used for crocheting and knot on fringes at the bottom of the crocheted

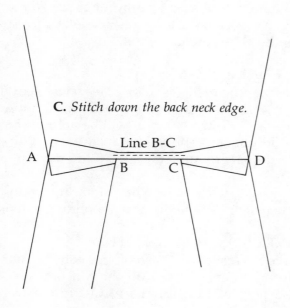

**C.** *Stitch down the back neck edge.*

Line B-C

A    B    C    D

**D.** *On the wrong side,*
*stitch down the shoulder tabs.*
*Stitch C-D (on 1 side of the shoulder seam),*
*then back on the other side of*
*the shoulder seam to C.*
*Stitch on from C-E,*
*then E-F, F-D, D-G, and G-H.*
*Repeat stitching*
*on the other shoulder.*

G
H
A    B    C    D
E
F

**163.** *Shepherd jacket. Sleeveless coat and vest (described in text)*

bands. Untie the edge knots on the vest so you can work the false fringe on the crocheting into the sequence of the warp fringe on the bottom of the vest.

Steam these added fringes over a teakettle to fluff them up. Do 2 rows of single crochet around each armhole. You do not need to go across the tab. Just start at the bottom of the armhole edge, crochet up over the shoulder, and down to the bottom of the other side of the armhole. Turn back, and retrace your edge to the beginning, making 2 rows. Finish it off, hiding the yarn ends on the inside of the vest.

### Pressing

If you pressed the vest piece with your hands as you put it out to dry, the only pressing it should need now is on the crocheted edgings. Use a wet cloth under an iron set at wool temperature, and steam the edges as needed. Allow the vest to lie flat until the edges are completely dry.

## ALTERNATE: LONG COAT

This vest can be made as a long sleeveless coat for spring and summer wear. Keep a good record of the amount of warp used for the short vest. Then you will be able to calculate the amount of additional warp to allow for weaving the extra distance between hem and underarm (all other measurements are the same).

The long coat, especially when done in white or a pale solid color, usually needs a good steam pressing to look its best.

## BABY BLANKET ON 38-IN. WIDTH

To weave the rest of the warp off in a baby blanket, tie onto the front apron where you cut off the finished vest material. Even off the warp with a few narrow strips of wool header material. You need from 8 to 10 in. of warp yarn to tie your fringes. If you want to weave a baby blanket that is longer than it is wide, skimp a little on the fringe at the beginning and end; as little as 6 in. will tie a single-knotted fringe. Allowing a generous 10 in. to begin and end, you may still find that you have a little longer weaving space than you needed to make it square, but that is better than running short.

For the 38-in. width of warp, you will probably get no more than 37 in. of a woven width, even if using a template. So a woven length of 40 in., measured with ratchet tension released, will probably work out to a fairly square blanket. When you have woven this much, measure the warp you have left. Allow 8 to 10 in. of it for the fringe. If you have any excess length of warp, you may want to weave a longer rectangle for the blanket.

### Removing Blanket from the Loom

When you have woven the desired length, allowing warp for fringe, weave in 2 or more narrow strips of header to keep the edge from loosening before you get the fringe knotted.

Then, wind your warp forward until you have the knots carefully pulled through the heddles and through the reed. Keep winding the warp forward until the knots (of the handspun warp to the permanent warp) are against the front of the breast beam of the loom. Attach your clamp about halfway between the knots and the reed.

Cut off the blanket next to the knots, leaving the knots attached to the handspun fringe and the permanent warp ends without knots. This way, you are ready for tying on your next warp.

### Knotting the Blanket Ends

Release the front ratchet, unwind the blanket, and untie the knots that fasten it to the apron. Remove all but the header closest to the woven edge. Now, removing it a little at a time, ahead of your work, tie the fringes in knots, 4 at a time. When you have 1 row done on the beginning, repeat this with the other end. Check your work for mistakes while you have only 1 row of knots tied. If you find a skipped thread, pull out that thread from the nearest end and correctly reweave it in, using a large blunt yarn needle. If you have allowed only 8 in. for fringe, you may want to settle for 1 row of knots.

### False Fringe on Blanket Edges

Here is where you can use up the leftover warp yarn from the armholes of the vest. Actually, it takes more yarn than those leftovers to make fringes on both selvedge edges of the blanket, but you can use up leftover yarn from other projects. If you mix it up well enough, it does not even have to be all the same size yarn. The lengths will need to be twice the length of the desired fringe. Take these snips 2 at a time, fold them over in the middle, and pull that center fold of yarns through the selvedge edge with a crochet hook. Slip the loose ends of that fringe through the loop, and pull it fast against the selvedge.

You do not need to loop fringe into every selvedge loop (the loops are just the turning back of each weft thread), but can tie a fringe into every other edge loop. Do this to the full length of both selvedge edges. Then trim the fringes around the whole blanket to about the same length, and it is ready for washing.

### Washing the Blanket

Completely dissolve detergent in quite warm wash water. Soak the blanket for 10 to 15 min., sousing it up and down a few times. Spin out the wash water in the separate spin cycle of your washing machine. Rinse the blanket and spin out the rinse water. If you do not have a separate spin cycle, just squeeze out the wash water and do 2 or more rinses to remove all the suds. Then roll it in towels to absorb excess water. Unroll it and lay it out on a blanket-covered table, pressing it into shape with your hands and smoothing out all the wrinkles. Leave it there until it is *completely* dry.

## LARGE VEST ON 44½-IN. WIDTH

This is the same project as the small vest except that it is on a wider loom and makes approximately a size 40 man's vest. You need a permanent warp to tie onto, with 5 threads per in. in a #5 reed (a total of 223 threads). Thread them through the heddles and reed, and roll the warp onto the loom.

### Handspun Warp

You need 223 threads of handspun warp, about 3½ yd. long plus a few extra inches. This can be 8 chains of 22 and 2 chains of 24, which would give you 1 extra warp thread, all sized and ready to use if you have a broken thread.

### Weaving the Vest

The large vest is woven like the small one except that you weave farther to the armhole (18 or 20 in.). It is also divided a bit differently for the back and shoulders.

End with your shuttle at the right-hand selvedge to make the armholes. Open your shed, count off 20 of the *top shed* threads, and pass your shuttle through that far, bringing it up through the top and resting it on the fabric. Count off 20 of the *top shed* threads from the left side, with the same shed open, and start there with a separate quill, emerging at the left selvedge. Now, count off 10 of the *top shed* threads from where the shuttle emerges from the right shoulder, and start your shuttle through the warp at that point to weave the back. It comes out at a point which is 10 top shed threads from where the quill entered for the left shoulder.

With the vest thus divided, weave these 3 sections (with the underarm sections remaining unwoven between them) up about 4 or 5 in. Stop there, and weave in the underarm tabs, as described in the small vest instructions, weaving across the number of threads allowed for the somewhat larger tab of the large vest. Overcast the end of the tab and then go back to weaving on up to the shoulders of the vest. This is a distance of about 14 in. from the beginning of the divided warp (from the armhole). Note in the small vest instructions how to pull in the selvedges to make a good fit.

### Overcasting the Edges

Overcast the edges as directed for the small vest. Wind your warp forward until the overcast edges are at the front breast beam. Then attach your clamp onto the warp threads, midway from the reed to the overcast edge. Cut it off about ½ in. from the overcasting.

Release the front ratchet and remove the vest from the loom. Stitch the overcast edges on the sewing machine, close to the edge. Tying the fringe, and washing, tailoring, and crocheting the large vest should be done the same way as was described for the small vest.

## PONCHO OR LARGE BABY BLANKET

Tie the remaining warp to the front apron, weave in 2 or 3 narrow header strips, and then weave a square for a poncho or baby blanket, following directions for the baby blanket on the narrower loom. Weave until it is about 46 to 47 in. long (measured with ratchet released) so that it comes out square after washing. Before washing, knot fringes onto the selvedges, as directed for the baby blanket.

After washing, lay it out to dry on a blanket-covered table, smooth it out flat with your hands, and stretch it a little in either width or length, if necessary, to make a perfect square. Leave it until it is *completely* dry.

## LOOM PLANS

This 48-in., 4-harness counterbalanced loom was designed specifically to be made from standard dimension lumber, which is available at lumber yards. With the exception of the optional ratchet for the front cloth beam, the loom can be constructed by using a table saw, drill press, and hand tools.

The tension assembly that is shown for the front beam adjustment will advance the beam about $3/8$ to $1/2$ in. each step, or about $1/36$ of the circumference of the front beam. A weaver wanting a finer adjustment may prefer the ratchet with 2 pawls, so it is included as an alternative.

While the loom is shown with 4 treadles, it can just as easily be made for a 6 treadle tie-up.

### Sectional Beam

The back warp beam can be converted to a sectional beam by constructing 4 separate, removable, sectional attachments out of $5/4 \times 3 \times 46$-in. lumber, with sectional pins (2-in. pins cut from welding rod) set at 1- or 2-in. intervals along the narrow side of each strip. These attachments can be fastened onto the back beam when needed for sectional warping.

### Canvas Apron

A front apron can be made from a 48-in. square of light canvas or heavy duck. One edge is tacked to the length of the front beam. The opposite edge is hemmed, encasing a $1/2$-in. metal rod that is 48 in. long. The hemmed edge can be notched at 1-in. intervals for tying your warp onto the front apron, but a better system is to have a second rod. This is fastened to the rod in the apron by loops of cord at about 6-in. intervals, and your warp is tied to the attached rod. In some countries, the custom is to hold the second rod in place by a single long cord that is laced back and forth between the 2 rods. However, this always seems to need some adjusting as you tie on your warp and can be a bother.

# 19
# Building a Floor Loom and Reel

On the back warp beam, we prefer a rod that is attached by several sturdy lengths of webbing instead of using an apron. A rod thus attached can also be used if the beam is converted for sectional warping. The webbing strips should be long enough that they can be tacked to the back beam, go once around the beam, and still extend up over the back of the loom, reaching almost to the heddles. Each strip is sewn back into a loop at that end, to encase the rod to which your warp (or permanent warp) attaches. The webbing length can be calculated so that, with sectional pieces in place, they let the rod come to within ½ in. of the edge of 1 of the sectional pieces when the webbing is wound up against the beam. This allows room for easy attachment of each section of warp threads.

**164.** *Floor loom – isometric illustration*

LIST OF MATERIALS FOR LOOM

| Nominal dimension | Actual dimension in inches except where marked | Quantity |
|---|---|---|
| 1 × 2 | ¾ × 1½ | 14 ft. 3 in. (linear feet) |
|  | ¾ × 2¾ | 4 ft. 7 in. |
| 1 × 6 | ¾ × 5½ | 3 ft. 6 in. |
| 1 × 10 | ¾ × 9½ | 4 ft. 6 in. |
| 2 × 2 | 1½ × 1½ | 18 ft. 5 in. |
|  | 1½ × 2 | 10½ in. |
| 2 × 4 | 1½ × 3½ | 37 ft. 4 in. |
| 2 × 6 | 1½ × 5½ | 40 ft. |
| 2 × 8 | 1½ × 7½ | 2 ft. 6 in. |
| 4 × 4 | 3½ × 3½ | 10 ft. 10 in. |
| 6 × 6 | 5½ × 5½ | 9 ft. 11 in. |
|  | ½ × 1½ | 33 ft. 4 in. |
| 4 × 8 | 3½ × 7½ | 5 ft. 2 in. |
| Dowel | 1⁵⁄₁₆ | 2 in. |
|  | 1 | 11 ft. 3 in. |
|  | ½ | 6 ft. ½ in. |
|  | ⅜ | 4 in. |
|  | ¼ | 7 ft. 2 in. |
| Garden implement handle | 1 to 1¼ | 5 ft. 4 in. |
| Hardware | ⅛ × 1½-in. mild steel | 2 ft. 8 in. |
|  | ¼-in. sash chain | 20 ft. |
|  | ³⁄₁₆-in. coated clothesline | 20 ft. |
|  | ⁵⁄₁₆- to ¼-in. thick harness leather | 6 sq. in. |
|  | ½-in. screw hooks | 64 |
|  | ¼ × 2-in. stove bolts with nuts and washers | 6 |
|  | #12 × 1½-in. wood screws with 2 washers each | 4 |

*Note: There is no allowance for cutting or waste in the above totals. Add 5 to 10%.*

## CUTTING LIST FOR LOOM PARTS

| Assembly | Nominal dimension | Length in inches | Number of pieces cut to this length | Notes |
|---|---|---|---|---|
| Loom frame | 2 × 4 | 60 | 1 | In addition to being cut |
| | | 54 | 1 | to the sizes on this list, |
| | | 53 | 2 | all pieces will |
| | | 42 | 2 | have additional |
| | | 31 | 2 | joinery to cut and fit. |
| | | 15 | 2 | Make sure there is a good |
| | 2 × 6 | 62½ | 2 | fit on all joints so |
| | | 60 | 2 | that the structure is sturdy |
| | | 33 | 2 | and works smoothly. |
| | | 25½ | 2 | |
| | | 25 | 2 | |
| | | 17½ | 1 | |
| | | 16½ | 2 | |
| | 2 × 8 | 15 | 2 | |
| | 4 × 4 | 58 | 1 | |
| | | 54 | 1 | |
| | 1 × 2 | 4½ | 6 | |
| | 1-in. dowel | 2½ | 12 | |
| | ½-in. dowel or mild steel rod | 11 | 1 | |
| | ¼-in. dowel | 1½ | 48 | |
| Warp and cloth beams | 6 × 6 | 59 | 2 | |
| Tension handles | 1 to 1¼ in. (implement handles) | 28 | 1 | |
| | | 24 | 1 | |
| | | 12 | 1 | |

| Assembly | Nominal dimension | Length in inches | Number of pieces cut to this length | Notes |
|---|---|---|---|---|
| Bench and supports | 1 × 10 | 54 | 1 | |
| | 2 × 4 | 49½ | 1 | |
| | 2 × 6 | 34½ | 2 | |
| | 1-in. dowel | 2½ | 4 | |
| | ½-in. dowel | 2 | 10 | |
| Treadle supports | 2 × 4 | 15 | 2 | |
| | 4 × 4 | 17½ | 1 | |
| | 1½ × 2 (actual size) | 3½ | 3 | |
| | ½-in. dowel | 3½ | 8 | |
| | ½-in. dowel or mild steel rod | 13½ | 1 | |
| Treadles | 2 × 2 | 40 | 4 | |
| Lams | 1 × 2 | 36 | 4 | |
| Heddle bars | ½ × 1½ (actual size) | 50 | 8 | |
| Roller assemblies | 1⁵⁄₁₆-in. dowel (e.g. closet rod) or similar rollers | 1 | 2 | Drill with ¼-in. hole in exact center |
| | 1-in. dowel | 44½ | 2 | |
| | ¼-in. dowel | 1½ | 2 | |
| | ¼-in. mild steel rod | 2 | 2 | Top roller axle |
| | ³⁄₁₆- to ¼-in. thick harness leather | 6 to 8 sq. in. | 1 | For end bearings on bottom rollers (see D) |

| Assembly | Nominal dimension | Length in inches | Number of pieces cut to this length | Notes |
|---|---|---|---|---|
| Hardware | ¼-in. sash chain | 20 ft. | | |
| | 3/16-in. coated clothesline | 20 ft. | | |
| | ½-in. screw hooks | 64 | | |
| | 1/8 × 1½-in. mild steel strap | 16 | 2 | Heated and bent 90° on end and drilled to accept stove bolts (see I) |
| | ¼ × 2-in. stove bolts with nuts and washers | 4 | | |
| | #12 × 1½-in. round head wood screws with 2 washers each | 4 | | |
| Beater assembly | 1 × 6 | 42 | 1 | Cut in half lengthwise in order to produce 2 pieces, ¾ × 2¾ × 42 |
| | 4 × 8 | 62 | 1 | Cut into 3 pieces, 2⅜ × 3½ × 62 |
| | ¾ × 2¾ (actual size) | 54¼ | 1 | |
| | 3/8-in. dowel | 2 | 2 | |
| | ¼-in. dowel | 2⅜ | 4 | |

Note: *All dimensions are in inches except where marked.*

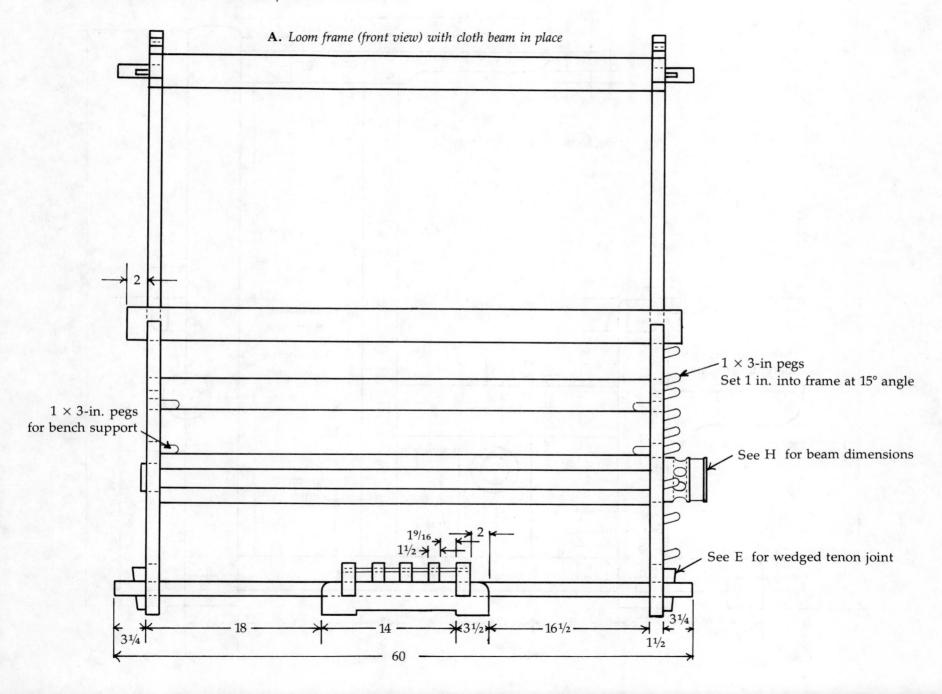

**A.** *Loom frame (front view) with cloth beam in place*

1 × 3-in pegs
Set 1 in. into frame at 15° angle

1 × 3-in. pegs
for bench support

See H for beam dimensions

See E for wedged tenon joint

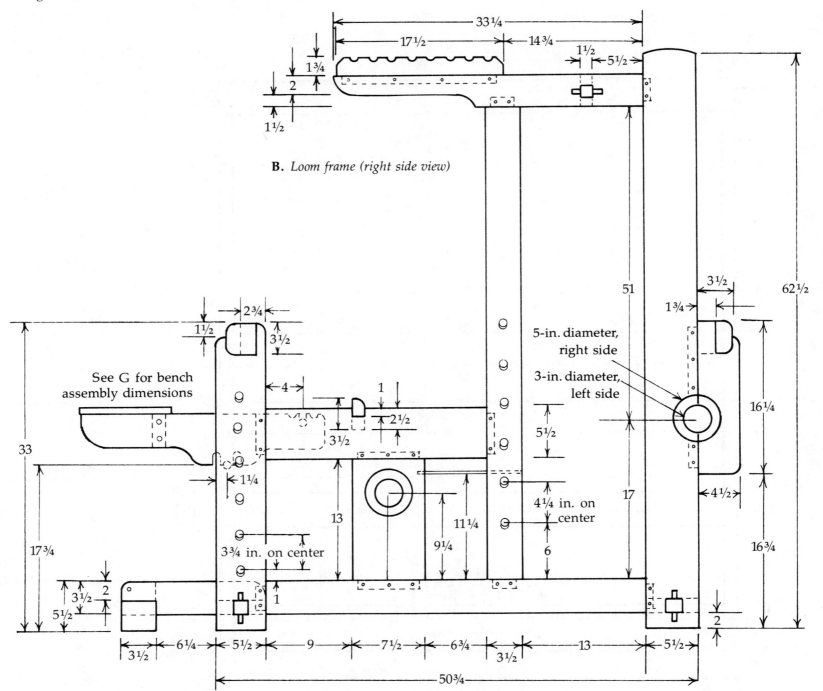

**B.** *Loom frame (right side view)*

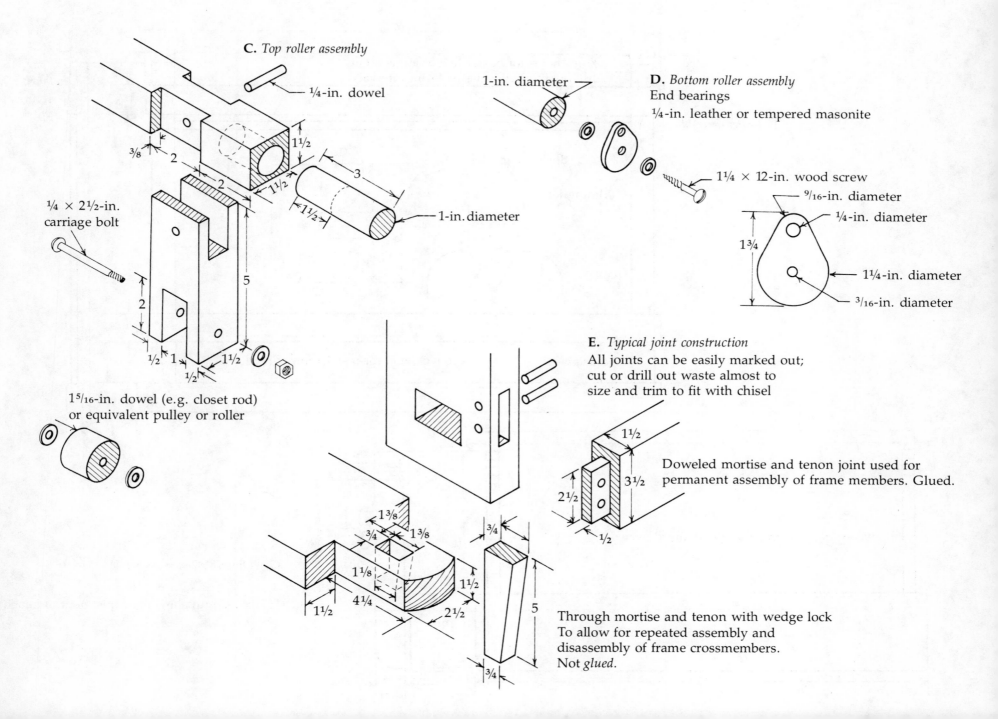

**C.** *Top roller assembly*

¼-in. dowel

1½

3

2

2

⅜  2

1½

1½

1-in. diameter

5

2

½  1

½

1½

¼ × 2½-in.
carriage bolt

1⁵/₁₆-in. dowel (e.g. closet rod)
or equivalent pulley or roller

1-in. diameter

**D.** *Bottom roller assembly*
End bearings
¼-in. leather or tempered masonite

1¼ × 12-in. wood screw

⁹/₁₆-in. diameter

¼-in. diameter

1¾

1¼-in. diameter

³/₁₆-in. diameter

**E.** *Typical joint construction*
All joints can be easily marked out;
cut or drill out waste almost to
size and trim to fit with chisel

1½

2½

3½

½

Doweled mortise and tenon joint used for
permanent assembly of frame members. Glued.

1³/₈

¾  1³/₈

¾

¾

1⅛

1½

1½

4¼

2½

5

¾

Through mortise and tenon with wedge lock
To allow for repeated assembly and
disassembly of frame crossmembers.
Not *glued*.

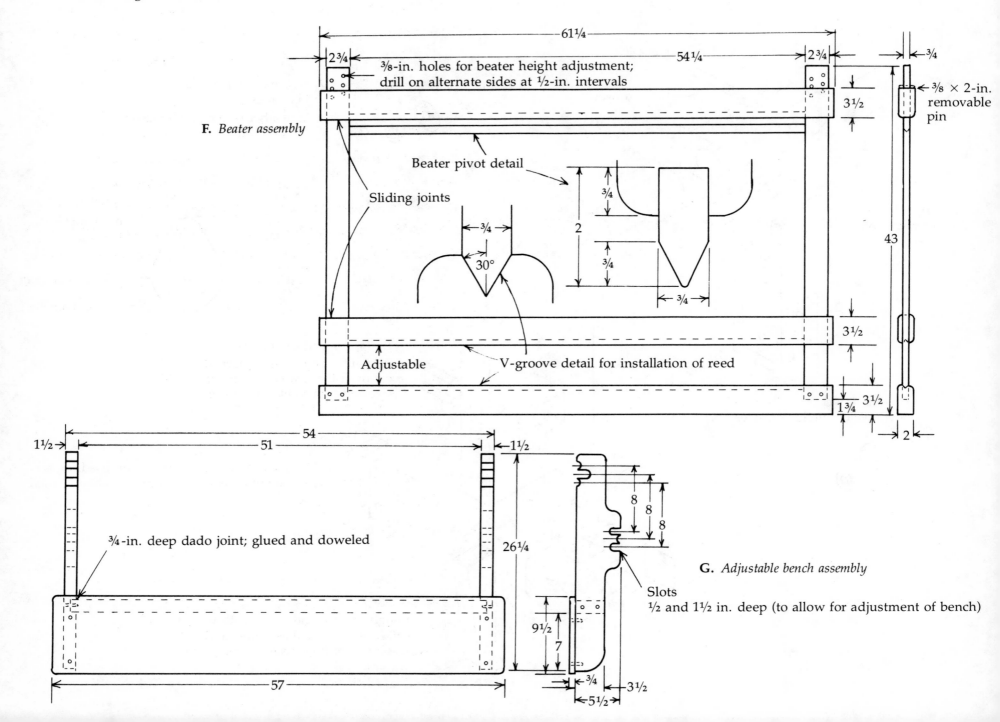

F. *Beater assembly*

3/8-in. holes for beater height adjustment; drill on alternate sides at 1/2-in. intervals

Beater pivot detail

Sliding joints

Adjustable

V-groove detail for installation of reed

3/8 × 2-in. removable pin

3/4-in. deep dado joint; glued and doweled

Slots
1/2 and 1 1/2 in. deep (to allow for adjustment of bench)

G. *Adjustable bench assembly*

**H.** *Warp and cloth beam detail*

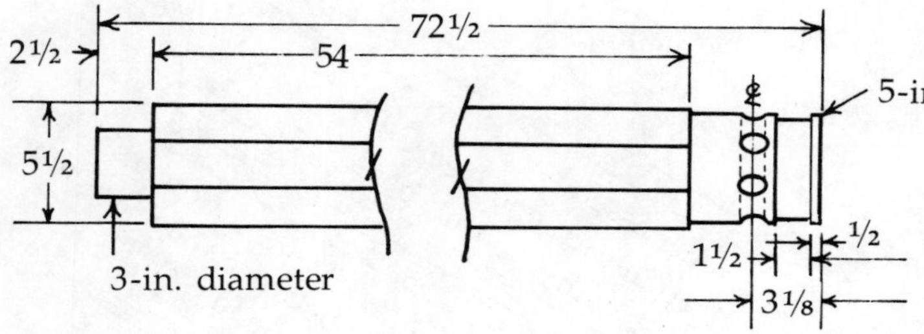

$72\frac{1}{2}$
54
$2\frac{1}{2}$
$5\frac{1}{2}$
5-in. diameter
3-in. diameter
$1\frac{1}{2}$
$\frac{1}{2}$
$3\frac{1}{8}$

The beams are cut from nominal 6 × 6-in. stock
and the square corners are cut and
planed to octagonal shapes.
The ends are carefully cut and
drilled with the holes
$\frac{1}{4}$ in. larger
than the handles to allow
for proper operation.
This assembly is a positive acting,
highly adjustable tensioning
device that replaces traditional
ratchet and brake devices.

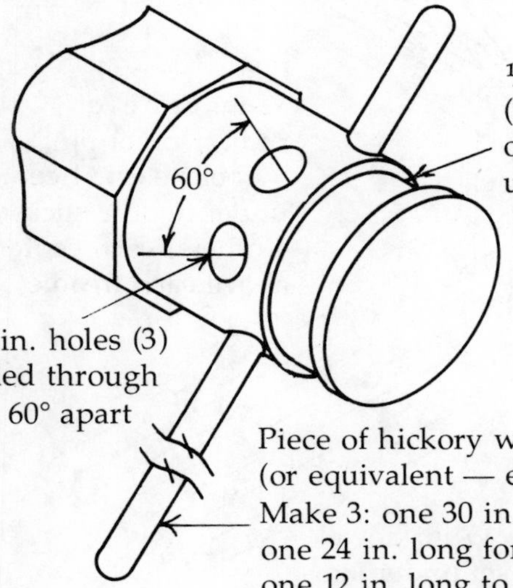

60°

$\frac{1}{2}$-in. deep recess optional
(to allow for wrapping
of end to prevent splitting
under heavy tension)

$1\frac{1}{4}$-in. holes (3)
drilled through
and 60° apart

Piece of hickory with 1-in. diameter
(or equivalent — e.g. garden tool handle)
Make 3: one 30 in. long for warp beam,
one 24 in. long for cloth beam,
one 12 in. long to assist in
tightening and releasing tension

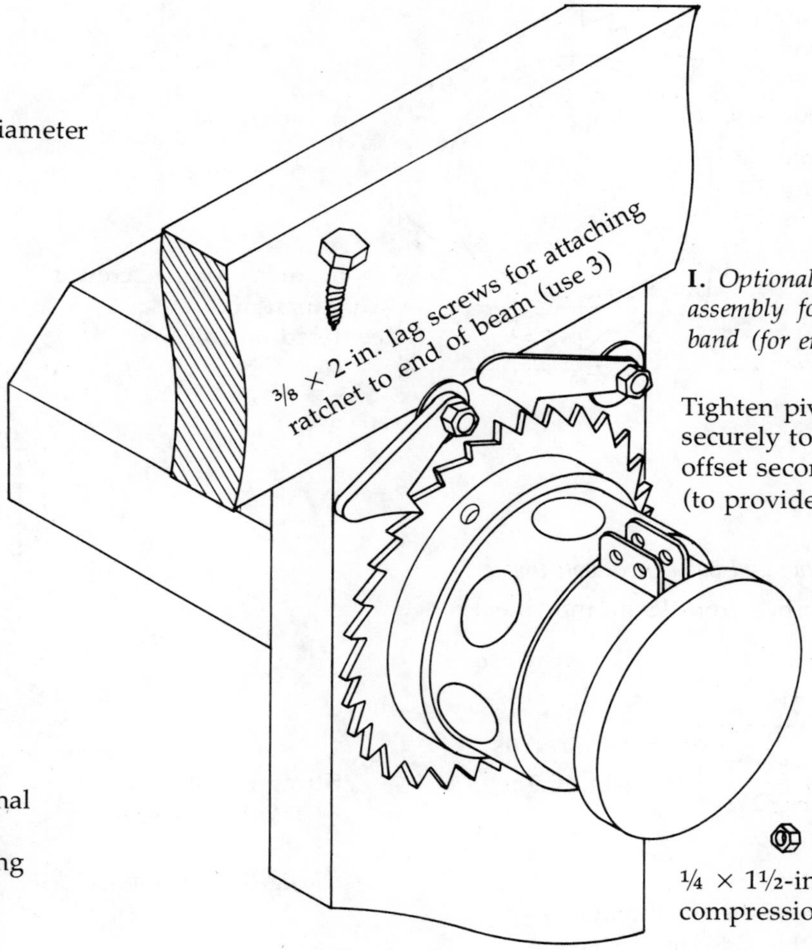

$\frac{3}{8}$ × 2-in. lag screws for attaching
ratchet to end of beam (use 3)

**I.** *Optional ratchet and pawl
assembly for cloth beam and compression
band (for ends of both beams)*

Tighten pivot bolts
securely to loom frame
offset second pawl one half-step
(to provide for finer adjustment)

$\frac{1}{4}$ × $1\frac{1}{2}$-in. stove bolts for tightening
compression band (use 2)

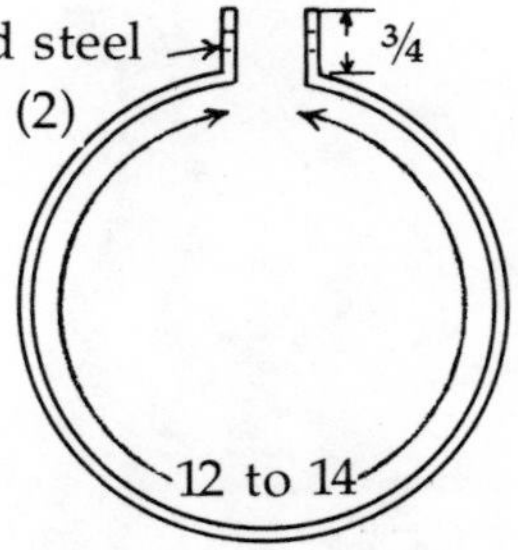

$\frac{1}{8}$ × $1\frac{1}{2}$-in. mild steel
$\frac{1}{4}$-in. holes (2)
$\frac{3}{4}$

**J.** *Compression band*

Size should allow for tightening
around the beam end
(to prevent splitting
when under heavy tension)

12 to 14

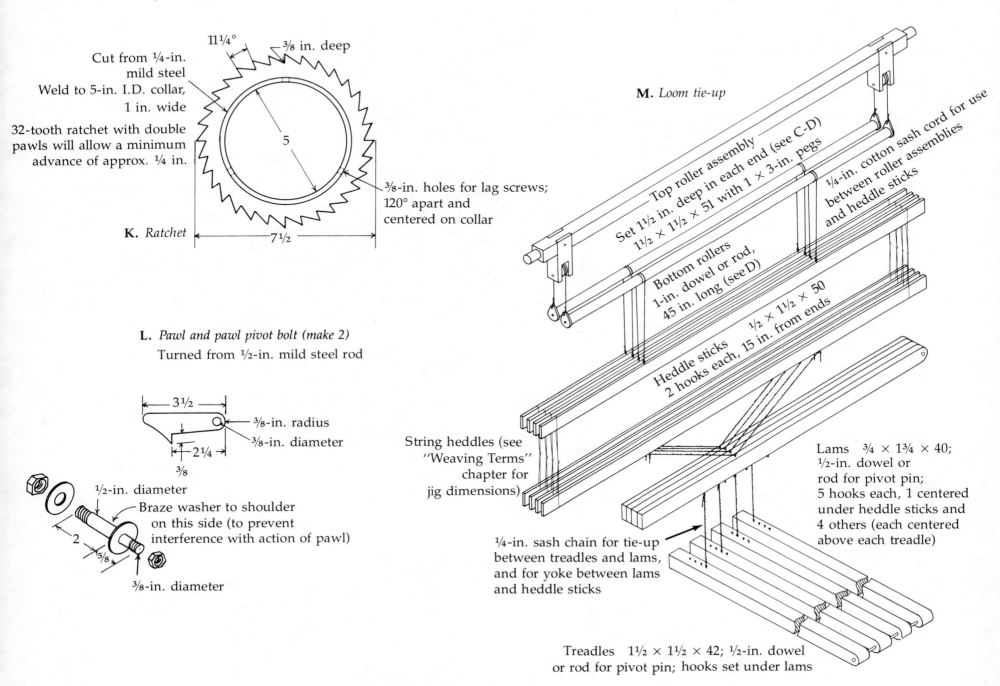

**K.** *Ratchet*

Cut from ¼-in.
mild steel
Weld to 5-in. I.D. collar,
1 in. wide

32-tooth ratchet with double
pawls will allow a minimum
advance of approx. ¼ in.

11¼°

⅜ in. deep

5

⅜-in. holes for lag screws;
120° apart and
centered on collar

7½

**L.** *Pawl and pawl pivot bolt (make 2)*
Turned from ½-in. mild steel rod

3½

⅜-in. radius
⅜-in. diameter

2¼

⅜

½-in. diameter
Braze washer to shoulder
on this side (to prevent
interference with action of pawl)

2

⅝

⅜-in. diameter

**M.** *Loom tie-up*

Top roller assembly
Set 1½ in. deep in each end (see C-D)
1½ × 1½ × 51 with 1 × 3-in. pegs

¼-in. cotton sash cord for use
between roller assemblies
and heddle sticks

Bottom rollers
1-in. dowel or rod,
45 in. long (see D)

Heddle sticks     ½ × 1½ × 50
2 hooks each, 15 in. from ends

String heddles (see
"Weaving Terms"
chapter for
jig dimensions)

Lams   ¾ × 1¾ × 40;
½-in. dowel or
rod for pivot pin;
5 hooks each, 1 centered
under heddle sticks and
4 others (each centered
above each treadle)

¼-in. sash chain for tie-up
between treadles and lams,
and for yoke between lams
and heddle sticks

Treadles   1½ × 1½ × 42; ½-in. dowel
or rod for pivot pin; hooks set under lams

## WARPING REEL PLANS

A warping reel is faster and more efficient than a warping frame or warping board.

Compared to a vertical warping mill, this horizontal warping reel takes somewhat less effort to turn, as its weight is supported at both ends. Also, the warp does not tend to slide off when the tension is released.

The arms of this reel can fold flat together while still on the base, allowing the reel to be stored near a wall where it occupies only a small space when not in use. For even smaller storage area, the base can be disassembled into separate pieces and stored together with the folded arms.

For warping methods needing a cross at both ends of the warp, make 2 of the wooden ends that are used for the cross, and position these at both ends of the reel, after determining the length of warp desired.

For warping methods using a cross at 1 end, as described in the "Weaving with Handspun: The Warp" chapter, use 1 of the wooden crosses. The other end of the warp then needs only a dowel placed at the desired position for the length of warp planned. For short warps, there are dowel holes in all the arms, both at the ends and at midway points.

**165.** *Warping reel*

*Note: Dimensions are in inches except where marked.*

**A.** *Reel sides (cut 4)*

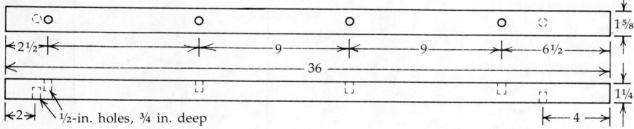

½-in. holes, ¾ in. deep

**B.** *Crossmembers (cut 4)*

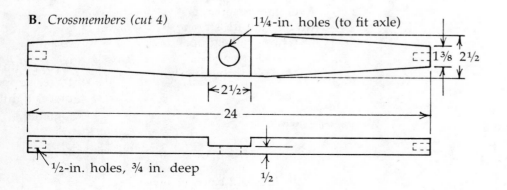

1¼-in. holes (to fit axle)

½-in. holes, ¾ in. deep

**C.** *Legs (cut 2)*

¼-in. slots (to fit axle spindles)

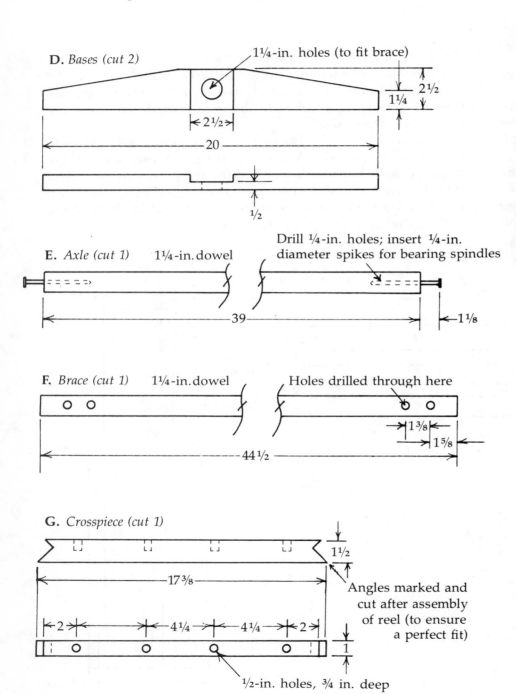

**D.** *Bases (cut 2)*

1¼-in. holes (to fit brace)

2½

1¼

2½

20

½

**E.** *Axle (cut 1)*    1¼-in. dowel

Drill ¼-in. holes; insert ¼-in. diameter spikes for bearing spindles

39    1⅛

**F.** *Brace (cut 1)*    1¼-in. dowel

Holes drilled through here

44½    1⅜    1⅝

**G.** *Crosspiece (cut 1)*

1½

17⅜

Angles marked and cut after assembly of reel (to ensure a perfect fit)

2    4¼    4¼    2    1

½-in. holes, ¾ in. deep

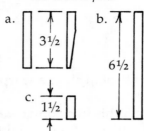

**H.** *Dowel pins*

a.    3½    b.    6½    c.    1½

a. Cut 4: 2 straight, sand wedge on 2
b. Cut 5: 4 are glued into crosspiece, 1 is inserted into reel sides (to determine length of warp)
c. Cut 8: glued between reel sides and crossmembers

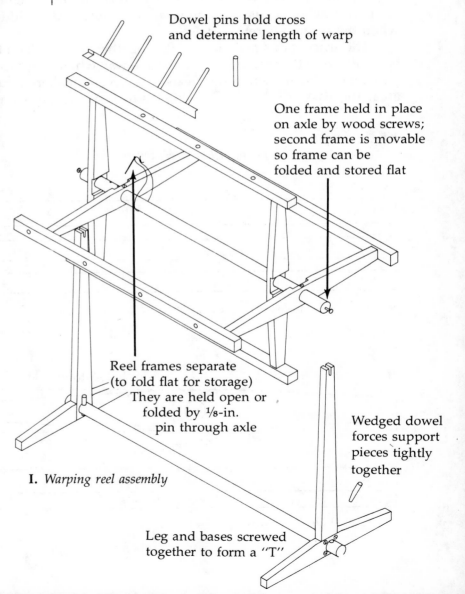

Dowel pins hold cross and determine length of warp

One frame held in place on axle by wood screws; second frame is movable so frame can be folded and stored flat

Reel frames separate (to fold flat for storage) They are held open or folded by ⅛-in. pin through axle

**I.** *Warping reel assembly*

Wedged dowel forces support pieces tightly together

Leg and bases screwed together to form a "T"

## 20
## Knitting with Your Handspun

### SINGLES OR PLY

Whether you knit with singles or ply them depends somewhat on how suitable the single ply is for your knitting project. A fine single ply that has too much overtwist is apt to take on a bias slant after it is knitted; plying the yarn tends to counteract the effect of the overtwist. A single ply that has too many thick and thin places for the item you want to knit can be plied, thus balancing out some of these irregularities and making the yarn more usable. And plying eliminates the need to spin varied thicknesses of yarn in order to have a variety of sizes of single-ply yarn.

On the other hand, the obvious advantage of a single-ply yarn is that you eliminate the extra spinning, which consists not only of spinning twice as much yarn, but spinning it a third time to ply it.

### ELASTICITY AND NEEDLE SIZE

To allow for the unusual elasticity of handspun, you need to use a knitting needle that is just a little larger than you use with an equivalent size of commercial yarn. When handspun is knitted on needles too small, it produces a hard, stiffened garment that is not pleasant to wear. Just knitting up a small swatch on the size needles you think you want to use does not always give an accurate picture. You should instead make up several swatches, each with one size larger needles, to determine how large a needle you could use without the knit being too loose for its intended purpose.

### STITCH GAUGE

Most knitting patterns rely on stitch gauge to tell you how many stitches to use for a certain size. Because of its irregularities, handspun is different from the commercial yarn for which the patterns are designed. It is hard to be accurate in counting the number of stitches per inch in a small swatch to determine the gauge. Yet it is the fraction-of-a-stitch difference

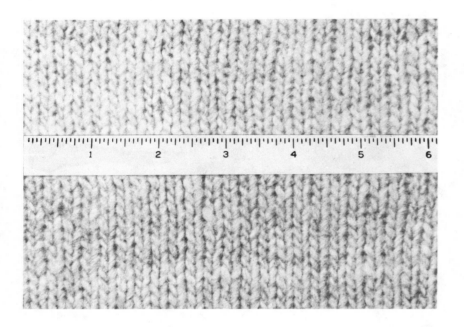

**166.** *Make a large swatch to determine the approximate stitch gauge.*

that can make up several inches difference in the size of a whole sweater.

For a more accurate count, if you need a stitch gauge to estimate the number of stitches to cast on, you should knit a swatch that is at least eight inches wide. To determine the approximate stitch gauge, count the number of stitches in the center six inches of that swatch and divide by six to get the approximate number per inch. On the average, you will have miscalculated by at least four stitches over a six-inch distance if you have settled for counting the stitches in one inch of a small swatch. Even though this stitch count produces more accurate results, it should be used only in a general way to determine if you want to try the exact number of stitches called for in the pattern or alter the number of stitches to get the size you want. Using a stitch gauge with handspun is not as reliable as using a tape measure to check on the size as you go along.

Do not knit "blind" and depend on a pattern completely. As you are knitting, compare the measurements of your work with the desired finished measurements. The use of a tape measure ensures a good fit, for if you see it is going to be too small or too large, you can rip back at once and start with more stitches or fewer stitches to make the correct dimensions.

If the piece is too large, do *not* change to smaller needles — just decrease the number of stitches. In handspun, the smaller needles can make it too firm, and the object is to find the best needle size to obtain a soft, wearable garment, which usually means using as large a needle as possible for the size of yarn.

FIT

In most instances, you should be careful not to make handspun sweaters with too tight a fit. A tight fitting, handspun sweater, when knitted on needles large enough to allow for the softness of the yarn, can show holes between the stitches when it is stretched too tight. The insulation is in the wool itself and it need not be a snug fit in order to be warm.

Use a tape measure to be sure your garment is knitting up in the size you want. This can be simplified by measuring the person for whom you are knitting or by measuring a garment that fits properly. Make a brown paper pattern with those dimensions, and compare the paper pattern to the knitted pieces as you knit them.

## DOUBLE-POINTED NEEDLES

When knitting around and around with double-pointed needles, there are gaps that sometimes show up as a series of loose stitches in a vertical line through your knitting, where you work from one needle to the next. These can be avoided by taking advantage of the special elasticity of handspun.

To tighten the stitches from one needle to the next, do not pull the yarn snug as you start to work the first stitch on the needle. Instead, tighten your yarn *after* the first stitch, when you insert your needle into the loop to make the second stitch. This prevents any gap between needles and makes a neat, even tension on watch caps, socks, or other articles knitted on double-pointed needles.

## THIN PLACES

Ordinarily, the thinner and thicker places in handspun will knit into a uniform, attractive texture. But when an unusually thin place in your yarn occurs directly above a thin place in the row below, the resulting thin area can be remedied. Just tear a wisp of yarn a few inches long off a spare ball or the other end of the ball you are using, and knit it *along with* the thin place in your yarn. The wisp of wool does not show once you have knitted past it on the next row as long as the wisp does not have a cut end.

Overly thick places in your yarn can be thinned down, if desired, by untwisting them a little and pulling them out so they are thinner. Just brace your hands against something to give you more control so you do not accidentally pull the yarn apart.

## JOINING ON

Do not tie a knot when joining a new ball of yarn. "Splice" it by knitting the first few inches of the new ball along with the last few inches of the last ball, with the yarn thus doubled for a few stitches. If it is broken instead of cut, you will not be able to find where you joined on the new ball of yarn.

## TAPERED ENDS

In using handspun for knitting (and weaving, too) it is always important to break it, not cut it. If it will not break easily, untwist it a little, then pull it apart. The difficulty with cut ends is that they eventually pop out on the surface.

## SLIPPING THE FIRST STITCH

Whenever it does not interfere with your pattern or garment shaping, *slip* the first stitch of each row. It makes a smoother, tighter edge on your work and eliminates any tendency toward a bumpy or loopy side edge. This is especially helpful when you are knitting something like a scarf or a stole, where those edges are exposed rather than sewn into a seam or finished off with a knitted band.

## ESTIMATING QUANTITY

Estimating the quantity of yarn needed for a knitting project is always a problem. However, if you spin all the skeins of uniform length, it will be easier to calculate how many are needed. When you are knitting with skeins of equal length and you have knitted up one or two skeins, you should be able to make an educated guess of how many more skeins you will need for the whole garment. There is another advantage of making uniform measured skeins — you can weigh the skeins to determine rather quickly whether they are all spun in approximately the same size.

The number of ounces of yarn needed for a specific project can vary depending on the amount of twist in the yarn, and can be affected by the breed of sheep (wool type) from which the fleece was obtained. A finer wool spins up to a different weight than a coarse wool, even when spun to the same diameter yarn. If you knit a sweater pattern once, it takes about the same amount of *yardage* to do it again, but in a different wool type, this yardage does not necessarily weigh the same amount.

The safe thing, in all instances, is to spin up more than you think you will need *before* you start knitting. That way, you have more assurance that you have a sufficient number of skeins of the same shade and yarn size.

BALL WINDING

Hand ball winders can be purchased, and we use one for all our knitting yarns, but for many years we used a much less expensive one — the cardboard tube from the center of a roll of toilet tissue. On it, you can wind a center-pull ball that looks as professional as if it were done on a real ball winder.

As the yarn comes from your skein on the swift (fig. 157), pull the end of it through the cardboard tube. Fasten it to the end of the tube with a paper clip or a bobby pin, or just wedge it into a short slit in the end of the tube. Wind the yarn around the center of the tube a few turns, then start winding it on the diagonal, turning the tube slowly as you do, and always going in the same diagonal direction. At the end of the skein, tuck the last bit of the yarn into the outside of the ball. Then unfasten the paper clip and remove the ball from the tube.

This makes a center-pull ball, and you start knitting with the end that sticks out of the center of the ball, the end that was fastened to the tube. Since the ball is wound over a tube, once the tube is removed there is no longer any tension on the yarn. This is easier on the yarn, and is more convenient for knitting than if you wound a solid ball and knitted from the outside.

**167.** *Ball winding. Step 1. Start winding yarn around the center of the tube.*

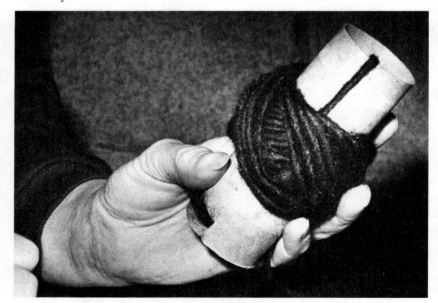

*Step 2. Wind it diagonally while rotating the tube.*

## RELIEVING OVERTWIST

In the beginning, everyone invariably has trouble with overspun yarn. The ultimate remedy, of course, is lots of practice and patience. In the meantime, overtwist makes it difficult to knit with the yarn unless there is some way to remove some of the twist. One simple way is to stick a knitting needle through your center-pull ball of yarn in such a way that you can loop the yarn in a half hitch over one end of the needle as the yarn comes from the ball. You can then suspend your ball of yarn occasionally, as necessary, and allow some of the twist to unwind as the ball rotates. When you have removed a sufficient amount of twist, you need only take out the needle in order to continue knitting.

## EDGINGS

If possible, knit edgings of sweaters and other items right along with the body of the garment rather than knitting them separately and sewing them on. Sewing them on always leaves a seam that is a little more rigid than the knitted handspun garment, while knitting them on gives edgings with the same elasticity as the rest of the knit. It also eliminates the chore of finishing and the possibility of a seam that is less than perfect in appearance.

## RAGLAN SLEEVES

The success of a sweater depends as much on how it is put together as it does on the knitted pieces. In handspun, a raglan sleeve fits best and also has a seam line that is much easier to sew. A knitted-in raglan sleeve is even better, as it has no seam at all and eliminates the inevitable restriction of movement that is felt at a sewn seam when wearing the sweater. The knitted-in raglan can be made by starting at the collar edge and knitting down, in which case you are increasing stitches along each sleeve seam line (see pattern book in "Sources" chapter).

When you start at the bottom of a sweater and knit upward (for a knitted-in raglan), the sleeves, back, and fronts can be knitted separately until they are all up to the armhole, then joined together on one circular needle. Knit up to the shoulder with all pieces together, decreasing stitches along the diagonal sleeve seam line. However, if the sweater is extra bulky (when made with yarn that must be knitted on #13 or #15 needles, for example), then you need to knit the pieces separately and sew them together. They would be too heavy on your needles if knit in one piece. For sewing the seams, spin up some of the matching wool into a finer-weight yarn.

*Step 3. The finished ball of yarn. Remove the tube and work from the center-pull ball.*

## SWEATER ZIPPERS

The zipper should be undetectable, or at least as inconspicuous as possible. This means that a front zipper in a sweater should not show at all from the outside of the sweater. To accomplish this, the front edges of the sweater must come completely together, hiding both the zipper tape and the zipper teeth. Sew it in with enough "seam allowance" that the teeth are not sewn into the seam and the zipper can still be opened and closed. This sewing can be done by hand, working from the wrong side of the sweater after either pinning or basting in the zipper. Use a back stitch and heavy carpet thread for a heavy sweater. In some knits, it can be done by machine, especially if your thread *exactly* matches your yarn color. Whether sewn in by machine or by hand, the outer edge of the zipper tape should then be caught lightly against the inside of the sweater by hand.

Another important consideration is the relation of the zipper length to the length of the front edge of the sweater. It should be just slightly shorter than the sweater edge. If the zipper is the same length as the sweater front or a little longer, it will cause the front edge of the sweater to ripple. Also, if your yarn has not been washed, it is best to wash the sweater before you sew in the zipper. Otherwise, if the yarn is not preshrunk and shrinks during the first washing, it will cause the same rippling effect.

If the front edge does ripple, either because of the zipper being too long for the edge or because of shrinking after washing, the zipper should be removed and shortened. Most metal zippers have teeth that can be pulled off. Use small pliers, gripping each tooth as close to the tip as possible. Do not have the zipper pull so close to the top end of the zipper that it slips off when you are removing teeth. Also removable is the tiny clamp at the top of the zipper that holds the zipper pull from coming off the end. Use a large darning or yarn needle, pushing it inside that clamp to spread it until it can be taken off. Save it, and clamp it on again with your pliers after you have removed the necessary number of teeth.

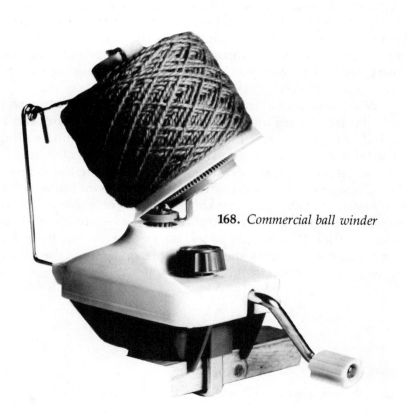

**168.** *Commercial ball winder*

## BLOCKING

You should aim to have your finished article as near to the desired size as possible. However, it can be blocked and stretched slightly larger or longer or to somewhat different measurements than it was when you finished knitting it. This is done by steaming. Do not use an iron directly against the wool. Instead, use a very wet cloth under an iron set at wool temperature. Unless you are trying to correct a very uneven texture, you do not need to press hard on the wet cloth. Just touch it with the iron enough to send the steam into the knit.

Sweater pieces can be pinned into shape, on a blanket or towel, until dry. A knitted baby blanket can also be steamed to its maximum size and held in shape until it is completely dry from the steaming.

## WASHING HANDSPUN KNITS

If you knit with preshrunk yarn, you do not need to worry about shrinkage in normal washing. In fact, it is more apt to stretch, unless handled carefully.

A wet sweater is heavy with water, and if held by the shoulders, unsupported, can get badly stretched. Ribbing can also get stretched out of shape if not handled gently. The sweater should, when wet, be picked up and supported on your hands. If you "spin" the water out of it, do not allow it to remain in a heap for any length of time for this "sets" the wrinkles in it. Lay it out flat to dry (at once) on towels or a blanket, and pat it into the correct shape, squeezing in the wrist and other ribbings so they dry in a gathered-in position.

Some sweaters will stretch in width when they have been worn for a time. This can be offset after washing by stretching them a little in length, while they are still damp, and letting them dry that way.

## TWO KNITTING PROJECTS
Pussyfoots
Small size (changes added for medium and large sizes).
Size #3 yarn (see "Designating Yarn Size" in "Learning on a Spinning Wheel" chapter).

Use #9 or #10 needles.
Start at top edge, cast on 32 (36, 40) st.
Row 1: p 1, *k 2, p 2, repeat from *, end with p 1.
Row 2: k 1, *p 2, k 2, repeat from *, end with k 1.
Repeat these 2 rows for 6 (6½, 7) in. Bind off.

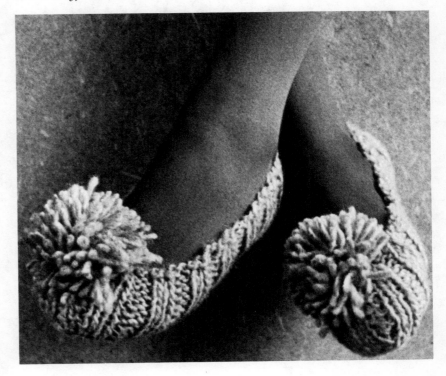

**169.** *Pussyfoots*

**170.** *Striped Ski Hat*

Finishing: Fold slipper in half lengthwise and sew ends together with an overcast stitch, being sure that the p-1 ridges meet on the right side to form a p-2 rib. Run double strands of elastic thread inside the top edge. Divide remaining yarn in 2 parts and use to make pom-poms. To make pom-pom, wind yarn over a 1½-in. cardboard. Tie at 1 end securely. Cut other end and trim it to rounded shape. Sew 1 pom-pom over an end seam of each slipper for toe ends of the slippers.

Striped Ski Hat
Size #4 yarn (see "Designating Yarn Size" in "Learning on a Spinning Wheel" chapter).
 60 yd. of main color (MC);
 30 yd. of contrasting color(CC).
Use size #11 needles for hat and #10 double-pointed needles for top.
With #11 needles and CC, cast on 25 st.
Row 1: Purl across, drop yarn, but do not break off.
Rows 2, 3, 4, and 5: With MC, knit.
Row 6: With CC, knit.

Repeat last 6 rows until you have 14 MC stripes, but do not break yarn. With CC, bind off, leaving about a 15-in. end. Use this end to sew cast-on edge to bound-off edge, leaving a small seam allowance. Using #10 double-pointed needles and with MC still attached to hat, pick up 2 st. in each MC stripe along top edge (28 st.). Divide on needles. Knitting loosely on the #10 double-pointed needles, knit 1 round without decreases. Then, shape top of hat by decreasing (k 2 tog) at beginning and end of *each* needle, until 10 st. remain. Draw end through st. and fasten off.

With large crochet hook and MC, crochet 1 row around bottom of hat, making 2 sc in each MC stripe and 2 sc in each CC stripe. Weave in ends. Hat will conform to head when worn, as shown in illustration.

PARTIAL LISTING OF SPINNING SUPPLY
CATALOGS (ORDERED BY MAIL)

Gordon's Naturals
P.O. Box 506
Roseburg, Oregon 97470

Greentree Ranch
163 North Carter Lake Road
Loveland, Colorado 80537

Handcraft Wools
Box 378
Streetsville, Ontario, Canada

The Handweaver
460 1st Street East
Sonoma, California 95476

Hide n' Hair
3311 University Drive
Durham, North Carolina 27707

The Mannings
R.D. 2
East Berlin, Pennsylvania 17316
*Catalog 50¢*

Oldebrook Spinnery
Mountain Road, Box 288 B
Lebanon, New Jersey 08833

Robin and Russ Handweavers
533 North Adams Street
McMinnville, Oregon 97128

Serendipity Shop
1523 Ellinwood
Des Plaines, Illinois 60016

Snug Valley Farm
Box 394, R.D. 3
Kutztown, Pennsylvania 19530

Spincraft
P.O. Box 332
Richardson, Texas 75080

Spin-It Weave-It Studio
2621 University Avenue
San Diego, California 92104
*Catalog $1.00*

Straw into Gold
5533 College Avenue
Oakland, California 94618
*Catalog 50¢*

Traditional Handcrafts
571 Randolph Street
Northville, Michigan 48167

Village Wools
3719 4th Northwest
Albuquerque, New Mexico 87107
*Catalog 50¢*

Wildflower Fibres
205 Northwest 2nd
Portland, Oregon 97209

Woodsedge Farmstead
P.O. Box 464
Kingston, New Jersey 08528
*Catalog 75¢*

PARTIAL LISTING OF FLEECES
(ORDERED BY MAIL)

Boyd, Ruth
R.F.D.
North Powder, Oregon 97867

# 21
## Sources

Colorado Fleece Company
516 West Ute
Grande Junction, Colorado 81501

Greentree Ranch
163 North Carter Lake Road
Loveland, Colorado 80537

Hathaway Wools
Route 3, Box 407
Kiger Island
Corvallis, Oregon 97330

Hedgehog Equipment
Forest Craft Centre
Upper Hartfield
East Sussex, England

Hide n' Hair
3311 University Drive
Durham, North Carolina 27707

Jones Sheep Farm
R.R. 2, Box 185
Peabody, Kansas 66866

Midwest Wool Cooperative
405 East 14th
Kansas City, Missouri 64116

Oldebrook Spinnery
Mountain Road, Box 288 B
Lebanon, New Jersey 08833

The River Farm
Route 1, Box 169 A
Timberville, Virginia 22853

The Shearing Shed
P.O. Box 585
Sisters, Oregon 97759

Sheepman Supply Company
P.O. Box 100
Barboursville, Virginia 22923

Straw into Gold
5533 College Avenue
Oakland, California 94618

Wells, Lorraine
18728 Southeast Cheldelin Road
Portland, Oregon 97236

## FLICK CARDS

*This is new equipment in the U.S.,*
*so most suppliers are overseas.*

Baillie and Watts Limited
Box 1512
Auckland, New Zealand

Hedgehog Equipment
Forest Craft Centre
Upper Hartfield
East Sussex, England
*(Also sells worsted flickers)*

Pipy Craft Limited
228 Wellington Street
Howick, Auckland, New Zealand

## DRUM CARDING MACHINES

Baillie and Watts Limited
Box 1512
Auckland, New Zealand

Cascade Looms
7364 Conifer Northeast
Salem, Oregon 97303

Green, Patrick
48793 Chilliwack Lake Road
Sardis, British Columbia V0X 1Y0
Canada

Hedgehog Equipment
Forest Craft Centre
Upper Hartfield
East Sussex, England

Mark IV by The Spinning Wheel Factory
Distributed by Something Special
5400 Park Lake Road
East Lansing, Michigan 48823

Ram Industries
143 Smith Street
Winnipeg, Manitoba R3C 1O5
Canada

*Drum carders also sold by most*
*spinning-weaving supply shops*

## CARD FILLET FOR DRUM CARDERS, RETAIL

*Sold by the following*
*(addresses listed under*
*"Drum Carding Machines"):*

Baillie and Watts Limited
Green, Patrick
Hedgehog Equipment
Something Special

## CARD FILLET FOR DRUM CARDERS, WHOLESALE

Critchley Sharp & Tetlow
Prospect Mills, Cleckheaton
West Yorkshire, England
BD19 3BL

## CARD CLOTHING SHEETS FOR DRUM CARDERS

Holdsworth, J. and Brothers Limited
South Brook Mills
Station Road, Mirfield
Yorkshire WF14 8NQ, England

Sellers, J. and Son Limited
Scholes Lane
Scholes Cleckheaton
Bradford BD19 6NJ, Yorks, England

The Spinning Wheel Factory
1666 Steeles Avenue West
R.R. 4
Milton, Ontario, Canada

## CARDING BOARD

Dutch Canadian Spinning Wheel Company
Box 70
Carleton Place, Ontario K7C 3P3
Canada

## CARDING AND SPINNING OIL, WHOLESALE AND RETAIL

Obadiah Tharp Company
8406 Southwest 58th Avenue
Portland, Oregon 97219

## HANDCRAFTED NIDDY-NODDIES

Joyous Song
Route 6, Bradley Chapel Road
Jones Cove
Sevierville, Tennessee 37862

The Meisterheim's
R.R. 5, Box 210
Dowagiac, Michigan 49047

## BEGINNER'S KIT (SPINDLE, WOOL, CARDS)

The Shearing Shed
P.O. Box 585
Sisters, Oregon 97759

Spincraft
P.O. Box 332
Richardson, Texas 75080

Wildflower Fibres
205 Northwest 2nd
Portland, Oregon 97209

## PARTIAL LISTING OF SPINDLES

Casa de las Tejedoras
1619 East Edinger
Santa Ana, California 92705
*Gillan's turkish spindle*

Fiber Craft Imports
P.O. Box 504
Lagunitas, California 94938
*Turkish spindle*

Handcraft Wools
Box 378
Streetsville, Ontario, Canada
*Drop and long lap spindle*

Joyous Song
Route 6, Bradley Chapel Road
Jones Cove
Sevierville, Tennessee 37862

Schacht Spindle Company
1708 Walnut Street
Boulder, Colorado 80302
*All kinds*

Straw into Gold
5533 College Avenue
Oakland, California 94618
*Turkish spindle*

## SPINNING WHEEL PLANS

Craftplans
Rogers, Minnesota 55374

Handweavers Guild of America
998 Farmington Avenue
West Hartford, Connecticut 06107

Old South Pattern Company
P.O. Box 11143
Charlotte, North Carolina 28209

University of Wisconsin — Stout
Industrial Teacher Education Department
Menomonie, Wisconsin 54751

## SPINNING WHEEL MANUFACTURERS

*(In addition to wheels and manufacturers presented in ''Available Spinning Wheels'' chapter)*

Bartholomew, Chet
2717 West Locust
Tacoma, Washington 98466

Blackburn, J. W.
R.R. 3, Caledon East
Ontario, Canada

Gudat, Eric
P.O. Box 12
Washingtonville, Ohio 44490

Hall, Norm
P.O. Box 648
North Norwich, New York 13814

Kelly, Carl
P.O. Box 95
Elcho, Wisconsin 54428

Kronenberg, Bud
Horse Fence Hill Road
Southbury, Connecticut 06488

Modern Spincraft
Route 2, Box 224
DeLeon, Texas 76444

Oak & Elm Handcrafts
Anthony and Vlasta Glaski
R.F.D. 1
Unity, Wisconsin 54488

The Oak Shop
Chris A. Bolton
1600 West County Road 10E
Berthoud, Colorado 80513

Reeves Woodworks
Box 34
West Amana, Iowa 52359

The Ricks
Route 1, Box 13
Friday Harbor, Washington 98250

Rognvaldson, R. and G.
R.R. 4
Acton, Ontario, Canada

Sather, L.
R.R. 3, Box 122
Northwood, Iowa 50459

Sievers Looms
Box 5
Washington Island, Wisconsin 54246

Spice of Life
Route 1, Box 119
North Glarus, Wisconsin 53574

Spinoakes Crafts
G. Lee Ericson
Route 2, Box 223
Berryville, Arkansas 72616

Tromp n' Treadle
Richard Loftun
41901 Woodbrook Drive
Canton, Michigan 48188

## PARTIAL LISTING OF LOOMS

Circadian Looms
2547 8th Street
Berkeley, California 94710

Countryside Handweavers
163 North Carter Lake Road
Loveland, Colorado 80537

Harrisville Designs
Harrisville, New Hampshire 03450

Herald Looms
118 Lee Street
Lodi, Ohio 44254

J. L. Hammett Company
10 Hammett Place
Braintree, Massachusetts 02184

Nilus Leclerc Incorporated
C.P. 69
L'Islet, Quebec G0R 2C0
Canada
*(Write for list of distributors)*

Pendleton Looms
Box 233, Jordan Road
Sedona, Arizona 86336

*Also sold at all spinning-weaving
supply shops and by
most mail order shops*

## LOOM PLANS

*Build Your Own Floor Loom (book)*
by Steve and Darlene Lones
Harbour Publishing
Box 119
Madeira Park, British Columbia, Canada
*About $4.00*

**Craftplans**
Rogers, Minnesota 55374
*Floor loom plans – about $2.50*

Sievers Looms
Box 5
Washington Island, Wisconsin 54246
*Floor loom plans – about $17.00*

Tom Turnbill Looms
4519 Kingsway
Mobile, Alabama 36608
*Jack-type loom plans – about $12.50*

Village Wools
3719 4th Northwest
Albuquerque, New Mexico 87107
*8-harness, 45-inch Jack floor loom*
*with double warp beams –*
*plans about $4.00*

Whitney Looms
514 Myrtle Place
Lafayette, Louisiana 70501
*Table loom plans – about $7.50 and $10.00*
*Tapestry loom plans – about $5.00*

## LOOM REEDS

Bradshaw Manufacturing Company
Box 425
West Columbia, South Carolina 29169

Whitaker Reed Company
90 May Street
P.O. Box 172
Worcester, Massachusetts 01602
*Steel or stainless steel*

## HEDDLE FRAMES

Earthwares
103 North Pleasant Street
Amherst, Massachusetts 01002

## LOOM PARTS (RATCHETS, HEDDLES, ETC.)

Robin and Russ Handweavers
533 North Adams Street
McMinnville, Oregon 97128

Village Wools
3719 4th Northwest
Albuquerque, New Mexico 87107

Wildflower Fibres
205 Northwest 2nd
Portland, Oregon 97209

## WARP SIZING, RETAIL

The Country Weaver
105 Meeker Southwest
Puyallup, Washington 98371

Magnolia Weaving
820 102nd Northeast
Bellevue, Washington 98004

Obadiah Tharp Company
8406 Southwest 58th Avenue
Portland, Oregon 97219

Robin and Russ Handweavers
533 North Adams Street
McMinnville, Oregon 97128

Snug Valley Farm
Box 394, R.D. 3
Kutztown, Pennsylvania 19530

*Some other mail order shops also*
*carry warp sizing, retail.*

## WARP SIZING, WHOLESALE

Paula Simmons
Box 12
Suquamish, Washington 98392

## HAND WRINGERS

Countryside
Route 1
Waterloo, Wisconsin 53594

Sears Roebuck
*(Listed under ''Clothes*
*Wringers'' in catalog)*

## YARN BLOCKERS

Cesaletti, Bill
c/o 10 North 12th Street
Hawthorne, New Jersey 07506

Hemlock Hill Handspinners
Box 48
Mount Airy, Maryland 21771

Pintler
Route 1, Box 28 F
Moxee City, Washington 98936

The Shearing Shed
P.O. Box 585
Sisters, Oregon 97759

## COMBINATION YARN BLOCKER–WARPING WHEEL

Dutch Canadian Spinning Wheel Company
P.O. Box 70
Carleton Place, Ontario K7C 3P3

## WOOL PICKERS

Green, Patrick
48793 Chilliwack Lake Road
Sardis, British Columbia V0X 1Y0

Pintler
Route 1, Box 28 F
Moxee City, Washington 98936

## PERMANENT MOTHPROOFING (MITIN F.F.)

Handcraft Wools
Box 378
Streetsville, Ontario, Canada

## BOOKS

*The Handspinner's Guide to Selling*
by Paula Simmons
Seattle: Pacific Search Press, 1978

*Handspinning, Art and Technique*
by Allen Fannin
New York: Van Nostrand Reinhold, 1970

*Making Simple Inexpensive Carding
& Spinning Equipment*
from Nancy Ellison
R.R. 2, Box 197
Hayfield, Minnesota 55940
*$2.50 plus postage*

*The New Key to Weaving*
by Mary Black
New York: The MacMillan Company, 1961

*Patterns for Handspun*
from Paula Simmons
Box 12
Suquamish, Washington 98392
*$1.35 plus postage*

*A Pictorial Guide to American Spinning Wheels*
from Dave and Beth Pennington
1993 West Liberty
Ann Arbor, Michigan 48103
*$4.00 plus postage*

*Raising Sheep the Modern Way*
by Paula Simmons
Published by Garden Way Publishing
from Paula Simmons *(see address above)*
*$6.95 plus postage*

*Spinning Wheel Building and Restoration*
by Bud Kronenberg
New York: Van Nostrand Reinhold, 1981

*Spinning Wheel Primer*
by Alden Amos
Published by Straw into Gold
5533 College Avenue
Oakland, California 94618
*$3.95 plus postage*

*Textile Tools of Colonial Homes*
by Marion Channing
Box 552
Marion, Massachusetts 02738
*$2.25 plus postage*

## GENERAL SPINNING AND WEAVING BOOKS

The Book Barn
Avon Park North, Route 44
Avon, Connecticut 06001

The Unicorn
Box 645
Rockville, Maryland 20851

## PUBLICATIONS

*Black Sheep Newsletter*
28068 Ham Road
Eugene, Oregon 97405

*The Crafts Report* (newsletter)
700 Orange Street
Wilmington, Delaware 19801

*Handwoven* (and *Spin-Off*, published annually)
306 North Washington
Loveland, Colorado 80537

*Naturally*
P.O. Box 506
Roseburg, Oregon 97470

*Shuttle Spindle and Dyepot*
998 Farmington Avenue
West Hartford, Connecticut 06107

*Warp and Weft*
533 North Adams
McMinnville, Oregon 97128

*Weavers Newsletter*
P.O. Box 259
Homer, New York 13077

*Yarn Market News*
50 College Street
Asheville, North Carolina 28801

# Index

Boldface numerals indicate pages on which photographs and drawings are located.

## OTHER BOOKS FROM PACIFIC SEARCH PRESS